The Four-Day Workweek

David M. Maklan

The Praeger Special Studies program, through a selective worldwide distribution network, makes available to the academic, government, and business communities significant and timely research in U.S. and international economic, social, and political issues.

The Four-Day Workweek

Blue Collar Adjustment to a Nonconventional Arrangement of Work and Leisure Time

PRAEGER SPECIAL STUDIES IN U.S. ECONOMIC, SOCIAL, AND POLITICAL ISSUES

Praeger Publishers　　New York　　London

Library of Congress Cataloging in Publication Data

Maklan, David M
    The four-day workweek.

    (Praeger special studies in U.S. economic, social,
and political issues)
    Bibliography: p.
    1. Four-day week—United States. I. Title.
HD5124.M3   1977   658.31'21   77-14308
ISBN 0-03-039916-5

658.3121
M235

PRAEGER PUBLISHERS
383 Madison Avenue, New York, N.Y. 10017, U.S.A.

Published in the United States of America in 1977
by Praeger Publishers,
A Division of Holt, Rinehart and Winston, CBS, Inc.

9   038   98765432

TO CLAIRE
FOR SHARING MY WORK AND LEISURE

64567

FOREWORD
Allan G. Feldt

Interest in the development of the four-day workweek and similar innovations such as flexible worker scheduling has grown consistently over the past decade. Most of this interest has focused upon its effect in the workplace itself and occasionally upon the new demands such types of scheduling might place upon various social services such as leisure and transportation.

In an urban society, however, all individuals are imbedded within a matrix of interactions with other individuals. The dimensions of the matrix are geographic place and the flow of time over daily, weekly, and annual cycles. Our network of social relationships is conditioned by those occasions when other individuals occupy the same position in time and space with us. Most have learned to accept and adjust to regular and systematic occurrences of such social contacts within a well ordered and unchanging matrix of time and space whose dimensions are commonly accepted and understood by others around us.

Then what happens to an individual who is suddenly provided new gradations to one of these dimensions, gradations differing from those around him with whom he has learned to live? How does one now handle the interpersonal contacts which evolved under the old constraints when they must be lengthened, shortened, or shifted to meet the demands of the new constraints? Most particularly, how does the individual readjust relationships to the family which may still be operating under the old matrix despite innovative changes at the workplace?

David Maklan addresses these questions in this work and provides the basis for developing answers. Modifying time schedules in an urban society is serious business and its implications spread well beyond the more obvious economic and managerial aspects which have received most of our attention thus far. In a careful and thorough examination of the impact of four-day-workweek innovations on the workers and their families, Maklan uncovers both the stresses and the promises these innovations provide. Through cautious comparisons of similar workers still following conventional schedules with those following four-day-week schedules, Maklan opens the door to a better and more complete understanding of what these recent experiments mean both to individuals and to the social world surrounding them.

vi

ACKNOWLEDGMENTS

This book would have been far more difficult without the contributions made by a number of people and organizations. First, I want to thank the faculty members of my doctoral committee. The independence with which they each encouraged me to proceed was an important boost to the self-confidence that this work required. John Robinson, with whom I worked most closely, provided expertise in survey research and helpful criticism along the way. In particular, his interest and experience in studies of time use added a valuable dimension to this work. Allan Feldt was always available when I needed him. His encouragement, good humor, and patience are appreciated more than he probably realizes. Being able to draw upon the divergent concerns and experiences of Lou Ferman and Fred Goodman facilitated the broad perspective that I hoped to maintain.

Special thanks are also due Professor Bev Driver. His interest in leisure and willingness to discuss the issues made him a great help in formulating the problem. My friend and former office-mate Joe DiMento also contributed useful ideas and reactions during the formative stages.

To Claire, my wife, I owe the greatest appreciation. Her own development and her continuing interest in my work provided constant intellectual stimulation and psychological support. I hope I shall be as understanding of her frustrations and as generous with my time.

Marija and Arpad Barath are two friends who contributed in no small way. Marija's diligence and cheerfulness made the long weeks of coding both more successful and pleasant. Arpad's statistical expertise, interest in the work, and inexhaustible willingness to help were very important.

Finally, financial assistance from The Canada Council and research grants from the U.S. Department of Labor and the Institute for Social Research made this book possible.

The material in this project was prepared under Grant No. 91-26-74-10 from the Manpower Administration, U.S. Department of Labor, under the authority of title I of the Manpower Development and Training Act of 1962, as amended. Researchers undertaking such projects under Government sponsorship are encouraged to express freely their professional judgment. Therefore, points of view or opinions stated in this document do not necessarily represent the official position or policy of the Department of Labor.

vii

CONTENTS

ix

St. Philip's College Library

LIST OF TABLES AND FIGURES

PART

I

**PLACING THE
STUDY IN CONTEXT**

CHAPTER

1

THE FOUR-DAY
WORKWEEK CHALLENGE

Technological changes have proved historically to be particularly explosive sources of second-hand social, economic and political changes that were never envisioned
(Raymond Bauer 1960, p. 4).

This book is concerned with an anticipated consequence of technological progress. As work has become easier and as dissatisfaction with it has grown, as incomes rise and the nonwork activities on
which it can be spent appear increasingly rewarding, the traditional
balance between labor and leisure has shifted. Industrial societies
are developing a leisure orientation.

Until recently, access to leisure and the possibility of making
meaningful choices among alternate creative and recreative free-
time activities were restricted to a relatively small number of people.
The masses of humanity neither had nor could afford large blocks of
free time. Instead, work dominated life; it constituted the individual's
central life domain. The workers' daily routine, and that of their
family, was organized around the job. What nonwork time remained—
and, during certain eras, it was plentiful—was severely constrained
by societal, religious, and peer-group norms. In no way could it be
viewed as discretionary time, for the individual lacked both the
requisite resources and knowledge of alternate modes of behaving.
So long as survival and the accumulation of basic life necessities
remained paramount in the collective mind, speculation concerning
the impact of leisure upon a society and its individual members
could safely remain on the backburner of society's consciousness.

This is no longer the case. During the past several decades,
this situation has undergone radical transformation. Indeed, part of

the traditional wisdom in any work-leisure debate is that the amount
of free time, and the uses to which this time is put, have been changing rapidly and will continue to do so in the future. Many reasons are
cited for this transformation—increasing productivity, rising incomes,
universal education, the "global village," and so on—but beneath all
these lies the drive of modern technology. For both good and ill,
advancing technique has reshaped the physical world, changed the way
we perceive its operations, and brought into existence new cultural
values, mechanisms, and social institutions to guide our perceptions.
The upheaval is felt in all aspects of modern life, but only in a few
areas are its ramifications more significant than in the changing
attitudes toward work and leisure and the resultant uncertainty surrounding their relative meaning and value.

In light of current popular sentiment about work, it is not surprising that several work-setting innovations are attracting the serious attention of both labor and management. This interest reflects
concern with the economic dislocation caused by absenteeism,
declining productivity, work stoppages, high turnover, vandalism,
and the other markers of poor morale and growing disenchantment
with jobs. It also reflects employees' feelings of frustration, boredom, and a general sense of being abused. Thus, both management
and labor are motivated to search for, and experiment with, various
means of coping with these and related problems.

From industry's new look at the nature of jobs, two distinct
courses of reform based on different perceptions of the scope of the
problem and the likelihood of successfully restructuring the routines
of work have emerged. The first set of innovations is largely internal
to the work place. In an effort to match more closely the demands of
jobs with the capabilities of employees, various organizations have
begun experimenting with the procedures and practices of work itself.
If jobs are somehow deficient in content and interest, then the obvious
solution is to upgrade them. Job enrichment, job enlargement, worker
democracy, and the planned-change (group process and feedback)
approach of consulting firms such as England's Tavistock Institute
and the National Training Laboratory in the United States represent
attempts to make the rewards of work more consonant with employees' needs and aspirations. The redesigning of Sweden's Volvo auto-
motive assembly line is among the most widely publicized examples
of the job-restructuring approach. Worker ownership of the Vermont
Asbestos Group and the International Group Plans Insurance Company
exemplifies the potential benefits to be derived from a democratiza-
tion of the work setting.

It is the second set of reforms, however, the instituting of a
variety of nonconventional workweek schedules, that has garnered
the lion's share of public interest and enthusiasm. Surveying news-

paper and magazine articles in one not-atypical week, Glickman and Brown (1974) found reports on the Washington, D.C. police department, which changed from a five-day, 40-hour schedule to overlapping ten-hour shifts; an advertising agency that remains closed on Fridays; and Lufthansa's "gliding work time" in which the worker self-selects his arrival and departure time within a 12-hour day.

Today's experiments with alternate work schedules are laying the ground for the work-leisure balance of the future. In great measure, these innovations find their thrust in the dual beliefs that (1) work, as presently organized, has negative effects on other life domains, such as family life and free time, and (2) meaningful change within the work setting is unlikely and/or unfeasible in the foreseeable future. Rather than expend their limited resources in efforts to rectify the psychologically damaging aspects of work, proponents of nonconventional work schedules advocate circumventing these problems whenever possible. Instead of job improvement, they call for a judicious removal of the individual from work's deleterious sphere of influence.*

To be sure, many people have long worked on schedules at variance with the standard five-day workweek about which much of urban life revolves. Many fuel-oil and gasoline delivery truck drivers, for instance, have worked a four-day week for over 30 years (Mortimer 1971). Only recently, however, has talk about such alternatives to the dominant mode been accompanied by an appreciable amount of serious action across a broad spectrum of the work system.

Historically, the demand for relief from the debilitating consequences of labor has focused upon decreasing the number of hours spent in the work setting. During the first half of this century, the length of the average workweek in private, nonagricultural industries declined from 60.1 hours per week to 39.8 hours (de Grazia 1964, p. 419). However, as Table 1.1 shows, there was only a slight change in the length of the average workweek during the next quarter century—from 39.8 hours down to 36.2 hours. Examining data for full-time workers in manufacturing—the most reliable figures for long-term work-hour trends—one finds a decline from 59 hours per week to 40.5 hours between 1900 and 1950 (Levitan and Belous 1977).

---

*Certainly, there are other not insignificant benefits to be derived from nonconventional work schedules. The four-day workweek, for instance, makes for (1) a 20 percent reduction in commuting time, thereby saving both time and money; (2) a possible reduction in work-related expenses such as babysitters and lunches out; and (3) a two-to-three-hour reduction in the workweek (Hedges 1973). More importantly, it is seen by many as a mechanism to shape the available work.

TABLE 1.1

Length of Average Workweek
In Private Nonagricultural Industries

Year	Hours	Year	Hours
1950	39.8	1963	38.8
1951	39.9	1964	38.7
1952	39.9	1965	38.8
1953	39.6	1966	38.6
1954	39.1	1967	38.0
1955	39.6	1968	37.8
1956	39.3	1969	37.7
1957	39.8	1970	37.1
1958	38.5	1971	37.0
1959	39.0	1972	37.1
1960	38.6	1973	37.1
1961	38.6	1974	36.6
1962	38.7	1975	36.1
		1976	36.2

Sources: 1950-54: U.S. Bureau of Labor Statistics, Employment and Earnings 19 (June 1973), Table C-1, p. 75; 1955-76: U.S. Bureau of Labor Statistics, Employment and Earnings 24 (March 1977), Table C-1, p. 93.

In comparison, the reduction for these workers during the following 25 years was minor even when increased holidays and vacations are taken into account. In fact, several industries recorded small increases in hours worked per week during this period. It appears, therefore, that during the past few decades, there has been little public support for further reductions in total working hours. Though there were minor fluctuations in average working time since the 1940s and early 1950s, these movements were around a 40-hour workweek.

Today, it is uncertain whether this stability in average weekly work hours will continue. While the long-term trend toward shorter hours has been interrupted in the post-World-War-II era, many of the social, demographic, and economic forces maintaining the standard workweek are weakening. With birth rates declining dramatically, educational attainment rising, productivity still increasing, and younger workers tending to prefer more leisure to additional income, renewed interest is being expressed in nonconventional patterns of working time. Whether these forces will result in strong pressure for reduced work time remains to be seen. Yet some change in this direction appears inevitable considering the abnormal short-term pattern of workers taking only 8 percent of the rise in productivity in the form of increased leisure time. The 12 extra paid days-off for each worker recently won by the United Auto Workers (UAW) for its Ford Motor Company employees indicates that such a tilt will probably occur. At the very least, new demands will emerge for greater flexibility in the arrangement of work and nonwork time. Moreover, as workers become more concerned with the quality of their leisure, as incomes rise and the number of wives in the labor market increases, and as more families exceed some minimum acceptable standards for the quality of life (inflation permitting), income considerations may be less dominant in decisions concerning the allocation of future increases in productivity between leisure and consumption. We should, therefore, anticipate "more striving for individual fulfillment in attractive ways that require more free time than income" (Glickman and Brown 1974, p. 2).

EMERGENCE OF THE FOUR-DAY WORKWEEK

The four-day, 40-hour workweek was selected for examination principally because of its immediacy and potential pervasiveness in the United States and Canada. This is the nonconventional work schedule most commonly adopted to date. As a result, it is the workweek experiment most readily accessible for evaluation. More importantly, it is the nonconventional schedule most likely to affect significantly the course of manpower planning (in the broadest sense of the term) for years to come.*

The four-day workweek is a recent work-scheduling phenomenon. While a few firms experimented with this arrangement of work time soon after the end of World War II, with the exception of the fuel oil and gasoline delivery truck drivers mentioned previously, these efforts were either of short duration or, as for Reader's Digest employees, seasonal in nature. As recently as seven years ago there were

---

*At least two other nonconventional work schedules, flexi-time and variable time, show signs of increasing popularity. To date, however, their growth has been limited mostly to North American subsidiaries of European firms. In Germany and Switzerland, these schedules have a wide following, while compacted work schedules such as the three- and four-day week are almost unknown.

only an estimated 40 companies and 7,000 workers on a weekly work schedule of four ten-hour days (Moore and Hedges 1971). By and large, these firms were small (under 500 employees), nonunion, non-urban, manufacturing concerns. Their primary interest in the schedule was as a mechanism for improving morale or for attracting higher-quality labor.

Since then, worker pressure and innovations in management practices have stimulated the drive for alterations in the configuration of hours and days worked. With increasing frequency, work-schedule changes are being used as strategies for problem solving (Hedges 1975). Scheduling by objective, for example, where the aim is to improve the functioning of the firm, may often result in the adoption of work schedules at variance with the standard workweek.* Whatever the specific objective, this problem-solving approach led, in the early 1970s, to the introduction of flexi-time and variable schedules. It also fueled the drive for schedules providing larger blocks of leisure. Employee problems with their work, inconvenient schedules, and excessive hours led to a further heightening of interest in these compacted workweeks.

The results were predictable. Larger, urban, unionized organizations such as banks, hospitals, municipalities, retailers, and insurance companies started adopting the four-day workweek. News-week magazine (August 23, 1971) estimated that as of mid-1971, over 500 American firms had switched to some variant of the 4/40 schedule. A year later, it was calculated that the figure had grown to approximately 2,000 companies, covering one out of every 840 workers (Wheeler, Gurman, Tarnowieski 1972). In 1973, the number of four-day firms was placed at closer to 3,000 (La Velle 1973). By May 1974, about 650,000 full-time wage and salary employees usually worked such a schedule (compared to 575,000 employees the previous year). When all full-time, nonfarm employees who regularly worked less than five full days a week are combined, they totaled around 1.1 million people or slightly less than 2 percent of the total number of full-time wage and salary employees (Hedges 1975). While this is a far cry from the revolution in working time expected several years ago (Poor 1970), it does indicate a growing interest in nonconven-

---

*Examples of objectives that could affect work hours would be (1) adjusting the flow of man-hours to match peak workloads, (2) increasing the utilization of plant and equipment, (3) improving customer service, (4) improving recruitment, (5) lowering absentee rates, (6) reducing turnover, or (7) raising worker morale and job satisfaction.

tional schedules, particularly in the four-day workweek.* Indeed, the Wall Street Journal (February 16, 1977, p. 1) estimates there may now be as many as 10,000 firms on this schedule.

Prospects and Obstacles

There exist several factors that bode well for the continued growth of the four-day work schedule. For one, 35 to 40 percent of the labor force is readily convertible to a compacted schedule (Nash 1970). It has also been suggested that much of American industry might be forced to adopt such a schedule either to enable the urban areas to comply with new federal pollution regulations, to reduce traffic congestion, to cope with the energy shortage, or to "share the work" in the event of a sustained downturn of the economy. Several cities—New York and Houston, for example—have already suggested to firms within their jurisdiction that they should consider adopting a four-day workweek.

The American Management Association has predicted that by the early 1980s, many, perhaps the majority, of American workers will be on a four-day or otherwise shortened workweek (Morse 1972). Significantly, the 1976 contract agreement between the Ford Motor Company and the UAW provided these workers with a potentially precedent-setting 12 extra paid days-off. The electrical, steel, and railway unions have already indicated their intention to demand shorter working hours for their members. For its part, the UAW has warned several times that the four-day workweek (but with less than a ten-hour day) will be high on its list of future contract priorities. Government interest in the four-day workweek has also showed signs of heightening. Legislation was introduced in Congress that would allow federal workers to experiment with both the four-day week and flexible daily schedules (that is, variable start-up and quitting times). This could ultimately affect 2.8 million workers. President Jimmy Carter recently suggested that government agencies and private industry temporarily adopt the four-day workweek to reduce natural gas consumption.

Despite its impressive growth potential, the future of the four-day workweek remains uncertain. Several major obstacles need to be overcome before more than marginal additional growth can occur. The first of these is legal. Several pieces of federal legislation cur-

---

*Flexi-time and variable schedules likewise show noticeable growth. To date, however, their acceptance has been largely confined to American subsidiaries of European firms.

rently exist that prevent millions of workers from shifting to this schedule. Both the Contract Work Hours and Safety Standards Act and the Walsh-Healey Public Contracts Act require premium pay for all work done after eight hours of labor each day for employees of all firms holding government contracts in excess of $10,000. The Federal Pay Act has a similar provision.* While some congressional committee discussions concerning the limitations that these acts impose on the further spread of the four-day workweek have taken place, little has come of them. The Department of Labor felt at the time that there was insufficient evidence to warrant recommending changes in these statutes to permit employers to adopt four-day workweeks involving more than eight hours of work a day without paying overtime (Federal Register, March 15, 1972, p. 5416).

The second obstacle is the opposition of organized labor to the 4/40 schedule. Though labor views increasing the amount of free time as one of its primary goals (Meany 1957), it nonetheless sees the ten-hour day as a regressive step. Speaking at a Labor Department hearing on adoption of a four-day, 40-hour workweek, an AFL-CIO economist stated labor's basic position:

> Organized labor has been the pioneer and the driving force in the reduction of working hours. We support the shorter workweek and shorter workday. We support labor-management efforts to reschedule working hours, through collective bargaining. But we are adamantly opposed to stretching out the workday and nullifying the eight-hour standard (Oswald 1971, quoted in Glickman and Brown 1974, p. 19).

It is a matter of principle; workers fought hard to reduce the workday and fear that the 4/40 schedule may be yet another attempt by employers to exploit them. There are grounds for these fears.

In general, it is management that suggests conversion to a four-day week. Indeed, it is not unusual for the decision to be presented to employees as a fait accompli (Poor 1970). Though the change may be, in part, undertaken for humanitarian reasons, any benefit accruing to employees from such a switch has often been a minor consideration. Depending upon the specific target, scheduling by objective can result

---

*Public Law 87-581, August 13, 1962; Public Law 74-846, June 30, 1936; and United States Code, Title 5, Chapter 61, respectively. Also relevant is the amended Fair Labor Standards Act (Public Law 93-259, April 18, 1974), which requires that employees involved in interstate commerce and in public administration be paid overtime for all work exceeding 40 hours a week.

in an arrangement of work and leisure time beneficial to the firm but detrimental to the employees. For example, a ten-hour day is one way to rationalize the use of equipment (for example, gasoline trucks that can be emptied in five hours of deliveries), thereby minimizing the need for overtime. Paradoxically, the four-day schedule can also be utilized as an insidious form of worker manipulation, designed to induce employees to work on their extra day-off as a way to fill time. This would negate the necessity to hire and train additional people. Whatever the reasons, organized labor perceives few benefits to be derived from relaxation of the eight-hour standard. One consequence has been their opposition to the proposed amendments to the Walsh-Healey Act and Contract Work Act. They have also supported a bill that would have amended the Fair Labor Standards Act to require premium pay after eight hours' work a day as for all work in excess of 40 hours a week. Forty-five million workers are covered under this act.

Perhaps the most serious barrier to widespread conversion to the four-day workweek is the attitude and position taken by many in the ranks of management. There are at least two often-stated reasons for their hesitation in adopting this schedule. First, many employers fear that the 4/40 week is but a wedge in the door to subsequent labor demands for shorter workweeks rather than rearranged working hours. They can point, for example, to UAW statements affirming a commitment to obtaining a four-day, 32-hour week. In addition to possible scheduling difficulties, management is concerned with potential increases in the cost of labor relative to gains in productivity that could result from adoption of shorter work hours. Assuming that take-home pay remained constant while work hours decreased, the bulk of the anticipated rise in productivity would have to be absorbed by the increase in hourly wage rates. History has shown, however, that under conditions of full employment (which is a major reason for labor's advocacy of shorter hours), unions are seldom satisfied with just maintaining real earnings. Few unions have been willing to delay wage increases in favor of reduced hours (Levitan and Belous 1977).

A second reason for management's opposition to shorter hours and nonconventional work schedules is that firms most readily convertible to a four-day week are those that are highly labor-intensive. For many companies, however, the nature and requirements of their productive processes—such as the need for continuous operation, heavy capital investment, and other special situations—create nearly insurmountable obstacles. Thus, while large, labor-intensive organizations—such as hospitals, insurance companies, and retail firms— are now experimenting with alternate work schedules, vast sectors of the economy must of necessity remain spectators. Due to the often staggering capital costs concomitant with their initiating a radical change in the hours of work, conversion to a compacted work schedule will await the accumulation of ample evidence as to the sagacity of this move.

Challenge to the Individual

The reallocation of time to work and nonwork is an act that speaks directly to the current uncertainty surrounding the meaning and place of work itself. By reordering the hours of labor and leisure, nonconventional schedules attempt to harmonize better the imperatives of society's productive processes with emerging life-styles. But in the course of liberating the individual from work's drudgery, they may place him in new contexts and force him to confront novel sets of behavioral demands. The individual's ability to adjust to these contexts will influence his general attitude toward his leisure. His ability to cope with these demands could affect his overall mental health (Linden 1958; American Psychiatric Association 1967).

Larger blocks of free time force the individual to make adjustments in his habitual pattern of behavior. At the very least, they create a time vacuum that must be filled. The person may try to expand the time he spends in activities that are already familiar. So long as he has access to resources and facilities that make this mode of adaptation possible, mental health is not threatened. In many cases, however, a more active form of adjustment may be required due to the new schedule's impact on the person's established hierarchy of values. Relatively dormant motivations may awaken, or new ones may come into play. For instance, the individual may develop an urge to take up vegetable gardening so as to beat inflation. While the activity may be relatively foreign to him, it is one made desirable by the economy and made easier by more functionally arranged time-off. As before, the success of his adjustment depends, at least in part, upon accessibility to requisite resources.

Another likely consequence of nonconventional work schedules is that a new set of behavioral demands may be directed at the individual by relevant others. A wife may now expect her husband to help out around the house and to become more involved with the children; his peers may encourage him to participate in civic affairs. While some of these activities are intrinsically satisfying to the individual, others are not. To the extent that participation is extrinsically motivated (that is, the desired rewards, such as prestige and esteem, are mediated by persons other than the focal person), the individual's satisfaction with his free time is dependent upon his doing things that others value. His happiness is thereby held hostage to his ability to meet their demands. Failure to live up to others' expectations may induce his wife to withhold her affection or cause his friends to lose respect. During periods of person-environment instability, such as may occur when one's routine is disrupted by new blocks of discretionary time, the contingent nature of extrinsic gratifications has the result that their attainment becomes increasingly variable and increasingly less predictable. Ironically, it is during just such times as these that solid social support and a steady supply of valued gratifications are most needed.

In an attempt to reestablish a measure of environmental certainty, the individual will generate his own set of demands for goods and services, both public and private. The degree to which these resources are accessible will help determine both his success in meeting the behavioral demands of others and his own level of satisfaction with his free time. If the needed resources are available, the individual should experience little difficulty in adjusting, provided that the demands made upon him are not abhorrent. On the other hand, if he lacks access to requisite goods and services, he may be unable to meet the expectations of those around him, which, in turn, could result in extrinsic gratifications being withheld. If the demands made by others are important to them, if the gratifications withheld are salient to the individual being denied, and if he cannot effectively remove himself from that setting, then his relationships with these others will eventually suffer. Unassisted, such a situation may cause the individual to adjust poorly to his new work-leisure schedule, leading to psychological stress and a decrease in general satisfaction with life.

It may be argued that most people who have switched to a non-conventional work-leisure schedule have, in fact, had little or no difficulty gaining access to needed resources, much less experienced severe adjustment difficulties or suffered psychologically. In their study of four-day workers, Nord and Costigan (1973) found that 80-85 percent did not report any difficulties adjusting to the new schedule. So, the present concern is, clearly, with a minority of workers—but a substantial and socially significant minority—those for whom novel arrangements of free time constitute a real problem.

Also to be considered is the fact that the number of people working nonconventional schedules remains quite small. The probability exists that as the number of firms adopting a shorter workweek grows, the number of individuals experiencing adjustment difficulties will grow apace. Further, a proliferation of these schedules would exert increasing pressure upon existing public and private resources. If demands for needed goods and services outrun the supply, the ranks of the potentially maladjusted can only be enlarged.

The common thread in this discussion is that increased free time, however organized, will almost inevitably require the development of leisure-related goods, services, and facilities. If individuals are to make the most of their nonwork time, to use leisure in a manner both wise and satisfying, assistance is necessary. We can no longer hope successfully to go it alone—for many of the activities we wish to engage in and, more generally, the quality of life and lifestyles we aspire to, are beyond the capacity of individual resources. The challenge of leisure is, therefore, quite clear: We must create new cultural mechanisms and social institutions adequate to cope with present and future problems arising out of growing amounts of leisure.

THE STUDY

Prospects are quite strong that a significant percentage of Canadian and American workers will soon be adopting novel work schedules, which necessitate adaptive adjustments in all their life domains. This study was designed to investigate selected responses of male, blue-collar workers currently on an official workweek of four ten-hour days. While this schedule's impact is explored in several life domains, the emphasis here is on the adjustments these men have made in their nonwork, primarily in their family, spheres of life.

A Study of Male Blue-Collar Workers

Male blue-collar employees were chosen for examination first because their occupations are so organized and located in the work system as to make them most readily convertible to a four-day or otherwise compressed work schedule. The second reason for selecing blue-collar workers is that several studies have shown their mental health to be worse than that of many other groups in society (Kornhauser 1965). Assembly-line workers, followed closely by occupants of other tedious jobs such as fork-lift operators, tool and die makers, and train dispatchers, reported not only the greatest boredom and job dissatisfaction, but also had the highest levels of anxiety, depression, irritation, and psychosomatic disorders (Caplan et al. 1975). Considering that a principal motivator behind the drive for nonconventional work schedule is the desire to provide workers with some relief from job-related stresses that imperil their mental health, it is essential that the effectiveness of this approach be examined.

The third reason for choosing male blue-collar workers is that many social scientists and social commentators believe these individuals to be among the least prepared to take advantage of increased free time (Dumazedier 1967; Schlesinger 1971). Nonconventional work schedules place the worker in new contexts that confront him with

novel problems. His ability to convert free time into genuinely satisfying leisure depends on his capacity to cope effectively with the situation before him. This capacity, however, is influenced by whether he
has the necessary resources available and can use them creatively,
whether his behavior pattern is not overly specialized, and whether
he has already mastered a wide variety of challenging problems. It is
the presence of just these factors among blue-collar workers that is
often questioned. Even if they have the basic material resources, so
the argument goes, they constitute the group least trained by education and environment to display their resources in a flexible and effective manner. If nothing else, these men tend to lack the repertoire
of diverse behavior patterns and social experience believed vital to
making either a satisfactory adjustment to leisure or a creative use
of free time. While an examination of the objective quality of blue-
collar workers' use of free time is beyond the scope of this study, an
attempt is made to measure their subjective adjustment to their four-
day workweek.

The fourth, and final, reason for selecting blue-collar workers
is more macroscopic in nature. Though workers located in different
social classes and/or belonging to different occupational groups face
their own unique sets of work-leisure problems, to the extent that
blue-collar workers constitute an underprivileged class with respect
to leisure, they should also provide us with clues as to the nature and
extent of the leisure problems before us.

Adjustment in the Family Setting

A major interest in this study is with individual adjustment to
the four-day workweek in the family context. While the relative merits
of eight-hour days versus three-day weekends have been debated from
several perspectives, the family perspective, though often raised, has
usually been given short shrift. This oversight is regrettable.

In their excellent study on shift work, Mott et al. (1965) found
that working the afternoon or night shift rendered the husband and
father roles more difficult to carry out. Though information is scarce,
there are indications that nonconventional work schedules have also
proved to be disruptive. A case in point is the 200 pharmaceutical
workers studied by Nord and Costigan (1973). In this, the only analytic
study undertaken to date with substantial longitudinal data, the researchers found that, after one-year experience with a four-day, 40-
hour schedule, workers with children living at home tended to see unfavorable consequences for their family life. Moreover, the proportion of negative reports on homelife increased significantly with time,
particularly among the male employees. Both Swados (1958) and

Meyersohn (1963) have pointed to boredom with the extra time spent at home as one of the negative consequences attendant to the nonconventional work schedules they examined.

Despite this potential for causing harm outside the work place—a conclusion reachable on logical if not yet empirical grounds—few systematic studies have seriously concerned themselves with the impact of nonconventional work schedules on the individual's nonwork life. Those that do usually offer minimal insight into what transpires in the family context.* They provide little in the way of solid evidence, or even educated guesswork, as to the extent of family disruption caused by these schedules, their severity, the types of families comprising the high-risk group, or the dynamics by which families come to suffer. Still unknown is whether the individual's adaptive processes are hindered or helped by differing patterns of family interaction and organization. It is not even known whether the difficulties the individual encounters in the family setting are, in fact, primarily due to the nature of the dynamics inherent to that setting. Several researchers have found, for example, that a favorable attitude toward one's experience with a nonconventional work schedule correlates positively with aspects of the individual's personality—his willingness and ability to plan his leisure, his ability to follow through on these plans (Meyersohn 1963; Swados 1958), and whether these plans tend to be task or recreation oriented (Nord and Costigan 1973).[†]

This failure to investigate the ramifications of alternate work-leisure arrangements within the family setting is noteworthy. It is quite probable that the adjustment the individual makes in this context, and the satisfactions he derives from it, will be major determinants of the long-run viability of nonconventional work schedules. This is especially true for relatively inflexible (compacted) schedules like the four-day week. Indeed, the need for research into this schedule's impact in the family setting has increased now that several studies indicate its effect within the work setting to be generally marginal and usually short-run.[††]

---

*In fact, scant research exists that seriously combines work (nonconventional or otherwise) and family life into a comprehensive whole. As Kasl (1974) notes, "research on work and the family has been quite segregated, and, indeed, it is quite rare to find a study that focuses on more than one role, . . . and the modest, positive correlations made by these studies are not very illuminating" (p. 187).

[†]Other factors so far implicated as affecting individual adjustment within the family, but not subject to its control, are age, regional location of the family (Wilson 1971), and occupational status (Nord and Costigan 1973).

[††]Wheeler, Gurman, Tarnowieski (1972) found that many managers anticiapted an improvement in productivity upon conversion to

The family context is viewed as important here for at least four reasons. The first and most basic of these is that people who are happy in their marriage and family life tend to be happy in general (Gurin, Veroff, Feld 1960). It has long been known that a positive relationship exists between marital happiness and the use of leisure time in the United States (Benson 1952; Burgess and Wallin 1953) and that this relationship is stronger for working husbands than for wives (Gerson 1960). By changing the hours of labor, the four-day workweek may cause the family to reorganize its leisure time, affect the satisfactions its members derive from it, and, possibly, influence the quality of their interpersonal relationships. Therefore, an evaluation of a novel work-leisure schedule that fails to take into consideration its ramifications within the family setting ignores potentially significant social consequences.

A second closely related reason for focusing upon the family is that, in both American and Canadian society, the conjugal and parental roles are perceived to be highly significant sources of personal joy and distress (Veroff and Feld 1970). With the possible exception of the work place, the family setting is the most salient one in the lives of most men. It is not surprising, therefore, to find that the majority of married men desire to spend most of their free time with their family (de Grazia 1964). This being the case, we would anticipate the family setting to be the one within which many, if not most, of the major ramifications consequent to a change in work-leisure patterns appear. Even if the family is not itself the source of the individual's adjustment difffculties, more than likely it is within this setting that his problem will become evident. Chrysler's recent experiment with the four-day workweek was discontinued in part because, when the summer vacation period came to an end and children returned to school, the primary benefits the family derived from this schedule ended (Detroit Free Press, September 21, 1974). The trade-off between the joy of a three-day weekend at home with the family and the additional strain engendered by this schedule on the job began to work to the Chrysler employee's disadvantage.

The third reason lies in the fact that, more frequently than is true of other social institutions, the family is capable of adapting its structure and activities to fit new environmental situations. It thus mediates between the changing goals and demands of society and the ongoing socialization/adjustment process of all family members (Vincent 1966). During periods of rapid sociocultural change, people tend

---

a four-day workweek. Only 3 percent reported a decline. They also reported a decline in absenteeism. Other studies, however, found that both productivity and absenteeism returned to normal, or near normal, levels after the novelty of the new schedule wore off—for example, see Conference Board in Canada (1973).

to become somewhat disoriented; they begin to lose sight of where
they are in social space. Ackerman (1958, p. 112) describes one
implication of this trend toward disorientation for the individual and
his family:

> One effect of this trend towards disorientation is that each
> person is thrown back upon his family group for restora-
> tion of a sense of security, belongingness, dignity and
> worth. The family is called upon to make up to its individ-
> ual members in affection and closeness for the anxiety
> and distress that is the result of failure to find a safe
> place in the wider world. Individuals pitch themselves
> back on their families for reassurances as to their lovable-
> ness and worth.

Being at variance with the standard mode, nonconventional schedules
like the four-day workweek may add to the individual's feelings of insecurity. The family's willingness and ability to provide him with the
assurances he needs could play an important role in preventing any
resultant breakdown. To the extent it does, the family plays an important role in determining both his attitude and the quality of his
adjustment to his nonconventional schedule.

The fourth reason for emphasizing the family is that it constitutes the major tension-management mechanism in our society (Hawkins 1968). The family is the individual's primary problem-solving
group (Hill 1949; Tallman 1970). Howard and Scott (1965) hypothesize
that in a given population, the degree of deviation (such as crime and
alienation) will correlate directly with the degree to which the problems confronting the people remain unresolved and the degree to
which legitimate means of relieving tension are blocked. If an environmental event, such as conversion to a four-day workweek, should
sufficiently disrupt the family's coping capacity by overloading its
problem-solving function beyond some critical threshold, then an
important mechanism for social integration could be put into serious
disarray. If the marriage partners should find themselves unable to
rectify this breakdown over an extended period of time, then the
central feature of their social and emotional life—their marriage—
may be jeopardized. This, in turn, could impair the individual's
capacity for maintaining satisfactory relations with his children
and others outside the family (Renne 1970). Consequently, the family's
patterns of internal organization, and the ability of its members to
provide mutual support during periods of disequilibrium, could play
an important role in determining both the worker's response to his
four-day work schedule and the long-run viability of that schedule.

SUMMARY

Widespread adoption of the four-day or some otherwise shortened workweek is not unlikely in the near future. These nonconventional work schedules create large amounts of free time, thereby constituting social events with the potential for dramatically affecting the lives of many individuals and the character of society at large. It is time, therefore, for the work-leisure controversy to be moved out of the realm of speculation and uncoordinated experimentation. We need to do more than just contemplate the coming situation; it is now time to commence planning for its arrival.

Two major planning problems emerge from new possibilities for work-leisure scheduling: (1) problems of individual adjustment to the new time schedule and (2) problems of gaining a measure of control over the sociocultural impacts. This study is directed toward the first of these problems. It describes the responses of individual men to a four-day work schedule, concentrating on specific adjustments in both their working and nonworking lives. The goal is to assist in the determination of whether alternate work-leisure schedules, like the four-day workweek, do indeed constitute social innovations of concern, to uncover some of the problems these schedules raise, and to aid in the identification of high-risk individuals, families, and environments. Thus, the book attempts to provide information of interest and value to planners, policy makers, social scientists, and others. This is particularly true with respect to the four-day workweek. Once such information becomes available, effective action can be initiated.

In order to plan for the future, it is first necessary to understand where one is and where one has been. "To enter the realm of the future," wrote Eric Hoffer, "is like entering a foreign country; one must have a passport, and one must be able to provide a detailed record of one's past" (1955, p. 48). Before we proceed to the specifics of the study, it is necessary to understand the historical relationship between work and leisure in advanced industrial societies, for both work and leisure—singly and interactively—will long continue, as in the past, to influence the form of our society and the quality of lives we live as individuals and family members.

CHAPTER

2

THE FOUR-DAY WEEK IN THE CONTEXT OF CONTEMPORARY WORK AND LEISURE

We do not live to work!

(Union Fighting Slogan)

The four-day workweek is an experiment in the scheduling of work that was all but unthinkable a few short years ago. It is an innovation made possible by dramatic changes in the norms and structures of work. Of equal, if not greater, significance, it is an innovation in the allocation of time for work and leisure made desirable by profound changes in cultural values. Two questions immediately present themselves. What will man in advanced industrial society do with this new arrangement of time? Perhaps of more importance, what will this new arrangement of work and leisure time do to man? The answers to both questions lie ultimately in the nature of the existing culture, and in the readiness of the people to undergo a period of cultural transformation.

"Culture," asserts Daniel Bell, "has been given a blank check and its primacy in generating social change has been firmly established" (1970, p. 18). In modern society, culture leads the process of social evolution; the social structure lags behind (Tiryakian 1967). As people have become wealthier, better educated, more mobile, and so on, their demands and life-style expectations have expanded. They have become increasingly sensitive to the wide range of opportunities in leisure time opening up before them. Inevitably their "way of life," or culture, changes too. On the other hand, the behavioral demands and normative expectations of the social structure have remained relatively stable. Preparing people for, and maintaining them in, work continues to be the guiding principle of most of our social institutions. The result is a growing schism between the society's social structure and its culture. Fundamental norms of the former are coming into ever sharper conflict with the emerging values of the latter. Speaking directly to this mounting culture-structure cleavage in the advanced capitalist state, Bell goes on to write (pp. 18-19):

> The social structure is ruled by an economic principle of rationality defined in terms of efficiency in the allocation of resources; the culture, in contrast, is prodigal, promiscuous, dominated by an anti-rational, anti-intellectual temper. The character structure inherited from the nineteenth century—with its emphasis on self-discipline, delayed gratification, restraint—is still relevant to the demands of the social structure; but it clashes sharply with the culture, where such bourgeois values have been completely rejected.

To be sure, Bell's characterization of the current status of bourgeois values could be challenged.* Nevertheless, all but the most casual of observations would bear out his central point; advanced industrial societies are experiencing an increasingly serious conflict between deeply rooted normative expectations integral to the social structure and a set of emerging sociocultural values evolving at variance with established ideology. To many, this cleavage signifies more than a condition of environmental and individual instability; it points to a shift, possibly a revolution, in individual and societal orientation.

> There is a revolution coming. It will not be like revolutions of the past. It will originate with the individual and with culture, and will change the political structure as its final act. It will not require violence to succeed, and it cannot be successfully resisted by violence. It is now spreading with amazing rapidity, and already our laws, institutions and social structures are changing in consequence. It produces higher reason, a more human community, and a new liberated individual. . . . It is both necessary and inevitable, and in time it will include not only youth but all the people in America (Reich 1970, p. 4).

---

*Indeed, many social analysts believe that our present inability to obtain satisfaction from our leisure—to use our leisure wisely—can be largely attributed to the penetration of such bourgeois personality characteristics as self-discipline and the need to feel productive into the realm of leisure.

While Reich's particular vision can be faulted on grounds of naive utopianism and excessive determinism, he is far from unique in his belief that society has entered a period of crisis, a time of cultural transformation, out of which there may arise, according to Bosserman (1971, p. 145), ". . . a new normative structure providing a new ordering of values, that is of the quality of being."

Can any predictions be made as to where our present condition may lead? Bosserman responds with a somewhat tentative affirmative. After reminding the reader that the "forces of fixity and persistence" are capable of stopping or diverting any process of social evolution, he adds what he believes to be a crucial, parallel aspect to Bell's analysis (p. 147):

> Culture is a way of life and leisure dominates the new culture. Leisure is becoming a way of life. To choose lifestyles implies having discretionary <u>income</u>, <u>time</u>, and hence <u>social behavior</u>. People—youth especially—increasingly want to be identified by their life-style and cultural tastes, rather than by occupation. Technology and scientific advances have made possible these three discretionary features. Their intersection is creating a new world perspective, a new consciousness, which is a hallmark of the "leisured society." . . . This is a new type of society.

Advanced industrial societies are thus in the process of creating a new social order, one governed by an increasingly leisure-dominated culture. Advancing technique* has democratized the distribution of

---

*All subsequent references to "technology" follow the lead provided by Jacques Ellul in his thought-provoking book <u>The Technological Society</u> (1964). He uses the word "technique" to make clear that his definition of technology encompasses far more than mere machinery. "It must be emphasized that, at present, technique is applied outside industrial life. The growth of its power today has no relationship to the growing use of the machine. . . . The machine is now not even the most important aspect of technique (although it is perhaps the most spectacular); technique has taken over all of man's activities, not just his productive activity" (p. 4).

Technique is an ensemble of means directed toward the goal of economizing. A technical operation, therefore, "includes every operation carried out in concordance with a certain method in order to attain a particular end. . . . In every case it is the method which characterizes the operation. . . . What characterizes the technical action within a particular activity is the search for greater efficiency" (pp. 19-20).

leisure to the point where a "leisured class," as defined by Veblen (1973), is almost nonexistent. Instead, both the time and material prerequisites for leisure are now available to workers of all classes in unprecedented numbers. So dramatically has technology altered the situation that in some occupations, retirement, education, vacations, holidays, and weekends now account, as a part of one's lifetime, for as much as or more than the time spent on the job. Moreover, the current trend toward automated production and extraction and the shift toward a service economy have often been cited as precursors to additional leisure yet to come (Brown 1971; Owen 1970).

Referring to the ubiquitous influence of modern technology on the hopes and aspirations of men, Kaplan states that "the new physical forces . . . provide man with new potentials for access to the goals he desires. The term leisure is a shortened way of viewing the new potentials" (1971, p. 24). Never before has the possibility for individual growth and well-being been as great as now. Never before has an opportunity for the development of a more truly humane society been as real.

Yet, for all the optimism expressed in Kaplan's statement, the key word here is potential. Man's environment has never been as unstable, and the infusion of additional leisure may serve only to exacerbate this instability. In an article concerned with the implications of increased leisure in the technotronic age, Schlesinger writes:

> The high technology has . . . wrought formidable changes
> in social organization, in social anxiety, human perception,
> and in the character of work. In particular, it has bestowed
> on man the astonishing gift of unprecedented amounts of
> free time; and it has done so at just the moment when man
> is intimidated and overwhelmed by the great organization,
> anxiety, and is in a time of transition in the way he im-
> poses his structure on his experience (1971, pp. 74-75).

Few settings remain wherein a person can securely maintain individual equilibrium—paradoxically for a work-centered social structure, perhaps least of all in his work. The routines and rhythms long associated with work derive from customs, beliefs, and conditions that are changing or disappearing altogether. The values adhering to work,

---

Under this definition, "organization," or what James Burnham (1941) called "managerial action," is technique applied to social, economic, and administrative life. Similarly, planning, whether it be disjointed incrementalism or long-range social planning, is also an example of technique and technical action.

which at one time provided a solid foundation for individual self-validation, have been seriously undermined, leaving many men and women adrift and disoriented.

Out of individual uncertainty and social instability may emerge a new society of high potential—a leisure society. Nothing, however, is less certain than the quality of the resultant culture. There is little in the shape of things today that makes self-evident the emergence of a more humane society tomorrow, one characterized by a new consciousness of a higher morality. For as Dumazedier reminds us: ". . . Leisure is a part of time made free by the growth of the productive forces, and is oriented towards rest, enjoyment, and improvement of the individual, and as an end in itself" (1971, p. 211). Leisure, therefore, has no inherent value; it is but the temporal framework for its cultural content, and that content is determined by the already existing standards, capabilities, knowledge, experience, and values of its creators. A new social order emerges only partially formed, still subject to the influence of its parent culture. And work, not leisure, is the core about which advanced industrial society and its culture revolve. Do we not often hear that the content and quality of our lives reflect the attitudes we hold with respect to work and the nature of our efforts to escape from it? Are we not often told that the decline of the work ethic is, if not actually responsible for it, the obverse of our growing interest in leisure? If the goals of men and women are, therefore, ever to be realized, then when we consider the potential inherent in leisure, we must reckon with the nature of modern labor and with the uncertainty and insecurity of life today.

This position is a classic in the study of leisure. It has most assuredly influenced those men and women behind the drive for nonconventional work schedules. If contemporary life is problematic and if a principal source of the difficulty lies in the work setting, then a logical approach to overcoming the abuses of modern labor is one that, whenever possible, liberates the individual from those detrimental normative and behavioral constraints inherent in our work-dominated social structure. The four-day workweek, with its longer, more functionally arranged blocks of free time accompanied by no decrease in take-home pay, represents just such an approach. It simultaneously maintains the worker's base of financial security while freeing him to participate more fully in the emerging leisure-dominated culture. Given these advantages, this work-leisure schedule should, at first glance, enhance the quality and happiness of the individual's life.

Proponents of the four-day schedule recognize the necessity of confronting the nature of work as a source of individual and societal disequilibrium. Their recognition that nonwork settings are increasingly salient sources of valued gratifications is an important first step toward the creation of a more humane society. But is it sufficient? Is it really logical to expect a basically passive approach to the problems of work to alter meaningfully the underlying relationships among work and leisure values and thereby bring about a transformation of the quality of life in postindustrial society? To answer these questions, we must first examine the nature of work under conditions of advancing technology to see if it does indeed constitute a serious social problem. We need then to determine whether removal from the work setting serves to liberate sufficiently the individual from its influence.

WORK AND ALIENATION

The Traditional Ethic of Work

I regard the five-day week as an unworthy ideal. More work and better work is a more inspiring and worthier motto than less work and more pay. . . . It is better not to trifle and tamper with God's laws.

(John E. Edgerton, president of the
National Association of Manufacturing, 1926)

Society has long tried to socialize the individual into believing that work is the socially acceptable and by far most satisfying long-run self-validating activity. Hard effort, diligence, and initiative, so the ethic goes, will pay off in social and economic advancement. Even Marx at first maintained that citizens of a communist state could become fully developed individuals in and through their work—individuals for whom, as he wrote in his Critique of the Gotha Programme, "productive labour is the first necessity of life" (quoted in Friedman 1964, p. 94). For their part, psychiatrists have long extolled work as a significant contributor to positive mental health:

Stressing the importance of work has a greater effect than any other technique of living in binding the individual more closely to reality; in his work he is at least securely attached to a point of reality, the human community. Work is no less valuable for the opportunity which it, and the human relations connected with it, provide for a very considerable discharge of fundamental libidinal impulses, narcissistic, aggressive and even erotic, than because it is indispensable for subsistence and justifies existences in society (Freud, quoted in Friedman 1964, p. 126).

Leisure, on the other hand, is something that has to be earned and re-earned.

> Seen as play for the child, recreation for the adult, and retirement for the old, both child and adult have to earn their rights—the child by growing and learning, the adult by working. Unearned leisure is something which will have to be paid for later. It comes under the heading of vice—where the pleasure comes first and the pain afterwards—instead of virtue, where the pain or work precedes the reward (Mead 1957, p. 11).

Clearly, then, men and women have been taught to value labor more than leisure and to view work as more than a mere necessity for individual survival. Rather, work, seriously undertaken and honestly done, is the essential activity of "moral" men and women. It gives meaning to their lives, a feeling of control over their destiny, and leads to a growing sense of social solidarity. Work is what distinguishes men from animals and lets them know that they are truly alive.

Yet the experience of working men and women has long run counter to these normative expectations. The social structure's promise of a "just reward" in return for one's labor has repeatedly failed to materialize. Advances in technique have remade the face of work; the work place has been totally redesigned, with tasks being reorganized in a manner necessitating a complete restructuring of the relationship between the individual worker and his tools, his product, and his cohorts. Technology's demand for ever greater efficiency in the allocation and utilization of manpower and material resources has led to a division of labor that specializes far beyond that required for a "functional" breakdown of work activity. All too often the drive for efficiency and technical rationality in production, transportation, and the servicing of goods and people in a market economy has crowded out concern for the costs that the system imposes on the men and women responsible for its continued smooth functioning. Social commentators have long been aware of the potential for harm in excessive specialization. Observing the growing demoralization of nineteenth-century English textile workers, Engels wrote a passage that has been re-echoed by Marxists, liberals, and conservatives alike:

> Nothing is more terrible than being constrained to do some one thing every day from morning until night against one's will. And the more a man the worker feels himself, the more hateful must his work be to him, because he feels the constraint, the aimlessness of it for himself. Why does

he work? For love of work? From a natural impulse?
Not at all! He works for money, for a thing which has
nothing whatsoever to do with the work itself. . . .
The division of labor has multiplied the brutalizing influences of forced work. In most branches the worker's
activity is reduced to some paltry, purely mechanical
manipulation, repeated minute after minute, unchanged
year after year (quoted in Wilensky 1969, p. 111).

The Division of Labor and Marx's Alienated Worker

Marx* saw the growing division of labor in industrial society as
causing estrangement of the worker from the product of his labor,
from the act of producing, and consequently, from himself.

On the worker's alienation from his product, Marx starts with
the premise that "the direct relationship of labour to its produce is
the relationship of the worker to the object of his production" (p. 99).
The central fact of this relationship is that the division of labor has
specialized the worker to the point where he has lost all knowledge as
to the essence of his product. Instead, the object of labor appears
before him "as something alien, as a power independent of the pro-
ducer" (p. 97). But the worker's estrangement from the product of his
labor is only one, and perhaps a less serious, aspect of the alienation
of labor. More damaging is the estrangement of the worker from the
act of production itself, and thus from his own humanity:

How would the worker come to face the product of his
activity as a stranger, were it not that in the very act
of production he was estranging himself from himself?
The product is after all but the summary of the activity,
of production. If then the product of labour is alienation,
production itself must be active alienation, the alienation
of activity, the activity of alienation. In the estrangement
of the object of labour is merely summarized the estrangement, the alienation, in the activity of labour itself (Marx
1969, p. 99).

Marx saw the skills and intelligence previously expressed by
craftsmen being built into the machines of the new factories. The
worker was thus left with jobs that were routine, monotonous, and

---

*Unless otherwise specified, Marx's quotes in this section are
from Friedman (1964). The page references refer to Friedman.

over which he had no control. Technology had come to dominate the worker, whose alienation was expressed in his relative powerlessness before it. Second, the division of labor produced jobs that were increasingly simple, diminished in responsibility, and requiring little or no understanding of the factory's total productive process. Work of this sort "fragmented the relation of the individual to his work [and] robbed him of a sense of purpose" (Blauner 1964, p. 3). Thus, to the alienation of powerlessness can be added that of meaninglessness. Last, due to his estrangement from his product, from the process of work, and, in a capitalist society, from the profits of his labor, little remained to motivate the worker to work with energy and intelligence. The worker is thus subjected to a third form of alienation, that of isolation from the system of production and from its goals.

As Marx saw it, the division of labor results in a lost sense of one's own humanity. The worker "no longer feels himself to be freely active in any but his animal functions . . . and in his human functions he no longer feels himself to be anything but an animal" (Marx 1969, p. 100). The worker is estranged from his body, from nature, and from that which constitutes his human aspect. He is also alienated from other men, their labor, and the objects of their labor. If this condition continued unchecked, Marx felt that a revolt of the proletariat would inevitably occur.

Marx at first believed that it was possible for the worker to become fully developed in and through his work. All that was needed was to provide him with both a theoretical and practical education and variety in his work. If this were done, it would "replace the detailed worker of today, crippled by life-long repetition of one and the same trivial occupation, and thus reduced to a mere fragment of a man, by the fully developed individual . . . to whom the different social functions he performs are but so many modes of giving free scope to his own natural and acquired powers" (Marx 1920, p. 494). Later on, however, Marx came to view the progressive division of labor, and the creation of increasingly specialized jobs, as an unalterable trend in industrial technology. Therefore, in his revision of the third volume of Das Kapital, he rejected work as a mechanism of human development. His emphasis shifted instead to that "realm of freedom" that, he declared, "only begins, in fact, where that labour, which is determined by need and external purposes, ceases," lying "outside the sphere of material production proper" (p. 94). In short, Marx came to view leisure, and not labor, as the principal source of hope for the full development of man.

The Division of Labor: Source of Solidarity or Anomie?

Like Marx, Emile Durkheim was quite aware of the disastrous effects of industrial specialization upon workers.

[The division of labor] has often been accused of degrading the individual by making him a machine. And truly, if he does not know whither the operations he performs are tending, if he relates them to no end, he can only continue to work through routine. Every day he repeats the same movements with monotonous regularity, but without being interested in them, and without understanding them. . . . He is no longer anything but an inert piece of machinery, only an external force set going which always moves in the same direction and in the same way. Surely, no matter how one may represent the moral ideal, one cannot remain indifferent to such debasement of human nature (1964, p. 371).

Durkheim, however, takes issue with the notion that this debasement of human nature is attributable to the division of labor per se. Rather, he argues that it is the result of external forces acting upon, and impeding, the normal evolution of the division of labor.

[The division of labor] does not produce these consequences because of a necessity of its own nature, but only in exceptional and abnormal circumstances. In order for it to develop without having such a disastrous influence on the human conscience, . . . it is sufficient for it to be itself, for nothing to come from without to denature it (1964, p. 372).

Durkheim saw the division of labor as essentially a source of social solidarity—if allowed to develop normally, the different interests and functions of a complex society operate smoothly and people experience a sense of moral solidarity. The "normal" division of labor "presumes that the worker, far from being hemmed in by his task, does not lose sight of his collaborators, that he acts upon them, and reacts to them" (1964, p. 372). Thus, Durkheim considered as pathological all forms of the division of labor that failed to realize this end.

In its "normal form," the different functions and interests are in harmony. When harmony is lacking, and the division of labor develops "abnormally," it is because these functions are improperly regulated. The division of labor is then "anomic." But this should occur only in exceptional cases for it implies a lack of coordination, an inadequate development of a system of rules and regulations for "determining the mutual relations of functions" (1964, p. 365). This could not occur naturally, for "in the normal state, these rules disengage themselves from the division of labour. They are a prolongation of it" (1964, p. 365). Thus for Durkheim, moral solidarity, rather than societal and individual disintegration, was the logical result of the division of labor.

Though Durkheim steadfastly maintained that the division of labor is a positive social force, he was aware of the potential for its abnormal forms to result in social turmoil. In Book 3 of the Division of Labour, he included among the most common abnormal forms those cases that have so enormously increased since his death.* In these chapters, he warns that "solidarity depends very greatly upon the functional activity of specialized parts. . . . Where functions languish, they are not well specialized, they are badly coordinated, and incompletely feel their mutual dependence" (1964, p. 390). Work must not be divided beyond what is necessary for efficient production and what is needed for worker satisfaction. If this principle is not adhered to, if "the work furnished is not only not considerable but even insufficient, it is natural that solidarity itself is not only less perfect, but becomes more and more completely faulty" (1964, p. 390). Eventually, "solidarity breaks down, incoherence and disorder make their appearance" (1964, p. 389).

While claiming that such an abnormality in the division of labor is exceptional, Durkheim shows that he is nevertheless willing to take the final step. Describing what for him must have been the ultimate travesty of normal social evolution, he wrote, "if no care is taken of them [the worker's tastes and aptitudes], if they are ceaselessly disturbed by our daily occupations, we shall suffer and seek a way to put an end to our suffering" (1964, p. 375). But if the division of labor is forced upon the worker, thereby providing him with little or no opportunity to obtain work better suited to his nature, then "there is no other way out than to change the established order and to set up a new one" (1964, p. 375).

Thus Durkheim, like Marx and Engels, viewed the emerging forms of the division of labor negatively. Like them, he saw in it the seeds of individual unhappiness and human debasement. If deflected too far from its normal course by external forces, it could lead to anomie on a massive scale, or even revolution. Whatever specific patterns the emerging forms of the division of labor might take, if they were not allowed to develop naturally, Durkheim viewed them with little optimism. Contemporary patterns would be, for Durkheim, "abnormal."

---

*Durkheim's inclusion of contemporary patterns of the division of labor among the "abnormal forms" is in part the result of his failure to consider the principles of technical rationality and efficiency as integral aspects of his doctrine. Had he done so, he would have realized that rationality and efficiency are part and parcel of the division of labor. They are what motivate technology to take on increasingly complex and special forms. Some authors see these principles as the prime motivators of all activity, human and otherwise (for example, see Ellul 1964).

The Contemporary Alienated Worker

Few students of American society still believe in the revolutionary potential of the working class. Yet, as Studs Terkel's (1974) conversations with workers make most evident, traditional images and present practices of labor often fail to meet the needs and expectations of today's better-educated worker. Even those jobs that may at one time have had the capacity to satisfy no longer do. Consequently, the belief that the modern social structure is anomic and that today's worker is alienated remains widespread.

In the modern context, alienation is viewed as a quality of personal experience that results from specific kinds of social organization.

> Alienation is a general syndrome made up of a number of different objective conditions and subjective feeling-states which emerge from certain relationships between workers and the sociotechnical settings of employment. Alienation exists when workers are unable to control their immediate work process, to develop a sense of purpose and function which connects their jobs to the overall organization of production, to belong to integrated industrial communities and when they fail to become involved in the activity of work as a mode of personal self-expression. In modern industrial employment, control, purpose, social integration and self-involvement are all problematic (Blauner 1964, p. 15).

Along with such writers as Fromm (1955) and Argyris (1957), Blauner assumes that the dignity and development of the individual is furthered by work that permits autonomy, responsibility, social connectedness, and self-actualization. Work that lacks these characteristics limits the fulfillment of potential and is, therefore, to be negatively valued. While recognizing that many contemporary jobs fall into this latter category, he nonetheless takes issue with the argument that leisure is a potential solution to the problems caused by work alienation and the decline of work as the central life interest for many workers. The leisure solution, he argues, underestimates the fact that work "remains the single most important life activity for most people, in terms of time and energy, and ignores the subtle ways in which the quality of one's worklife affects the quality of one's leisure, family relations, and basic self-feelings" (Blauner 1964, p. 183). For Blauner, the four-day workweek would not be an acceptable solution to the problems of work. Instead, he pins his hope on a restructuring of the work setting, and in particular, upon further automation. These, he claims, will result in "meaningful work in a more cohesive, integrated industrial climate" (1964, p. 182).

But are contemporary workers really alienated? Are there any indications that their alienation is increasing? In other words, are the complaints about the nature of work sufficiently widespread to constitute a serious social concern?

The extent of employee alienation today remains an open question. That it exists, however, would be difficult to refute. The symptoms and consequences of serious worker dissatisfaction can be observed throughout the work system. Passive withdrawal from work—tardiness, absenteeism, turnover, and inattentiveness on the job—are commonly cited expressions of worker alienation. Chinoy (1955) found, for example, that the frequent dreams and fantasies of automobile workers acted as a safety valve for their frustrations. More active expressions of alienation, such as pilferage, sabotage, deliberate waste, assaults, bomb threats, and other disruptions of work routine occur with alarming, though underreported, frequency (Walton 1974). Some workers have been known deliberately to damage equipment in an effort to make their tasks more complex and challenging. Public demonstrations have taken place, and underground newspapers have appeared in large organizations protesting company policies. More recently, employees have cooperated with newsmen, congressional committees, agencies, and protest groups in exposing objectionable practices. To be sure, worker alienation is especially prevalent in those industries most extensively penetrated by the norms and requirements of technological rationality, particularly those adhering to F. W. Taylor's "time and motion" functionalist approach to work. Yet increasingly, blue- and white-collar workers tend to dislike their jobs, resent their bosses, and rebel against their union leaders. This dissatisfaction reflects the excessive social and psychological costs incurred by the nature of many jobs. At a minimum, it measurably diminishes the productive output of the system, while its impact outside the work setting remains largely undetermined. In short, worker alienation exists and constitutes a serious social problem.

Active attack and passive withdrawal, however, constitute only the dramatic extremes of worker dissatisfaction. Their greater significance lies in the fact that they are symptomatic of a far larger, ongoing shift in individual orientation away from work. The fragmentation, routinization, and monotony inherent in many jobs today challenge belief in the sanctity of work. As labor becomes physically less taxing, real incomes rise, and the hours devoted to work decline, a growing number of people throughout the social structure have come to feel that their working lives are somehow deficient in content and interest. They have, as a result, begun to question, to criticize, and, on occasion, to reject outright, many of the traditional norms and standards of conduct and belief pertaining to work. One worker testified to his feelings of betrayal this way: "All we are left with is the deadend job . . . that offers little challenge to the more educated worker, little chance for advancement and hardly any chance to participate as a worker" (quoted in Kennedy 1974, p. 398).

In his article "Alienation and Innovation in the Workplace," Walton (1974) places the responsibility for the worker's alienation squarely on management, which he challenges to design new, more rewarding work systems. He lists six major work place conflicts between the evolving expectations of employees and the demands, conditions, and rewards of employing organizations:

1. Employees want challenge and personal growth, but work tends to be simplified and specialties tend to be used repeatedly in work assignments. This pattern exploits the narrow skills of a worker, while limiting his or her opportunities to broaden or develop.

2. Employees want to be included in patterns of mutual influence; they want egalitarian treatment. But organizations are characterized by tall hierarchies, status differentials, and chains of command.

3. Employee commitment to an organization is increasingly influenced by the intrinsic interest of the work itself, the human dignity afforded by management, and the social responsibility reflected in the organization's products. Yet organization practices still emphasize material rewards and employment security and neglect other employee concerns.

4. What employees want from careers, they are apt to want right now. But when organizations design job hierarchies and career paths, they continue to assume that today's workers are as willing to postpone gratifications as yesterday's workers were.

5. Employees want more attention to the emotional aspects of organization life, such as individual self-esteem, openness between people, and expressions of warmth. Yet organizations emphasize rationality and seldom legitimize the emotional part of the organizational experience.

6. Employees are becoming less driven by competitive urges, less likely to identify competition as the "American way." Nevertheless, managers continue to plan career patterns, organize work, and design reward systems as if employees valued competition as highly as they used to (pp. 229-30).

This is not to say that the majority of jobs, including many labeled "blue-collar," don't offer the individual access to substantial extrinsic rewards (such as money, security, and prestige) that are highly valued in their own right. Workers are now paid much more for working much less than they did at the beginning of the century, and their work conditions have improved immeasurably. Rather, these rewards by themselves often fail to satisfy. For while many of the extrinsic aspects of work have improved, the intrinsic aspects—that is, what the workers actually do—have not changed appreciably. House (1972) demonstrated, for instance, that intrinsically motivated blue-collar workers whose jobs deny them adequate intrinsic compensation for their efforts feel frustrated, dissatisfied, and have a lower level of self-esteem. To obtain missing gratifications, they accept supervisory positions that carry greater pressure and responsibility, a step that serves only to exacerbate their conditions still further. The additional gratifications received are outweighed by the added stress. Extrinsically motivated workers, on the other hand, indicate little attachment to their jobs. They look upon the job as a necessary evil, preferring, instead, to take those rewards that are most readily available and to then forget about work. "Perhaps," wrote Zweig, "most men believe that the function of a job, even an interesting job, is primarily to provide money for the comforts, amenities and pleasures of life" (1952, p. 97).

Devoid of opportunities for autonomous action, challenging activity, and a meaningful relationship to product and cohort, work fails to supply a sufficient stream of salient intrinsic gratifications to sustain its historic centrality in the worker's complex of values. Indeed, many blue-collar workers "find the meaning of work as often as not a negation rather than an affirmation of a basic sense of worthiness" (Shostak 1969, pp. 58-59). By "severing the organic connection between production and consumption, between effort and gratification," modern technique sets the stage for a purely instrumental attitude toward work (Blauner 1964, p. 27). This is a far different outcome than the "binding [of] the individual more closely to reality" envisioned by Freud. Indeed, Arendt (1958) emphasizes this factor as the basic precondition of alienation.

Counter-Argument and Refutation

But, many students of work argue, it is not at all clear that workers are as concerned about the allegedly dehumanizing intrinsic aspects of work as they are about such extrinsic concerns as money, fringe benefits, and job security. What about the impressive array of evidence from the many job-attitude surveys? Do not findings such as those summarized in Figure 2.1 indicate that workers are at least moderately satisfied with the context of their working lives? Indeed, if any conclusion should be drawn from the information conveyed by

FIGURE 2.1

Percentage of "Satisfied" Workers,
Based on Eight Gallup Polls
(men only, ages 21 through 65)

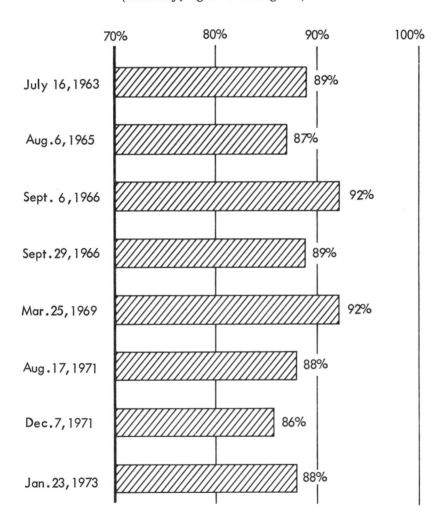

Source: Robert P. Quinn, Graham L. Staines, Margaret R. McCullough, "Job Satisfaction: Is There a Trend?" Manpower Research monograph no. 30, U.S. Department of Labor, Manpower Administration (Washington, D.C.: Government Printing Office, 1974), Figure II, p. 5.

this figure, it is this: Not only do the vast majority of workers express satisfaction with their jobs, the percentage of workers doing so may actually be on the increase. In addition, when asked whether they would continue to work if economic need were no longer a factor, 66 percent of all workers sampled by Quinn and Sheppard (1974) in 1973 responded in the affirmative. Although 86 percent of middle-class men and 76 percent of working-class men so responded 18 years previous (Morse and Weiss 1955), the 1973 figure still represents a sizable majority and does indicate a fairly strong motivation to work. Findings such as these, therefore, have led many writers to discount the conclusion that today's generation of workers is rejecting the world of work. In a statement that describes their position well, Machinists' Vice-President William A. Winpisinger said that "the real significance of studies showing that one worker in five finds fault with aspects of his job is that 80 percent are satisfied" (quoted in Strauss 1974, p. 41).

This interpretation is too simplistic to be readily accepted. It fails to take into account other significant factors against which the data should be read. Consequently, it has resulted in the drawing of an erroneous conclusion—the "myth of the happy worker" as Harvey Swados (1962) called it. First, a report of job dissatisfaction constitutes an expression of dissatisfaction with oneself. This is because an admission to having an unsatisfying job, in this society of individual responsibility, implies a measure of personal culpability. It is, therefore, an admission difficult to make. Instead, the worker will rationalize his condition in an effort to place himself in a better light. This is especially likely when alienation takes the passive form. Moreover, as Fromm (1955) pointed out, whatever the level of expressed dissatisfaction with work, it is bound to be higher if the unconscious depths are taken into account. Also to be considered is the general cultural bias toward expressing contentment (Robinson, Athanasiou, Head 1969). Thus, to the extent that such rationalization occurs, all simple verbal measures of job satisfaction are biased upward and, accordingly, need to be viewed with a measure of skepticism.

This skepticism is reinforced when one examines the distribution of responses to the following question: If you had the chance to start your work life over again, would you choose the same kind of work as you have now? The data, presented in Table 2.1, were brought together by Blauner (1964) and Wilensky (1961). As can be seen, when we parcel out the constraints on expression of job dissatisfaction imposed by the fact that the respondent's present job is probably the best he can find, large differences among occupations become quite apparent. While at least three-quarters of all skilled white-collar workers said they would try to get into a similar occupation if they could start over again, less than half the respondents in the remaining job categories (except skilled printers) felt that way.

TABLE 2.1

Proportions Among Occupational Groups Who Would Try
to Get into Similar Type of Work If They Could Start
over Again (Blauner 1960; Wilensky 1961)

Professional and Lower White-Collar Occupations	Percent	Working-Class Occupations	Percent
Urban university professor*	93	Skilled printers	52
Mathematicians	91	Paper workers	42
Physicists	89	Skilled auto workers	41
Biologists	89	Skilled steelworkers	41
Chemists	86	Textile workers	31
Firm lawyers*	85	Blue-collar workers*	24
School superintendents	85	Unskilled steelworkers	21
Lawyers	83	Unskilled auto workers	16
Journalists (Washington correspondents)	82		
Church university professors*	77		
Solo lawyers*	75		
White-collar workers*	43		

*All probability samples or universes of six professional groups and a cross-section of the "middle mass" (lower middle class and upper working class) in the Detroit area, stratified for comparability with respect to age, income, occupational stratum, and other characteristics (Wilensky 1961).

Source: Adapted from John P. Robinson, Robert Athanasiou, and Kendra B. Head, Measures of Occupational Attitudes and Occupational Characteristics (Ann Arbor, Mich.: Survey Research Center, Institute for Social Research, 1969), p. 28.

Clearly, these data indicate that people both in lower skilled white-collar jobs and working-class occupations generally are somewhat less than wholly satisfied with the context of their labor.

Skepticism is still further enhanced when inquiry is made into the reasons why people express a desire to continue working once economic factors are removed. For example, Quinn and Sheppard (1974) found that, when asked to explain why they felt this way, half their respondents mentioned boredom as the reason (49.8 percent). This is in marked contrast to the 9.7 percent who, because they enjoy working, would not stop. Interestingly, only 16.2 percent of the respondents felt that "work supplies direction in life." This finding provides yet another sign that the centrality of work in the individual's value structure is on the wane. Using data such as these and the information summarized in Table 2.1, one's estimate of the prevalence of job satisfaction becomes far more conservative.

The second counter-argument pertains to the phenomenon of "habituation"—getting used to a disagreeable job. Highly mechanized and specialized work is boring. The greater one's intelligence and education, the more severe the boredom. While boredom can act as a catalyst to action, it can also lead to lethargy and apathy. The individual becomes inured in the monotony of his simple, repetitious task and develops a dislike for changing work habits. He seems to adjust to his unchallenging environment. Once it becomes habitual, the worker is less likely to view his job in strongly negative terms. He does his job mechanically, without imagination. While such workers may not express overt dissatisfaction, they still are not highly motivated.

This view is supported by the research of Herzberg (1966) who concluded that work satisfaction and dissatisfaction are two distinct dimensions. Dissatisfaction is a function of extrinsic factors such as company policy, incompetent supervision, and unpleasant working conditions. While "hygienic measures" such as fringe benefits and group dynamics training for management and foremen can modify the intensity of work dissatisfaction, they will make workers not satisfied, but only apathetic. Satisfaction is a function of the intrinsic factors of work—that is, of achievement, challenge, and responsibility. In the modern work place, hygienic and extrinsic factors are relatively easy to improve. Intrinsic ones are far more difficult. Consequently, survey findings that appear at first glance to indicate moderate satisfaction, may, in fact, be partly a reflection of the workers' overall apathy and general lack of causes for overt expression of dissatisfaction. A statement made by Riesman seems particularly appropriate here:

> The great victory of modern industry is that even its victims, the bored workers, cannot imagine any other way of organizing work, now that the tradition of the early nineteenth century Luddites, who smashed machines, has disappeared with the general acceptance of progress (1958, pp. 372-73).

A third argument against the "myth of the happy worker" is that the very simplicity of the work tasks themselves serves to minimize expressions of hostility by creating a condition of insecurity due to the interchangeability of workers on jobs. Fried (1973), for example, found that 77 percent of the West End men he sampled preferred job security over a chance to get ahead. These men realized other jobs may be better but were unwilling to transcend their situation by actively engaging and transforming their environment. Instead, like House's (1972) extrinsically motivated workers, they accepted their jobs with good grace, if not with great satisfaction.

The last and perhaps most telling argument is that behavior—as compared with a response to a global, structured survey question—is the better indicator of attitude. Surely, the number of strikes over the past decade or two, particularly the increasing incidence of wildcat strikes, points to something other than widespread satisfaction with work. Granted, working men and women perceive a wider range of job-related gratifications than many social researchers would have us believe. Nevertheless, these rewards often fail to measure up to the individual's expectations, skills, and potentialities. Active opposition, after all, even in this violence-prone society, remains an extreme measure resorted to by only the most frustrated and angered of individuals.

If the work ethic is not yet dead, it is, assuredly, in a serious state of ill health. People are ambivalent toward work. Although they may be unable to specify what it is they are searching for and what it is they desire out of life, many have already decided it is not a steady diet of labor. They have little motive and find few opportunities to use occupational identity as a status-winning device or to elaborate the work role beyond the work place. In economic terms, the perceived marginal utility of added labor, and in many instances of the last unit of labor as well, is declining.* In short, people are turning away from the world of work, preferring to look elsewhere for that something that will provide them with the direction and meaning they feel their work lives now lack.

For many individuals, contemporary labor constitutes a serious personal problem. A small but growing minority of workers express their displeasure in the active hostility they direct toward the context of their labor. Many others express it in their passive withdrawal from work and, at times, from reality. The majority of workers survive; they approach their jobs sometimes with apathy, usually with good grace, generally without great satisfaction. Observing the growing disquiet, more than one writer has reached the decreasingly radical conclusion that "the once familiar ticket of life—work—seems in danger of having outlived its acceptability" (Kaplan 1971, p. 26). Perhaps

---

*A striking instance of this phenomenon was the auto industry's problem with massive absenteeism on Mondays and Fridays prior to the recent recession.

Kasl is on the right track when he advises that for the sake of the mental health of "those who must perform jobs that are difficult to make intrinsically interesting, a leisure-based culture may be necessary and attachment to the leisure role may be more satisfying" (1974, p. 175). Nonconventional work-leisure schedules like the four-day workweek may indeed be a step in the right direction.

CONTEMPORARY LEISURE

Concomitant with diminishing the attractiveness and potency of the work place as a source of reward and self-definition, modern technology has made possible a progressive expansion of the individual's sociocultural horizons. Relative affluence, a higher level of education, social and geographical mobility, combined with ubiquitous media of information and persuasion, have provided discontented workers with experiences (often vicarious) of alternate modes of behaving and, hence, of alternate life-styles. Consequent to their search for new sources of gratification and identification, there has resulted a broadening of the criteria against which people evaluate their society and the quality of their lives. For many people, this change is made manifest in a heightened consciousness of their own leisure. Those rewards perceived as obtainable through nonwork activities and associations have taken on added meaning and value. In contrast to the time spent on the job, many workers see in their periods of free and/or family time a veritable cornucopia of opportunities for creative, recreative, and expressive gratification. Increasingly, they wish to be identified by their life-styles and cultural tastes rather than by their occupations or some other method of social ordering.

Thus leisure is gaining acceptance both as a source of valued gratification and as a domain from which one may derive purpose and direction in life. This change in sociocultural orientation is clearly evident, for example, in a two-page Ford Motor Company advertisement run several years ago in Life magazine. Displaying keen insight into many aspects and trends of modern life, it depicted a shiny Lincoln standing in front of an elegant house. Attached to this attractive image of the "good life" were these words of advice to potential consumers:

Your house has glass walls
Your kitchen is a technological marvel
Your clothes and furniture are the height of functional beauty
Work easily, play hard

(quoted in Friedman 1964, p. 152; emphasis added)

Pointing to the growing significance of leisure today does not imply that either the individual or the society as a whole will soon become totally leisure oriented. Social standing still derives largely from one's occupation or profession, and, for many, work remains the most important source of self-identity (Wrenn, 1964). Moreover, the family is still organized around economic activity (Furstenberg 1974). Finally, as Kahn (1972) points out, the physical and social environment of the work setting is often more attractive than one's home and neighborhood. Productive activity should, therefore, long remain as an important, if not the dominant, determinant of behavior and lifestyle. If nothing else, the individual's financial requirements assure that the routines and rhythms of work will continue to function as the backdrop against which the activities of other life domains are organized. Rather, the situation described here is one in which the activities engaged in, and the rewards accrued during the periods of discretionary nonwork time, become sufficiently salient in their own right to serve as powerful motivators of behavior. Increased free time, for example, has made it possible for many families to develop their affectional relationships more extensively (Blood 1972). Consequently, the home, once the setting where recuperation from work fatigue occurred and in which a limited amount of recreation as reward for hard work was sanctioned, is now being transformed into a central reason for existence and increasingly provides much of the justification for work itself. It is in this far more restricted sense that both society and its individual members are referred to here as becoming increasingly leisure oriented. Perhaps Mead captured the essence of this position best when she observed that "as once it was wrong to play so hard that it might affect one's work, it is now wrong to work so hard that it may affect family life" (1957, p. 15).

How Much Leisure?

If advanced industrial societies are becoming increasingly leisure oriented, then the first question concerns the amount of free time that will be made available to the individual. Not surprisingly, prognosticators often disagree considerably on this point. The best premise is that in advanced industrial states there will be increasing amounts of leisure in years to come. Fourastié (1965) predicted an average workweek of 30 hours by 1985, with a guaranteed vacation of 12 weeks. Workers in the postindustrial society will also spend two-thirds of their lives studying or in retirement; work will occupy but one-third of their life span. Assuming a constant annual gain in per capita GNP of 3 percent, Krebs (1968) calculated that in 1985 American workers could have either a 22-hour workweek or a 27-week work year.

Recently, this premise has come into question. Wilensky (1961) suggests that the decline in the number of hours worked during the twentieth century has been grossly exaggerated by selective comparisons with the 12- to 14-hour day common in the 1800s. He estimates that the skilled urban worker of today may in fact have annual and lifetime leisure comparable to that of his thirteenth-century counterpart.

Since World War II, there has been little apparent interest in increased free time, at least as indicated by further reductions in the average number of hours worked per week. Between 1900 and 1968, the length of the straight-time workweek declined from 53 to 37.1 hours. But, of this decline, only 0.5 percent took place after 1956. Moreover, even this amount was more than offset by a rise in overtime from 2.8 to 3.6 hours per week (Moore and Hedges 1971). From an average allocation of 30 to 40 percent of increased productivity prior to World War II (Zuzanek 1974), the rate of growth in free time diminished to only 8 percent of GNP in the United States during the 1960s (Moore and Hedges 1971). A reanalysis of Hedges' (1975) data indicates that, in May 1974, fewer than 9 percent of all nonfarm, full-time wage and salary workers worked less than 40 hours per week on their primary job, while 24 percent still worked in excess of 40 hours (Table 2.2). While this last figure represents a decided decrease from the one-third of the labor force who worked 41 or more hours per week in 1963 (Northrup 1965), much of this decline can be attributed to the cutback in production, and the attendant shortening of work hours and overtime, resulting from the energy crisis and its attendant reces-

TABLE 2.2

Number and Percent Distribution of Nonfarm Wage and
Salary Workers Who Usually Worked Full Time, by
Usual Number of Hours Worked per Week, May 1974

Hours per Week	Total Reporting (in thousands)	Percent Distribution
35 or more	59,187	100.0
35 to 39	5,090	8.6
40	39,868	67.3
41 to 45	4,178	7.1
46 to 50	5,749	9.7
51 or more	4,301	7.3

Source: Adapted from Hedges 1975, p. 30, Table 1.

sion. Finally, as Zuzanek (1974) concludes in his summary of work and leisure trends in industrial societies: "Since the forties and early fifties, there have been minor fluctuations, but the movements were around 40 working hours per week" (p. 294).*

Though the future of the drive for more leisure is uncertain at present, the demand for more functionally arranged leisure through increased flexibility in the scheduling of work has only begun. However, if the four-day workweek is to be a viable solution to the problems of work, two assumptions held by its supporters must be borne out: (1) leisure and work must constitute two distinct life domains, for if leisure is highly influenced by the nature of work, it will provide no real escape; and (2) contemporary leisure must in fact be a more satisfying domain than work, for if it is not, the three-day weekend and the eight-to ten-hour day may prove more damaging to the individual's happiness than the alienating aspects of the work he is attempting to escape.

The balance of this chapter focuses upon these two basic four-day workweek assumptions. In the discussion that follows, a summary of the case of those who find fault with them is presented; the defense will not be discussed.† The reason for this one-sided approach is the belief of this writer that it is the responsibility of advocates of social changes to consider the possible shortcomings of their proposals and either refute or remedy them. This book is not designed to defend the four-day workweek but to evaluate certain ramifications of its adoption. Consequently, the emphasis is upon those aspects that are potentially troublesome.

The Four-Day Workweek Assumptions in the Context Of Modern Perspectives on Work and Leisure

The four-day-workweek solution assumes that the individual can sharply separate what transpires during his working time from what

---

*As discussed in Chapter 1, this situation may change as a result of the United Auto Workers' recently achieved progressive reduction in work hours. In addition, there is increasing talk on the part of several unions to include adoption of the four-day workweek as one of the future contract demands.

†It is important to note that there is a paucity of hard evidence either to support or to refute these assumptions—speculation certainly, but not reliable data. This is indicative of an almost total absence of research into the entire issue of leisure and its relationship to work. Systematic research has barely begun, and even descriptive information is lacking. Indeed, it is only within the last few years that the problems and dilemmas raised by increasing leisure have been taken seriously. Kaplan (1971) estimates that their visibility today is still no greater than that of ecology 20 to 30 years ago.

occurs outside the work setting. While a few writers feel that such compartmentalization does occur (for example, see Roberts 1970), this view is held by a decided minority of those concerned with the work-leisure relationship. Zweig summarized one aspect of the majority position when he wrote: "A man is not one person at home and a different person at work, he is one and the same man. He projects his personal worries, frustrations and fears on his workplace, and vice versa from workplace to home" (1952, p. 97). Examining the relationship between work and leisure from the perspective of "time," de Grazia adds a second factor. "Our kind of work, though freer of toil, requires a time-motion that makes our spare time free time and thereby links it inescapably to work. Aristotle was right about recreation. It is related to work, and given and taken so that work can go on. Thus it is with modern free time. . . . Free time has no independence of its own" (1964, p. 311).

Of the modern writers, perhaps Engels provided our main leads in this area. Alert to the fact that work routines and rhythms affect behavior outside the work place, Engels was pessimistic about the styles of life he saw emerging. He described the after-work activities of English laborers this way:

> On Saturday evenings, especially when wages are paid and work stops somewhat earlier than usual, when the working-class pours from its own poor quarters into the main thoroughfares, intemperance may be seen in all its brutality. . . .

> Next to intemperance in the enjoyment of intoxicating liquor, one of the principal faults of English workingmen is sexual license. But this, too, follows with relentless logic, with inevitable necessity, out of the position of the class left to itself, with no means of making fitting use of its freedom. . . . Working men in order to get something from life, concentrate their whole energy upon these two enjoyments, carrying them to excess. . . .

> The failings of the workers in general may be traced to an unbridled thirst for pleasure, to a want of providence and of flexibility in fitting into the social order, to the general inability to sacrifice the pleasure of the moment to a remoter advantage (quoted in Wilensky 1969, pp. 111-12).

In these passages, two major hypotheses that have been restated many times by contemporary writers can be recognized. These hypotheses are graphically summarized by Wilensky this way:

The "Compensatory" Leisure Hypothesis: In an up-to-date version the Detroit auto-worker, for eight hours gripped bodily in the main line, doing repetitive, low-skilled, machine-paced work which is wholly ungratifying, comes rushing out of the plant gate, helling down the superhighway at eighty miles an hour in a second-hand Cadillac Eldorado, stops off for a beer and starts a bar-room brawl, goes home and beats his wife, and in his spare time throws a rock at a Negro moving into the neighbourhood. In short, his routine of leisure is an explosive compensation for the deadening rhythms of factory life. . . .

The "Spillover" Leisure Hypothesis: Another auto-worker goes quietly home, collapses on the couch, eats and drinks alone, belongs to nothing, reads nothing, knows nothing, votes for no one, hangs around the home and the street, watches the "late-late" show, lets the TV programmes shade into one another, too tired to lift himself off the couch for the act of selection, too bored to switch the dials. In short, he develops a spillover leisure routine in which alienation from work becomes alienation from life; the mental stultification produced by his labour permeates his leisure (1969, p. 112).

Modern writers see the worker's experience on the job as penetrating and influencing his pattern of activity and his psychological well-being in other settings. They fear that the behavior patterns learned and the discontent engendered during work time are all too readily transplanted into free time, and this transfer, they feel, is psychologically nonproductive. In his analysis of several theories linking the concept of work-generated alienation to a radical criticism of the quality of modern leisure, Bacon distinguishes three different types of coherent expectations concerning the connection between work alienation and the way people use leisure time:

Alienated work and generation of false consumption obsessions. People who experience their work as a calamity, who find it is meaningless and strips them of their innate creative powers, will compensate for this degradation by an obsessive leisure time preoccupation with false consumer needs. . . .

Alienated work and the generation of passive leisure life styles. People whose work does not reward their motivational investment, who experience a lack of interest, control, or autonomy in their work, learn the lesson of retreatism. This is carried over into the nonwork sphere. Consequently, the leisure of alienated workers is characterized by passive, home-centered idle amusement; the purported aim is fun, relaxation, and a good time. In fact, the reality is the empty purposelessness of modern living.

Alienated work and generation of violent compensatory leisure behavior. People whose work is undemanding, repetitive, and unrewarding build up a reservoir of frustration and disaffection within themselves. This tension generates a very violent reaction in the sphere of leisure. Traditionally, this has resulted in an excess of intemperance or sexual license; in its more modern form it may result in aggressive behavior on the roads, or violent aggression against minority groups (1975, pp. 180-81).

Bacon concludes that a general theme runs through these theories: "Alienated work has serious consequences and is a social disturbant. It generates a number of abhorrent life styles which either threaten to undermine the stability of industrial society, or threaten the promise of a civilization based upon a dramatic expansion in leisure time interests and activities" (1975, p. 181).

Behind these theories lies the fear that leisure cannot become socially productive, or be otherwise used with wisdom and real enjoyment if the individual's ability to choose among alternative life-styles and behavior patterns is sharply limited by the nature of his work: "If we are not encouraged to think for ourselves at school and at work, we are not likely to have the mental resources to think for ourselves in leisure time" (Parker 1971, p. 14).

Segal (quoted in Glickman and Brown 1974, p. 49) hypothesizes,

Individuals who have learned to commit energies toward goal achievement will characteristically find minimum difficulty in making commitments, within the constraints of the social structure, as they choose employment, chore, leisure and free time activities, while individuals who have experienced developmental difficulties in learning to commit energies toward goal achievement will show a consistent inability to make such commitments in any area; or inconsistency and unrealiability over time from area to area.

In modern industrial society, the work setting remains the principal location for the development and fulfillment of the individual's drive for goal achievement. Yet it is just here that many workers express frustration—that their hopes and expectations are most explicitly blocked. They are denied in their work the very learning opportunities most necessary to the development of those skills and attitudes required for successful goal achievement in leisure or elsewhere. As a result, the individual may not find the refuge from his job he seeks in his free time, for the content of his leisure reflects the nature of his labor. Thus the first assumption made by advocates of the four-day workweek—that work and leisure constitute distinct life domains—appears, if not unsound, at least subject to considerable question.

Social critics differ in their perceptions of man's preparedness to use leisure wisely and to obtain satisfaction from it. A few are relatively optimistic. In a prediction perhaps most noteworthy for its inaccuracy, Ernst (1955, quoted in Kaplan 1960, p. 303) looked forward to the leisure of 1976:

> . . . close to one half of our people will, all through their
> adult lives, take courses by correspondence, or otherwise
> and effectively explore those aspects of life and the unknown
> which excite their curiosities. The new exciting leisure
> will establish prestige values of unorthodoxy; . . . millions
> of us will go abroad. . . . Our own people will learn at
> least three languages in childhood, as the Swiss do; . . .
> the cravings for narcotics and excessive alcohol will decline
> as people need fewer spurs for courage, and less forgetful-
> ness; . . . our spiritual road map [lies] this way—Energy,
> Leisure, Full Rich Life.

Dumazedier (1971) sees in the weekend activities of France's young people, artists, and intellectuals cause for mild optimism (also see Fourastié 1965; Burch 1971).

Most writers, however, feel otherwise. Though they also see in increased leisure the potential for a partial amelioration of current social exigencies, or for at least some attenuation of the frenetic pace of daily life, they nonetheless express profound pessimism as to the ability, even the willingness, of society to actualize leisure's full promise. Quoting Denney and Riesman:

> Certainly, it is arguable that we have gotten too "rich"
> too fast, in our quantities of time off, and behave with the
> discomfort and lack of grace common to parvenues. And
> it is evident that many people, consciously seldom, but
> unconsciously often, flee back to artificially strenuous
> work—or even war—in order to escape the perplexities of
> choice presented by abundant leisure (1964, p. 401).

Wolfenstein decried what she claimed was the emergence of a "fun morality." "Fun, from having been suspect if not taboo, has tended to become obligatory. Instead of feeling guilty for having too much fun, one is inclined to feel ashamed if one does not have enough" (1958, p. 86). But, in another way, people can no longer enjoy their periods of free time, for judgments of personal achievement and self-esteem have become too prominent.

Fromm (1965) saw in the freedom of leisure a danger to our cherished democratic values and institutions. More ominously, Gabor (1964) warns us that along with nuclear war and overpopulation, leisure is a major threat to civilization. Marcuse (1964) and Ellul (1964) go so far as to question the meaning and possibility of free choice, leisure or otherwise, in the modern technological society. Extreme as these views are, they differ only in degree from the worst fears of many other observers of the modern scene (for example, see Brightbill 1960; Charlesworth et al. 1964; Clawson 1959; de Grazia 1964; De Rosis 1951; and Smigel 1963).

Mesthene (1971) states what is apparently the gut concern for most of these critics—mankind's continuing inability to live up to the Periclean ideal. He feels that we are bothered by leisure because the activities engaged in during free time do not satisfy. Advances such as improvement in television technology and the proliferation of community art centers, orchestras, and sport franchises, appear to be palliative. "We miss the involvement we seek because it all lacks reality somehow, because it is not really leisure we are dealing with, but with the filling up of free time" (p. 52). One is immediately struck by the similarity of the sentiment expressed in this statement with that of Marx's "filling up of the pores" or gaps in the working days. Perhaps these writers fear the possibility of today's workers becoming alienated from their leisure as well as from their work. "A perpetual holiday" wrote C. P. Snow, "is a good working definition of hell."*

Repeatedly, critics of contemporary leisure point to the fact that for many people free time leads to boredom (Heron 1957), and that boredom, in turn, has been linked to psychological maladjustments of varying forms and severity (Greenson 1953). Such terms as "weekend neurosis," "vacation neurosis," and "Sunday neurosis" have already entered the psychiatric lexicon (see, for example, Grinstein 1955; P.A. Martin 1967b). More importantly, increased free time has been implicated as a

---

*Burch (1971) takes strong issue with what he perceives as the elitist-based pessimism of his colleagues. With more than a touch of sarcasm he writes that "the enlightened modern has made leisure standard fare in our literary cafeteria of despair" (p. 160).

cause of more severe forms of mental illness (Linden 1958; A. R. Martin 1964; P. A. Martin 1967a). Referring to those retirees with too much dead time on their hands, physicians and psychologists speak of "retirement syndrome" as a recognized medical entity that can even result in early death (Dubos and Pines 1965). A rise in the incidence of marital discord is yet another commonly cited negative consequence of unwanted leisure. For these and other related reasons, at least one president of the American Psychiatric Association has emphasized to his colleagues the need for community mental health services "to get at known social causes of mental health in the high-risk population" (Rome 1965, quoted in P. A. Martin 1967a, p. 5).

In view of these findings, the four-day-workweek advocate's assumption that leisure is a more satisfying domain than work, at least for many people, is certainly subject to doubt. This is not to say that this work schedule won't prove satisfying for the majority, only that this outcome is less assured than its proponents might assume. Furthermore, if adoption of the four-day workweek becomes widespread, special attention needs to be given to those who may suffer adjustment difficulties.

CONCLUSION

The nature of many blue-collar jobs in contemporary society has been shown to constitute a serious individual and societal problem. As was anticipated by Marx, Engels, and Durkheim, labor has been divided in a manner that limits the worker's opportunities for achieving full human development and happiness. This has resulted in the emergence of new sociocultural orientations toward work and leisure, and a growing cleavage between the work-dominated social structure and the ways of life, or culture, of the population. Clearly, for both moral and stability reasons, steps need to be taken to rectify this situation.

Though work may be in the process of being eclipsed by emerging leisure-oriented values, it remains the dominant aspect of culture. Because the work and nonwork spheres of life are interfacing and interacting, work colors and limits behavior and attitudes in all domains. Consequently, proposals that ignore the effects of this reciprocal influence leave much to be desired.

The four-day workweek constitutes a potential case in point. This approach attempts to rectify, albeit only partially, those problems arising from worker frustration and disquiet with the context of their labor through the provision of a more functional arrangement of work and leisure time. An extended weekend, its proponents argue, will enhance the worker's access to personally valued nonwork gratifications and to salient self-validating activities. Yet in attempting to solve the problems associated with modern labor by finessing the setting in which they arise, this solution almost completely by-passes the underlying causes of worker discontent, thereby leaving them intact. It virtually ignores those factors in the work setting responsible for the workers' lack of job satisfaction. Of perhaps greater immediate importance, the four-day-workweek solution fails to reckon sufficiently with either the influence that work activities may have on determining the practical scope of the individual's freedom of choice among alternate leisure pursuits, or more basically still, the problematic nature of free time for many people.

It is difficult to deal with the problems of work by invoking values associated with leisure. "Indeed," writes Dumazedier (1967, p. 87), "the humanization of work through the values of leisure is inseparable from the humanization of leisure through the values of work." Leisure, however, is but the temporal framework of its cultural content. Its quality reflects the standards, capabilities, and experience of its creators. Of blue-collar workers' leisure pursuits, Shostak writes:

> Blue-collarites choose leisure pursuits that have the power to affirm acquired wisdom rather than provide any confrontation with novel and possibly taxing matters. They choose leisure pursuits that have the power to "massage" rather than for any message the medium might contain. They also use their leisure as a source of relief from strain, a response to the enervating character of much of their work. And, finally, they see to it that leisure helps resonate the general blue-collarites' culture (1969, p. 208).

If Shostak's description is accurate, then working a four-day week is unlikely to result in a significant improvement in the blue-collar workers' overall quality of life. What is there, after all, in this work-leisure innovation that serves to promote the workers' engaging in novel activities capable of transforming the content of their culture? Nothing except the rearrangement of time itself. To be sure, the four-day schedule will, on the average, be looked upon favorably, for it does provide added flexibility in the scheduling of extra work (overtime, second-job-holding), as well as nonwork activities. But already established patterns of behavior should remain predominant.

**STUDY DESCRIPTION
AND METHODOLOGY**

This study is viewed as a first, exploratory attempt at measuring and gaining some understanding of the responses of blue-collar workers to a four-day, 40-hour workweek. Its aim is to examine selected consequences of the worker's adjustment decisions, both for himself and upon his relationship to, and functioning within, the work and family settings. Reflecting this, the primary objectives of the study are as follows: (1) To describe the worker's behavioral and affective responses to the four-day workweek in the work setting. (2) To describe the worker's behavioral and psychological responses to the four-day workweek in the family setting, particularly those responses that manifest the quality of his conjugal and parental role adjustments. (3) To describe changes in the use of time and leisure time consequent to working a four-day week, and to explore the relationship among marital satisfaction, satisfaction with free time, and the way time is used. Last and most important: (4) To evaluate the viability of the four-day workweek as an alternative to conventional work schedules.

CONCEPTUAL APPROACH:
THE STUDY OF PERSONS IN ENVIRONMENTS

The worker's social, psychological, and behavioral adjustment to his nonconventional schedule, whether it provides him with opportunities for personal growth or distress, is viewed in this research as a function of the conjunction between environmental variables and characteristics of the person. The argument is that if the four-day schedule improves the quality of the worker's life, this is due to an improved match between his needs and the enhanced rewards supplied by the new arrangement of work and nonwork time. Concomitantly, if the individual experiences difficulties due to his work schedule, this too should be a reflection of the match, or in this case the lack of it, between his needs and the possibilities for satisfying them. A concept of person-environment fit is, therefore, used as the immediate predictor of individual response or adjustment.

Many aspects of the four-day workweek's impact on workers can be evaluated independently of the theoretical approach used in this study. Indeed, in several of the following chapters, the impact of this schedule in several important life domains is examined without reference to person-environment interaction. However, in an attempt to obtain a better understanding of the dynamics involved in the worker's adjustment in the family setting, the Person-Environment (P-E) Fit model developed by French and his associates (1974) is particularly useful and has been adopted.

The P-E Fit model organizes the following major concepts: (1) the person's abilities; (2) the person's needs (motives, values); (3) the environment's demands upon the person (role demands); and (4) the environment's supply of opportunities and gratifications.

"Fit" is measured by discrepancies between needs and supplies, and between demands and abilities. A worker's response to his non-conventional work schedule can thus be viewed in terms of either his abilities and needs, the demands and supplies of his environment, or the degree of fit among these. What the P-E Fit model assumes is that, measurement difficulties aside, "the interactive product of relevant properties of persons and situations" (French et al. 1974, p. 1) is the best predictor of adjustment. To clarify by example, one might anticipate greater satisfaction with the new work schedule, all things being equal: (1) the greater the worker's desire to affiliate with his family, (2) the more the family situation provides him with opportunities for such affiliation, and (3) the better the match between the worker's affiliative desire and his affiliative opportunities. Certainly, a greater degree of satisfaction with the new schedule would be predicted in a situation characterized by "perfect fit" of affiliative desires and opportunities compared to one characterized by desired affiliations that are not supplied.

Much of the study's interest is focused on selected dimensions of the person or "person characteristics." These dimensions include (1) affective states, such as general marital satisfaction, role-performance satisfaction, and overall satisfaction with use of free time, and (2) needs, such as motivations, including the desire for affection from one's spouse, the desire to affiliate with one's children, and the desire for authority in one's conjugal and parental role relationships. To define these person characteristics, individuals can be located on each of these dimensions. Particularly with regard to motivations, it is assumed that these attributes are not subject to change or should change only slowly, as a result of switching to a four-day workweek. Thus, adjustment, or satisfaction, is viewed here as primarily a function of one's environment—the individual's access to those resources necessary for meeting his role demands, and the nature and extent of gratification he receives in return for fulfilling them. Because the interest is in assessing changes in affect, this study focuses on needs (motivations) and supplies (gratifications).

The major objectives and variables discussed above are reflected in the conceptual framework adopted. Figure 3.1 presents the major categories of variables to be treated and their hypothesized position in the causal sequence. It also indicates one of the conceptual complexities of the study—namely, that many of the characteristics of the person also serve as dependent variables or "responses."

For each set of relationships represented, the response is either a single variable or a number of interrelated effects. The possible determinants of the responses fall into three categories: (1) person's characteristics, (2) characteristics of one or more environments, and (3) interactions between person and environment. Each arrow in the figure indicates a set of testable hypotheses about causal sequence. As indicated earlier, the initial expectation was that some of the person characteristics and some of the environment characteristics would show at least part of their effects directly (arrows 1 and 2, respectively). However, it was anticipated that much of the explained variance in the responses studied will result from the interaction between these two categories of determinants. This set of relationships is indicated by the sequence of arrows through the "person-environment interaction" box (arrows 3, 4, 5).

HYPOTHESES

The development of a set of explicit hypotheses for this study was problematic. Hypothesis testing assumes the existence of a body of knowledge concerning the relationship among specific categories of relevant variables. In the field of leisure, especially adjustment to leisure, such a body of knowledge is just what is lacking. At best, insights may be gained from studies on unemployment and retirement. More help is to be found in the family literature, but even this is limited. Neither the person-environment-fit approach to marital adjustment nor the male's marital motivations have attracted much research attention. Consequently, this study is largely exploratory in nature. It raises questions about the impact of the four-day workweek and then examines the influence of several potentially significant control variables upon the nature, direction, and extent of the individual's adjustment responses.

FIGURE 3.1

Conceptual Framework with Major Categories of Variables

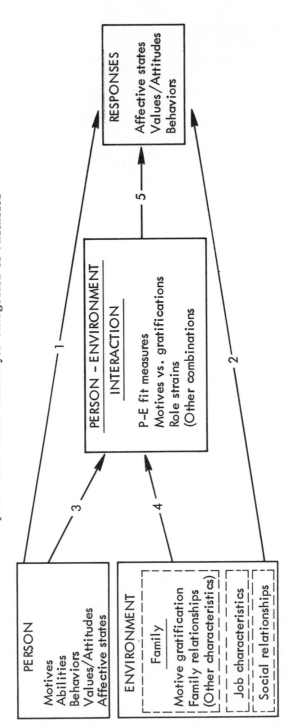

Note: All responses treated in this framework are characteristics of persons, and virtually all of them can be viewed as causes of other responses. Accordingly, all variables listed as RESPONSES are also listed as PERSON variables. In any specific analysis, a variable can serve as either a PERSON dimension (that is, a predictor variable) or as a RESPONSE, but it cannot serve as both simultaneously.

Source: Compiled by the author.

54

Nevertheless, several hypotheses of varying degrees of importance can be specified. What follows are the major hypotheses the study explored. While this constitutes a large number of hypotheses for a single research endeavor, many of them are closely related or overlapping as to both the measures employed and the implications of the results uncovered. Next to each hypothesis, the reader will find a reference to the chapter in which it is tested.

The first hypothesis concerns the four-day workers' response to their nonconventional schedule. Due to the relatively greater flexibility in the use of time inherent in working an official four-day week:

(1) Four-day workers will express greater satisfaction with their compacted work schedule than will a comparable group of five-day workers with their standard workweek (Chapter 4).

A second, closely related hypothesis states:

(2) The longer the experience with the four-day workweek, the less favorable the attitude toward it. These workers will, however, remain more satisfied with their schedule than a comparable group of five-day workers (Chapter 4).

In part, this hypothesis represents an attempt to replicate a similar finding by Nord and Costigan (1973) in their longitudinal study of workers' response to a four-day schedule.

With the basic nature of the job remaining unaffected by adoption of the four-day workweek, little, if any difference is expected between the levels of expressed job satisfaction by four-day and five-day workers. The possibility exists, however, that as a result of their processes of comparison between gratifications received within and outside the work setting, four-day workers may express somewhat less job satisfaction. Thus:

(3) The level of expressed job satisfaction by four-day workers will be equal to, or lower than, that expressed by a comparable group of five-day workers (Chapter 4).

With respect to overtime:

(4) Four-day workers will put in more overtime than will workers on a five-day schedule (Chapter 4).

A primary concern of this study is the relationship between the family setting and the attitude of four-day workers toward their nonconventional schedule. The intent is to determine the extent to which their attitude is influenced by their adjustment in the family setting. Workers will report difficulty of varying severity. A minority will express dissatisfaction with their four-day schedule. This brings us to the first of the "family" hypotheses:

(5) When difficulties are reported, they will most frequently occur in the family setting (Chapter 4).

Despite these difficulties, however:

(6) Four-day workers will report greater conjugal and parental role-performance satisfaction, and overall marital satisfaction, than a comparable group of workers on a five-day schedule (Chapter 5).

The study attempts to provide some understanding of the dynamics involved in the determination of the worker's response and the quality of his adjustment to his schedule in the family setting. To this end, the study examines the interaction among such family-related control variables as motivation, gratification, family pressure, and family organization, and the relationship between these variables and various response measures, notably, marital and role satisfaction, satisfaction with the four-day workweek, and reported behavior patterns. Employing the Person-Environment Fit model of adjustment, the following relationships (across individuals) are empirically expected for four-day workers (Chapter 5):

(7a) As marital motivation increases, opportunities for its gratification also increase due to the more functional arrangement of discretionary time) producing a positive correlation between each motivation variable and its corresponding gratification variables.

(7b) As marital motivation increases, the discrepancy between motivation and the environment's supply of gratifications remains constant (gratification opportunities increasing approximately proportionately): hence, conjugal and parental role-performance satisfaction and overall marital satisfaction will remain constant—that is, motivation is essentially unrelated to the level of "fit" between motivation and gratification, and thus is unrelated to these measures of adjustment in the family context. If, however, it is assumed that gratification of a higher level of motivation is more satisfying than gratifying a lower level of the same motivation, then greater conjugal, and parental role-performance satisfaction, and marital satisfaction should result.

(7c) As marital motivation increases, opportunities for dealing with family pressures also increase (due to alternative behavioral patterns being made feasible by the more functional arrangement of discretionary time); hence, conjugal and parental role-performance satisfaction, and overall marital satisfaction increases. This is, motivation will correlate positively with these measures of adjustment in the family context.

For five-day workers the following empirical relationships across individuals are expected (Chapter 5):

(7d) As marital motivation increases, opportunities for its gratification remain constant (or randomly variable), producing a near-zero correlation between each motivation variable and its corresponding gratification variable.

(7e) As marital motivation increases, the discrepancy between the motivation and the environment's supply of gratifications is likely to increase (gratification opportunities not increasing proportionately); hence, conjugal and parental-role performance satisfaction and overall marital satisfaction decreases. That is, motivation is negatively related to the level of fit between motivation and gratification and thus is relatively related to these measures of adjustment in the family context.

(7f) As marital motivation increases, opportunities for dealing with family pressures remain constant (due to time limitations and social norms); hence, conjugal and parental role-performance satisfaction, and overall marital satisfaction decrease. That is, motivation will correlate negatively with these measures of adjustment in the family context.

The last two family-related hypotheses are concerned with the influence of marital orientation and the wife's attitude toward her husband's four-day work schedule respectively:

(8) Individuals on a four-day workweek holding a "traditional" as compared to a "compassionate" marital orientation will express greater dissatisfaction with the four-day workweek and with family setting (Chapter 5).

(9) The worker's attitude toward his four-day work schedule will relate positively to the attitude toward it held by his spouse (Chapter 6).

Turning finally to the impact of the four-day workweek on the use of free time, the three-day weekend should enable workers to make more satisfying use of their free time. Therefore:

(10) Four-day workers will express greater satisfaction with their use of free time than will a comparable group of five-day workers (Chapter 7).

In addition:

(11) Four-day workers who engage in task-oriented activities during their free time (for example, repairs around the house) will report greater satisfaction with their use of free time and with their work schedule than those who engage in recreation-oriented activities (Chapter 7).

However:

(12) Four-day workers will not exhibit novel leisure behavior patterns but will, instead, expand already established job, family, and free time patterns (Chapter 7).

In terms of the data collected in this study, this means that four-day and five-day workers will participate in the various discretionary activities in approximately equal proportions. It is not anticipated, for example, that significantly more or fewer four-day workers will engage in either educational or organizational pursuits.

MEASURES AND METHODOLOGIES

In order to examine the above hypotheses, the study follows a cross-sectional format and utilizes two primary sources of data. Information concerning the characteristics of the person—his subjective perceptions of his family relationships, of his work, and of his free-time activities—was collected by means of a structured, personal interview with each of the sampled blue-collar workers. Objective behavioral data were obtained from time-budget diaries in which respondents recorded their activities for one workday and the preceding or following nonwork days. The diary provided information concerning activities engaged in, their duration, and whether they involved other members of the family.

In order to obtain the desired data and test the P-E Fit model, the following tasks had to be undertaken: (1) construction and validation of instruments designed to measure men's motivations, gratifications, satisfactions, and stress in marriage. These instruments had to be developed because a search of the family literature failed to uncover satisfactory measures compatible with a structured questionnaire of limited duration and which quantified concepts commensurately; (2) design and feasibility testing of a time-budget diary; and (3) selection of a sample comprised of both an experimental group of blue-collar workers currently on an official weekly work schedule of four ten-hour days, and a control group of men on a standard five-day week; the latter group provides a point of comparison for the responses of four-day workers and a handle on chance environmental fluctuations and other disturbances that could otherwise distort the results. The balance of this chapter describes how these tasks were completed.

Selection and Description of Marital Motivation Variables

Adjustment within the family is indicated by the individual's satisfaction with his marriage and with his role performance. These, in turn, are functions of the fit between the motivations he brings to the family setting and the extent to which they are satisfied by other family members.* This approach to marital adjustment finds ample support in the marriage and family literature. Katz et al. (1963), for example, conclude that at least for men their data "strongly support the general hypothesis that the degree to which personality needs are satisfied in marriage is reflected in one's evaluation of, and ability to interact effectively with, the spouse" (p. 213).†

---

*The willingness of these significant others to satisfy the focal person's needs and motivations is, of course, largely predicated upon his ability to satisfy their own needs and expectations. Thus, in theory, both sides of the exchange process should be measured so as to derive an accurate picture of adjustment and of the dynamics involved. This, however, requires in-depth interviews with these others as well as with the focal person, a step that could not be undertaken by this study. Consequently, only the worker's person-environment fit is examined.

†Also see Gurin, Veroff, Feld (1960), Kirkpatrick (1962), and Clements (1967).

According to Biddle, role theory

> may be said to deal with patterns of behavior or other characteristics which are common to persons and with a variety of cognitions held about those patterns by social participants. The conceptual distinctions of role theory center around a description of the patterns or of the cognitions. The propositions of role theory are concerned with the effects of the patterns upon the cognitions or of the latter upon the former (1961, p. 2).

If one adopts this perspective, the family can be viewed as a social institution comprised of an enduring association of individuals, each of whom occupies culturally defined roles in a setting of reciprocal expectations. These expectations place certain basic role obligations (role demands) upon each of the family members, and each anticipates receiving, in return, valued rewards (or gratifications). Since this study focuses upon married men, the concern is with the roles of husband and father, and with their concomitant conjugal and parental role relationships.

Unfortunately, in the marriage and family literature, there is little consensus on what the most significant marital motivations and satisfactions are. Both the concepts used and the measurement approaches adopted vary widely across studies. A search of the literature uncovered none that were readily adaptable to the requirements of both the role theory approach and the P-E Fit theory employed in this study. Consequently, it was necessary to construct new measures of marital motivation and gratification.

Though many of the basic conjugal and parental role obligations are culturally determined in rough outline (for example, financial support of the family, the taking care of children), more than ample scope remains for the expression of individual family differences. What this means for research is that the dynamics of family life can be approached from many directions and in many ways. However, in their review of the marriage and family research literature, Hicks and Platt (1970) found that researchers tend to use two basic, yet distinct, models of marriage—the institutional and the companionate. The former emphasizes the instrumental aspects of family roles and concentrates on the formulation of norms for guiding the husband and wife toward what has long been considered the major function of the family: child bearing and child rearing. Adherence to traditional sex-role specifications, customs, and mores are considered most significant to a successful marriage and family life. In contrast, the companionate model makes little distinction between independent and dependent variables. Instead, it emphasizes the affective aspects of family relationships and tries to describe the dimensions of interactions characteristic of a satisfying relationship. Though basic role specifications are largely taken for granted in the companionate family, new ones are often added. But no matter what the specifications are, the family members expect, even demand, much more of each other than would be the case in a traditionally oriented (that is, institutional) family.

This study is concerned with five basic marital motivations, two derived from the institutional model and three from the companionate model. The institutional model's failure to specify any of the relationships in the home makes the selection of salient motivations relatively difficult. Nonetheless, it is quite apparent that marital satisfaction is viewed by the model's adherent as being significantly affected by the extent to which the conjugal (and to a lesser degree the parental) role relationship satisfies at least two marital motivations of men. This body of research stresses the importance of the husband maintaining a positive self-image (for example, Katz et al. 1963). This in turn requires a congruence of the husband's self-concept and that held of him by his wife (Luckey 1960; Taylor 1967). More simply stated, many men need reinforcement as to how well they are meeting their wife's expectations. Meyerowitz (1970), for instance, found in a study of 407 expectant couples that the husband's self-image and marital satisfaction, while certainly related to aspects of his socioeconomic status, were especially related to his wife's continued confidence in him as a good husband and father. These findings yield the first motivation included in this study—the motivation toward conjugal esteem.

The second motivation derived from the institutional model concerns the desire on the part of many men to retain the male's traditional position of centrality in the family. In return for providing the family's financial support, they expect to receive the respect and the authority traditionally given a person who occupies the husband and father role. Shostak (1969) notes that this orientation is particularly prevalent among men who are poorest paid, least educated, and lowest in the job echelon. There is significant research support for the importance of this motivation. Aller (1962), for example, found that too great a capacity for independent thinking, aggressiveness, self-centeredness, or dominance in wives threatened the self-concepts of their husbands and adversely affected marital adjustment. Nye (1961) and Axelson (1963) reported similar findings among men with working wives. On the basis of these findings, the motivation toward conjugal authority was derived.

Deriving salient motivations from the companionate model is comparatively easy. Itself explicitly concerned with the quality of interpersonal relationships in the family and with the positive gratifications the family members receive from these relationships, this model has led researchers to explore a wide variety of personality and interpersonal relationship variables. Emotional maturity (Dean 1966; Dean 1968), isolation and depression (Renne 1970), and power (Tallman 1970) are a few of the variables research has identified with marital adjustment and marital satisfaction. Of the many factors studied, however, marital companionship appears central; it both affects and reflects adjustment. Hawkins (1968) uncovered a moderate association between this aspect and marital satisfaction. When Luckey and Bain (1970) asked the 38 satisfied and 34 dissatisfied couples in their sample, "What do you consider the greatest satisfaction that your marriage has given you so far?" 82 percent of the husbands and 84 percent of the wives in the satisfied group mentioned companionship. In the dissatisfied group, this aspect was mentioned by only 47 percent of the husbands and 41 percent of the wives. More specifically, Navran (1967) found that both verbal and nonverbal communication was better among happily married couples. The importance of companionship for marital satisfaction is widely supported by the findings of many other researchers (for example, see Gurin, Veroff, Feld 1960; Burr 1970). This brings us to the three motivations derived from the companionate model included in the study. Following Hawkins, who defines marital companionship as "the degree of marital expression by the spouses of affectionate behavior, self-revilatory communication, and mutual participation in other informal non-task recreational activities" (1968, p. 647), this study measures the strength of the men's motivations toward conjugal affection, conjugal affiliation, and conjugal communication.

Up to this point, the concern has been largely with the specification of conjugal motivations. The five motivations presented, however, also have relevance for parental role relationships. Hill (1949) distinguishes two types of fatherhood—developmental and traditional. The former is analogous to the companionate model of marriage; a father of this type tries to understand his children and is interested in all their activities. He lets them set their own goals and obtains satisfaction from playing a part in their growth. Such a father would certainly be motivated toward parental affection, parental communication, and parental affiliation. The traditional father, on the other hand, feels he knows what is best for his children. He makes little effort to understand them and is only interested in their activities when they cross over into what he considers to be the limited domain of his parental responsibilities. The child is seen as owing the father a debt that is paid off in obedience and respect. It would be very surprising if men so oriented did not exhibit strong motivations toward parental authority and parental esteem.

Table 3.1 organizes the ten motivation variables according to the family role to which they pertain and the model of marriage and

TABLE 3.1

Organization of Marital Motivations, by Family Role and
Model of Marriage and Family Life

Role	Companionate–Developmental Model	Institutional–Traditional Model
	I Motivation Toward Conjugal Companionship	II Motivation Toward Conjugal Role Status
Husband Role	1. Motivation Toward Conjugal Affection 2. Motivation Toward Conjugal Communication 3. Motivation Toward Conjugal Affiliation	1. Motivation Toward Conjugal Authority 2. Motivation Toward Conjugal Esteem
	III Motivation Toward Parental Companionship	IV Motivation Toward Parental Role Status
Father Role	1. Motivation Toward Parental Affection 2. Motivation Toward Parental Communication 3. Motivation Toward Parental Affiliation	1. Motivation Toward Parental Authority 2. Motivation Toward Parental Esteem

Source: Compiled by the author.

63

family life from which they are derived. In an effort to obtain stable motivation measures that tap a wide variety of the specific needs men bring to their family setting, each motivation was measured separately by a multi-item index and was then to be collapsed into the four composite motivations represented by the cells of Table 3.1: (I) motivation toward conjugal companionship; (II) motivation toward conjugal role status; (III) motivation toward parental companionship; and (IV) motivation toward parental role status. The first and third adhere closely to Hawkins's definition of a companionate marital relationship presented above. The second and fourth composite motivations are quite similar to the conceptualization of "status" advanced by Davis (1949) in his study of work.*

Table 3.2 presents a concise definition of each of the conjugal and parental motivation variables. These definitions were presented to a panel of seven social scientists along with a set of Likert-type items measuring these variables. Based on their judgments, items were added, revised, and deleted. They were then tested empirically in two pretests, and the surviving items appeared in the final survey instrument. In all, there were 34 items attempting to measure ten motivation variables.

Prior to their inclusion in the evaluation effort, extensive analysis was undertaken on both the motivation and gratification measures to test for evidence of discriminant validity derived from correlation and factor analysis. The object was to develop reliable, stable measures and then to test for validity at the variable rather than the item level. The results of this analysis are reported in detail elsewhere (Maklan 1976). Chapters 5 and 6 present evidence of construct validity in the classical sense (Cronbac and Meehl 1955)—that is, the extent to which measures relate to other variables in ways predicted by the theory that underlies the measures.

Based on these results, it was concluded that measures satisfactory for the purposes of this study had been developed for the following motivation and gratification variables: (1) conjugal affection, communication, affiliation, authority, and esteem; and (2) parental affection, communication, affiliation, and authority. Table 3.3 presents the items that comprise each of these nine motivation indexes. The gratification items are not given, for they are commensurate with those composing the motivation variables. These indexes were

---

*Davis (1949) divided "status" into two aspects—esteem and prestige. The definition of esteem used in this study is based upon his concept of esteem, while there is some similarity between his notion of "prestige" and the definition of "authority" used here. Much of the difference is due to the different nature of the two settings studied.

TABLE 3.2

Conceptual Definitions of Conjugal and Parental Motivations in Marriage

Conjugal Motivations

1. Motivation Toward Conjugal Affection:
   Conjugal affection refers to the degree of love, warmth, tenderness, etc., which is present in the husband-wife relationship, from the husband's point of view. A man who is motivated toward conjugal affection places a high positive value on being loved by his wife and seeks her expression of it. He is interested in experiencing a high level of conjugal affection.

2. Motivation Toward Conjugal Affiliation:
   Conjugal affiliation refers to the companionship, friendship, and/or the sharing of experiences, etc., a person feels as a result of engaging in activities or otherwise spending time with his wife. A man with this motivation places a positive value on the company of his wife and seeks to engage in activities or otherwise spend time with her. He is interested in experiencing as much conjugal affiliation as possible.

3. Motivation Toward Conjugal Communication:
   Conjugal communication refers to the degree of openness, self-expression, understanding, etc., which is present in the husband-wife relationship. This is assessed relative to the husband's felt needs rather than against any universalistic criterion. The husband who is motivated toward conjugal communication seeks a husband-wife relationship within which he feels he is free to express himself and convey his personal ideas, opinions, and problems. He wants his wife to really know and understand him.

4. Motivation Toward Conjugal Esteem:
   Conjugal esteem refers to the approval, respect, recognition, etc., a man receives for being a good husband. The approval is given for good role performance in the husband role rather than for merely occupying that position. The person with this motivation seeks to be approved and esteemed by his wife for his conjugal role performance. He is interested in gaining as much conjugal esteem as possible and wishes constantly to feel evidence of his conjugal esteem.

5. Motivation Toward Conjugal Authority:
   Conjugal authority refers to the obedience, deference, respect, etc., which is ascribed to the position of "husband" and automatically inherited by its occupants. Traditionally, an American husband has relatively greater authority than his wife. The person with this motivation seeks to be obeyed and respected by his wife and is interested in gaining and maintaining a high level of authority.

6. Motivation Toward Parental Affection:
   Parental affection refers to the degree of love, warmth, tenderness, etc., which is present in the parent-child relationship, from the father's point of view. A man who is motivated toward parental affection places a high positive value on being loved by his children and seeks their expression of it. He is interested in experiencing a high level of parental affection.

7. Motivation Toward Parental Affiliation:
   Parental affiliation refers to the companionship, friendship, and/or the sharing of experiences, etc., a person feels as a result of engaging in activities or otherwise spending time with his children. A man with this motivation places a positive value on doing things with his children and seeks to engage in activities or otherwise spend time with them. He is interested in experiencing as much parental affiliation as possible.

8. Motivation Toward Parental Communication:
   Parental communication refers to the degree of openness, self-expression, understanding, etc., which is present in the father-child relationship. This is assessed relative to the father's felt needs rather than against any universalistic criterion. The person who is motivated toward parental communication seeks a parent-child relationship within which the children feel free to express themselves and convey their personal ideas, opinions, and problems. He is interested in really getting to know and understand his children.

9. Motivation Toward Parental Esteem:
   Parental esteem refers to the approval, respect, recognition, etc., a man receives for being a good parent. The approval is given for good performance on the parent role rather than for merely occupying that position. The person with this motivation seeks to be approved and esteemed by his children for his parental role performance. He is interested in gaining as much parental esteem as possible and wishes constantly to feel evidence of his parental esteem.

10. Motivation Toward Parental Authority:
    Parental authority refers to the obedience, respect, deference, etc., which is ascribed to the position of "father" and automatically inherited by its occupants. In the parent-child relationship, the father has by far the greater authority. A person with this motivation seeks to be obeyed and respected by his children and is interested in gaining and maintaining a high level of authority.

Source: Compiled by the author.

65

TABLE 3.3

Component Items of Conjugal and Parental Motivation Indexes

Variables and Items

1. Motivation Toward Conjugal Affection:
   F1-a How true is it that a loving, sympathetic wife is important to a marriage?
   F1-z How true is it that a wife should often let her husband know that she thinks he is a good husband?
   F2-e How much would you like to receive affection from your wife?

2. Motivation Toward Conjugal Communication:
   F1-b How true is it that it is important for a man to be able to talk to his wife about very personal matters, no matter what they are?
   F1-l How true is it that being able to talk to your wife about many different things is important to a marriage?
   F1-x How true is it that it is important to a marriage that the man be able to talk to his wife about things that are important to him?

3. Motivation Toward Conjugal Affiliation:
   F1-c How true is it that having many opportunities to be with your wife is important to a marriage?
   F1-q How true is it that a wife should try to arrange her schedule so that she has free time to spend with her husband?
   F2-a How much would you like to spend time with your wife?

4. Motivation Toward Conjugal Authority:
   F1-d How true is it that a wife should keep her wedding vow of obedience to her husband?
   F1-m How true is it that a man has the right to expect his wife to obey him?
   F1-w How true is it that when a man asks his wife to do something for him, it is her duty to do it?
   F2-f How much would you like to get your wife to accept your suggestions about how the family should be run, without argument?

5. Motivation Toward Conjugal Esteem:
   F1-n How true is it that it would not bother you much if your children didn't come to you when they were worried or had a problem they couldn't solve?
   F1-o How true is it that living in a nice house or an apartment is not important to you?
   F1-r How true is it that if your wife didn't recognize the efforts you make to be a good family man, it would not bother you much?

6. Motivation Toward Parental Affection:
   F1-j How true is it that there are many things more important to a man than having his children often show their love and affection for him?
   F2-h How much would you like to get your children to hug you or show their affection for you in some other way?

7. Motivation Toward Parental Communication:
   F1-e How true is it that a father and his children should have a lot to talk to each other about?
   F1-k How true is it that one of the most enjoyable things about being a parent is having the chance to see the world as your children see it?
   F2-d How much would you like to spend time talking to your children about the things that interest them?

8. Motivation Toward Parental Affiliation:
   F1-t How true is it that it is important for a father to spend a lot of time with his children?
   F2-g How much would you like to take your children places—to movies, sports events, places like that?
   F2-k How much would you like to do things with your children—such as play with them, throw a ball around, things like that?
   F2-l How much would you like to do interesting and different things with your family?

9. Motivation Toward Parental Authority:
   F1-h How true is it that a father should not be satisfied with his children's behavior unless they always do as they are told?
   F2-j How much would you like to get your children to always do as they are told?

Source: Compiled by the author.

then combined to form satisfactory composite motivation and gratification measures of conjugal companionship, parental companionship, and traditional role status. The latter index was formed by combining the measures of conjugal authority, parental authority, and conjugal esteem.

Unfortunately, the analysis also demonstrated that the sensitive P-E Fit measures could not be constructed from the motivation and gratification indexes developed. While the findings offer some support for French, Rodgers, and Cobb's (1974) intuitively logical P-E Fit theory of adjustment, it was decided to discuss adjustment to the four-day workweek in the family setting in terms of motivations and gratifications alone.

Design and Construction of Instruments

The aim in designing the questionnaire was to construct interval scales that would reliably and validly measure the social-psychological variables of interest. Maximum reliability in the sense of internal consistency was sought so as to maximize the amount of common or valid variance (as opposed to item-specific or error variance) in the social-psychological measures. Great care was also taken to minimize the effect of response set by using both negatively and positively worded statements wherever possible. Although inclusion of reverse items tends to lower the average inter-item correlation, it serves the purpose of reducing the contribution of response set, hence making the attained variation on the scales a function more of their underlying content than of methodological artifact.

Two pretests were conducted as part of the process of index construction. The samples approximated reasonably well the final sample, though in the second pretest, several low-level white-collar workers were also included. The purposes of the first pretest were (1) to develop indexes of conjugal and parental motivations and satisfactions, (2) to assess the reaction of the respondents to a card sort technique for measuring these variables, (3) to develop indexes of family pressures, and (4) to test the format and approach developed for the time-budget diary. The second pretest was concerned primarily with further development and validation of the new measures of conjugal and parental motivation, satisfaction, and family pressures. Correlation analysis showed that motivation, gratification, and family pressure measures related to each other and to other variables in the pretest in the expected fashion.

The Time-Budget Survey

The design of the time-budget survey was guided from the outset by three general, albeit often conflicting, goals: to obtain time-use data that would (1) be representative of the individual's total range of activity, irrespective of work schedules (2) be reasonably sensitive to fairly small differences in time-distribution patterns of four- and five-day workers and (3) maintain an acceptable degree of precision and accuracy in the respondent's reports.

The first task was to determine the optimal period of time covered by the survey instruments. The trade-offs here were clear: the more days included, the more representative are the results of the person's activity range and the greater the sensitivity to small differences in these patterns between groups. On the reverse side of the coin, the longer the period of coverage, the less the accuracy and precision, and the greater the potential sample loss. Adherence to the first two guidelines quickly ruled out the possibility of employing a one-day "yesterday" interview of any form. The four-day, 40-hour workweek mandates changes in the individual's allocation of time to activities on at least his four regular workdays due to the compulsory nature of the extra two hours of daily labor. As for the additional day-off, only by working eight hours of overtime, or by second-job-holding for a like duration, could a person maintain a routine here similar to that of the fifth standard workday of his five-day counterpart. Furthermore, while differences between groups in time-use patterns on any given day of the week may be modest, when examined in terms of, say the entire week, they may well prove substantial. A one-day interview would, thus, tend to mask the very differences being searched for. This is particularly true given the small and fairly heterogeneous nature of the sample in question.

The following compromise was decided upon: The survey would cover all of the worker's days-off in the week following the personal interview plus a "typical" workday. Operationally, the latter was defined as either the day preceding or the day succeeding the respondent's days-off. Each group was split in half as to which workday they reported. Practically, this meant that the survey period for four-day and five-day workers was comprised of four and three contiguous days, respectively.* While this decision compels the treatment of all respondents within each of the two cells as interchangeable units, it was felt that this period of coverage would provide a good feel for even relatively small differences in time usage of four- and five-day workers. It also had the advantage of making the construction of a hypothetical, or "typical," week for each group of men possible, a procedure that facilitates intergroup comparisons.

---

*In cases where the days-off were of the pattern—off, off, work, off—the respondent was instructed to report on a workday other than the one bounded by his days-off.

In designing the survey instrument, several steps were taken to increase precision and accuracy. First, in an effort to minimize reporting errors due to inaccurate or incomplete recollection, a self-administered, open-ended time-budget diary was chosen as the measurement instrument. The respondents were instructed to record their daily acitivities at the end of each day. While "yesterday" interviews when supplemented by recall aids in the hands of a trained interviewer yield more reliable results than does the present approach without the aid of the interviewers (Scheuch 1972), it was nonetheless deemed superior where not one, but up to four, days had to be recalled after the fact.

The instructions accompanying the diary were specific and the interviewers went over them in detail with the respondents until they were understood. In the few cases where the respondent omitted a day, a telephone call-back was made and an attempt at reconstructing the missing day was undertaken. Lastly, to encourage accuracy and completion of the diary, each respondent was provided with a $5 gratuity.

SELECTION AND COMPOSITION OF THE SAMPLE

Selection of the Sample

The study design called for two comparable samples of blue-collar workers—men working an official four-day, 40-hour week and a second (or control) group of men on a standard five-day schedule. To obtain comparability, the following sample selection procedure was used. Within the geographical limits of the two midwestern states, Michigan and Minnesota, a list of organizations that were known to have adopted a 4/40 work schedule and employed more than 20 individuals was compiled. Management from a subset of these organizations were then contacted, and their cooperation in supplying lists of male employees was requested. When cooperation was obtained, a search was undertaken to identify a similar, but five-day, concern. For purposes of comparability, this second employer had to be (1) in the same industry with workers performing similar functions as those in the four-day plan, (2) located in the same community, town, or (if in a large metropolitan region) within reasonable proximity to its four-day counterpart, and (3) be of approximately the same size. Only when such paired firms could be identified, and the participation of both secured, was either organization included in the sample. A list of men holding similar jobs was then compiled from the employee rolls for each firm, and these men became part of the sample. Mari-

tal status and job similarity were determined from company records
and from personal conversations with members of management, union
representatives (where present), and supervisory personnel.

Because of the interest in undertaking analysis within the sample
of four-day workers, and particularly among subgroups with different
marital motivations, it was decided to employ a larger sample of four-
day than five-day workers. The study aimed, therefore, for 100 complete interviews with five-day workers and 200 complete interviews
with four-day workers. The total sample size of 300 individuals was
felt to be adequate for multivariate analysis, while the separate samples of 200 and 100 units would allow for some simple correlation
analysis within subgroups.

The actual selection of the sample, however, proved far more
difficult than had been originally anticipated. Two factors accounted
for most of the trouble. First, when the field phase of the study was
about to commence, the 1973 Arab oil embargo took place and brought
in its wake economic uncertainty and instability, which severely affected the normal operations of two large organizations that had
agreed to cooperate in the study. Consequently, both firms had to be
excluded and substitutes located. However, since the energy shortage
and the general bleakness of the economy at that time could have produced responses markedly different from normal, the postponement
was advisable. By mid-April 1974, the cooperation of additional
organizations had been secured and the complex of energy-related
problems appeared (at the time) to have bottomed out sufficiently to
allow interviewing to commence. Fortunately, though the economy
never really recovered, the full impact of the recession held off until
after completion of the field work. Nevertheless, the reader is ad-
vised to keep in mind the economic uncertainty characterizing the
succeeding few months.

The second difficulty that arose provided an interesting insight
into one of the obstacles to future expansion of the four-day workweek.
Initially, it was feared that it might be difficult to find and gain the
cooperation of eligible four-day organizations. There are, after all,
only a limited number of firms on a 4/40 schedule, with blue-collar
jobs and also located near comparable five-day organizations. As it
turned out, this fear was largely unfounded. While such organizations
are relatively scarce, on the whole those that were approached were
interested in the study and offered cooperation. Only 3 of the 12
firms contacted refused to participate. Consequently, a prospective
sample of 206 four-day working men could be drawn. Finding matching
five-day organizations was another matter. The management of two-
thirds of the 15 five-day companies approached declined involvement.
Six of the ten that so decided indicated that their refusal was due, in
part, to their opposition to the four-day workweek and their fear that

interviewing their employees about it might result in new demands within their own organization—demands that at that time they were not prepared to meet. As a result, a control group of male, five-day workers of the desired number could not be obtained since, in two instances, five-day organizations of suboptimal size had to be used. Only 77 five-day workers were found for inclusion in the sample.

In the end, men from 12 employing organizations were included in the prospective sample. Flint and Lansing, Michigan, and Minneapolis, Minnesota, supplied two organizations each. Ann Arbor, Michigan, contributed one, with both four-day and five-day employees. Five firms came from the Detroit metropolitan area.

Of the 283 men selected for the study, 15 were subsequently excluded from the sample lists by prior definition. These men had either left the firm, were on an extended sick leave, changed jobs within the same firm (for example, became foremen), or had changed place of residence to a different community. The overall response rate among the remaining 268 men was a satisfactory 86.9 percent, composed of 179 four-day workers (90.9 percent) and 54 five-day workers (76.1 percent).*

One hundred forty-nine four-day workers and 46 five-day workers initially agreed to fill out the time-budget diary, which works out to 83.7 percent of the men interviewed. Of these, 127 actually completed it for a 65.1 percent completion rate. The rates for four- and five-day men were almost identical (64.4 percent versus 67.4 percent, respectively). It is not surprising that only 54.5 percent of the men interviewed filled out the diary, for it was a somewhat time-consuming undertaking if done properly. Indeed, the author was gratified to find that two-thirds of the men who had initially agreed to complete the diary actually did so.

Composition of the Sample

Because the primary concern here is with the responses of four-day workers outside the work place, and especially in the family setting, there was less concern with obtaining homogeneity of workers on jobs than would be the case if adjustment in the work setting were emphasized. Consequently, a range of blue-collar jobs is represented in the sample. As is noted above, and can be seen in Table 3.4, the job-matching effort did not prove wholly successful. In particular, there

---

*While the figure is not available, it is known that several of the men sampled went south several weekends a month during the interviewing period. These men possibly account for a not insignificant portion of those who could not be reached.

TABLE 3.4

Demographic Composition of Sample
(in percent)

Control Variables	Four-Day Workers	Five-Day Workers
Occupation:		
Truck driver	43.3	27.8
Assembly line	5.6	25.9
Machine operator	27.0	18.5
Metal products fabrication	1.7	5.6
Mechanic	4.5	9.3
Utility maintenance	3.4	3.7
Maintenance, janitorial	5.1	0.0
Foreman	9.6	9.3
	100.2	100.1
	(N = 178)	(N = 54)
Work Shift:		
Day shift	73.0	87.0
Afternoon shift	15.2	7.4
Night shift	11.2	5.6
Other	0.6	0.0
	100.0	100.0
	(N = 178)	(N = 54)
Number of Years with Firm:		
Less than one	7.3	11.9
One to two	9.9	9.5
Two to three	6.0	4.8
Three to five	10.6	4.8
Five to seven	9.3	11.9
Seven to ten	15.2	9.5
Ten to 15	10.6	19.0
Fifteen to 20	7.3	2.4
Twenty or more	23.9	26.2
	100.0	100.0
	(N = 151)	(N = 42)
Income (total family):		
Less than $9,000	3.4	9.8
$9,000 to $10,000	6.8	4.9
$10,000 to $12,000	11.6	14.6
$12,000 to $15,000	20.5	26.8
$15,000 to $20,000	38.4	17.1
$20,000 to $25,000	14.4	19.5
$25,000 or more	4.8	7.3
	99.9	100.0
	(N = 146)	(N = 41)
Education (no. years completed):		
Less than high school	9.3	4.8
One or two years of high school	23.3	14.3
Completed high school	55.3	54.8
One or two years of college	10.0	26.2
Three or more years of college	2.0	0.0
	99.9	100.1
	(N = 150)	(N = 42)

72

Control Variables	Four-Day Workers	Five-Day Workers
Age:		
Less than 25	10.3	13.7
25 to 29	16.5	25.5
30 to 34	10.7	15.7
35 to 39	14.8	13.7
40 to 44	11.3	4.0
45 to 49	12.5	9.8
50 to 54	13.0	4.0
55 to 59	5.0	9.8
59 or more	5.7	4.0
	99.8	100.2
	(N = 176)	(N = 51)
Number of Children at Home:		
None	23.5	24.1
One	22.9	20.4
Two	24.0	25.9
Three	13.4	14.8
Four	8.9	9.3
Five	3.9	3.7
Six or more	3.3	1.9
	99.9	100.1
	(N = 179)	(N = 54)
Length of Experience with the Four-Day Workweek		
Less than one year	14.9	—
One to two years	12.4	—
Two to three years	24.2	—
Three to five years	14.3	—
Five to seven years	8.1	—
Seven to ten years	6.2	—
Ten to 15 years	9.3	—
Fifteen or more years	10.6	—
	100.0	
	(N = 161)	
Life-Cycle Stage:		
Under 45, married, no children at home	5.0	9.3
Married, children— youngest under age five	30.2	29.6
Married, children— youngest age five to 14	31.3	33.3
Married, children— youngest age 15 or over	13.4	13.0
Over 45, married, no children at home	14.0	7.4
Over 45, divorced or separated, children at home	1.1	0.0
Other (generally divorced, separated, has children but not at home)	5.0	7.4
	100.0	100.0
	(N = 179)	(N = 54)

Source: Compiled by the author.

73

are relatively more truck drivers working a four-day week (43 percent versus 28 percent) and vice versa for men on an assembly line (6 percent versus 26 percent).

The assembly line has long been recognized as among the least satisfying and most stressful of blue-collar jobs. Driving a truck, on the other hand, is thought to provide more opportunities for independent action (for example, the pacing of work) and for affiliation. If the theories of alienation are correct, we would anticipate this inequity in the sample to exacerbate the differences between four- and five-day workers on such variables as schedule, job, and leisure satisfactions. To account for this possibility, and to bring the samples more in line with each other, the four-day assembly-line workers were weighted by a factor of 4, and the five-day truck drivers by a factor of 1.5.

Examination of the balance of Table 3.4 reveals that the two groups of workers are almost identically distributed on the two family variables (number of children living at home and life-cycle stage). They are also fairly close with respect to age and education though the four-day workers tend to be slightly older—39.5 years as compared to 35.9 years for the five-day workers—and have completed half a year less formal education. The similarity continues when one compares the number of years the two groups of workers have been with their employing organizations, with the average for both being 4.7 years. No statistically significant differences were found between four-day and five-day workers on any of the variables.

On two of the remaining variables, however, some differences do appear. Though 76 percent of the total sample work the day shift, the proportion of four-day men working the afternoon or night shift was approximately twice that found in the five-day group (26.4 percent versus 13 percent, respectively). However, because the differences between the two groups on this variable are not major, the sample was not weighted to take it into account. Four-day workers also tend to have a higher family income than their five-day counterparts—a difference that cannot be attributed to variance in the number of working wives. To be sure, some of this difference is the result of the relative oversampling of four-day truck drivers and five-day assembly-line workers. Preliminary analysis, however, indicated that the four-day workers' greater earning capacity may also be a consequence of their four-day schedule, namely, the opportunities it provides for additional overtime. When these two variables (job structure and overtime) are taken into account, it is felt that the two groups are reasonably comparable with respect to income. Consequently, no weighting was done on this variable.

The final variable presented in Table 3.4 shows the length of the four-day workers' experience with their nonconventional schedule.

As can be seen, their experience runs from less than one year (14.9 percent) to more than 15 years (10.6 percent). The median length of time on the four-day workweek is approximately three years.

Though not included in the table, one additional demographic variable requires mention. In drawing the sample, the issue of race arose early. The study design called for the exclusion of nonwhite workers, yet 16 black and Mexican-American men were interviewed. Preliminary analysis for these respondents showed no major differences between these men and the balance of the sample. Therefore, it was decided that their inclusion would not distort the analysis.

PART

II

IMPACT OF
THE FOUR-DAY
WORKWEEK

CHAPTER

4

WORKERS VIEW
THEIR FOUR-DAY WEEK:
GENERAL RESPONSES AND
IMPACT IN THE
WORK SETTING

A basic issue in an evaluation of a social innovation is whether the people directly affected respond to it favorably. The intention of the first half of the chapter is to examine this question. In it, the attitudes expressed by four-day and five-day workers toward their respective work schedules are described, followed by a brief discussion of how they would change their hours of work and leisure if given the opportunity. Also included here is a look at the relationship between the four-day workers' satisfaction with their schedule and the length of their experience with it. Presented next are several of the benefits and disadvantages attributed to the four-day week by the men working this schedule. Following this is an exploration of how schedule satisfaction varies according to the workers' education, income, and age and by the four-day workers' perception of why their employing organizations adopted this schedule. Finally, the influence of several of the study's major independent variables on schedule satisfaction are reviewed in light of the task in the second half of this chapter and in the three succeeding chapters—describing and explicating the ramifications of this innovation in the arrangement of work and leisure within specific settings and on the use of time.

RESPONSE TO THE FOUR-DAY WORKWEEK

When asked to evaluate their work schedule in general terms, the men working an official four-day week reported significantly greater satisfaction than did the men on the standard workweek ($\overline{X}_4$ = 1.87 versus $\overline{X}_5$ = 2.94, p <0.01). As Table 4.1 shows, when they are grouped according to whether they were "completely satisfied," "mod-

79

erately satisfied," or "dissatisfied" with their work schedules, more than 63 percent of the four-day workers expressed complete satisfaction compared to only 28 percent of their five-day counterparts. Clearly, for this sample, the compacted work schedule made for a relatively satisfying alternative to the standard workweek. Indeed, the five-day men were themselves not unaware of the benefits to be gained by working a compacted schedule; when asked how they would change their own schedules, 39 percent indicated a preference for the four-day workweek.

In Chapter 3, it was hypothesized that the longer the experience with the four-day schedule, the less satisfied the workers would be with it. Upon testing, this hypothesis had to be rejected. Rather than becoming less satisfied with the schedule as his experience with it increased, schedule satisfaction was positively, though not significantly, correlated with the number of years the person had been working a four-day week (Gamma = 0.09). The relationship would have been stronger but for the greater dissatisfaction expressed by men who have been on the four-day week for three to five years. The dissaffection of these men could not be accounted for in terms of the variables measured in this study. Considering the small sample size, however, it is quite possible that this finding is a quirk of this particular study.

When the four-day workers were asked how they would change their work schedule if given the opportunity, their suggestions distrib-

TABLE 4.1

Satisfaction with Work Schedule
(in percent)

Schedule	Completely Satisfied*	Moderately Satisfied*	Dissatisfied*
Four-day workers (N = 209)	63.6	30.1	6.2
Five-day workers (N = 53)	28.3	49.1	22.6
Total	56.5	34.0	9.5

*The original response alternatives consisted of a seven-point Likert scale. These responses were combined to form three categories: completely satisfied (1), moderately satisfied (2-4), and dissatisfied (5-7).

Source: Compiled by the author.

uted as follows. While the majority were happy with their work schedule as presently established (55 percent), a not-insignificant 12 percent indicated a desire to return to the standard eight-hour day, five-day workweek. On the other hand, 9-10 percent of the men in the four-day group were already imagining an even shorter workweek of one form or another. A second change often suggested was having one's days-off overlap those of the rest of the working population (7 percent). This was raised on account of several of the men's "weekend" falling on traditional workdays. Surprisingly, the shortened lunch and coffee breaks, changes adopted by several of the firms when they went on the compacted schedule, were rarely mentioned (2 percent). The remaining changes suggested were minor, consisting, in the main, of slight shifts in the start-up time of work (7 percent), presumably to minimize the longer workday's interference with other valued activities.

The four-day workers were also asked what they liked and disliked about their work schedule. Their responses were recorded according to whether they were related to (1) recreation, (2) finances, (3) family, or (4) something else. Only one answer per respondent was coded into each of the four categories.

Not surprisingly, the answers were dominated by recreation-oriented responses. More than 87 percent of all four-day workers considered the extra day-off to be a distinct benefit. Of these men, 13 percent mentioned their increased opportunity to take short vacations, and another 8 percent felt they could do more of the things they wanted to do in their free time. When criticisms were raised, they all pertained, in one way or another, to the inhibiting effect the ten-hour workday has upon the individual's social and recreational opportunities (5 percent), particularly during the evening.

Turning next to financially related reasons, approximately 12 percent of the men felt the four-day workweek increased their opportunity for earning additional income, either through working overtime or by second-job-holding. A few men, however, did complain that they had to work too many hours before receiving premium pay or felt that this pay should be higher (4 percent). Two workers said the ten-hour day cut into their chances for landing a second job. Only slightly over 3 percent of the four-day workers mentioned that their schedule reduced their transportation costs. Finally, higher spending during free time was a financial problem raised by but a single respondent.

Almost as many men gave direct family-related reasons for liking their schedule as gave financial reasons. Fifteen percent of the total four-day sample stated that the compacted work schedule enabled them to spend extra time with their family, with a third of these specifically mentioning their children. The only family-related disadvantage had to do with one husband-wife pair whose work schedules conflicted. It should be noted that only those workers who expressed satisfaction with their work schedule provided any family-related responses.

Finally, we turn to the potpourri of advantages and disadvantages that could not be clearly fitted into the above categories. As expected, the compacted work schedule made it easier for many men to do their chores, particularly around the house (16 percent). Several workers also felt the schedule provided them with the opportunity to accomplish errands on traditional workdays (6 percent). As for the negative comments, most of the complaints directed against the four-day workweek are to be found here. Of all four-day workers, 14 percent felt the ten-hour day to be too long while an additional 10 percent said the long workday forced them to get up too early. Seven percent stated that management was exerting too much pressure for additional overtime. The final complaint—that days-off were split—was mentioned by several workers whose extra free day fell between workdays. However, only one of the men who indicated marked dissatisfaction with their schedule listed this as a cause.

The responses of those men indicating dissatisfaction with their four-day schedule were examined in the hope of finding cause for their negative attitude. Less than half the disaffected workers reported any advantages to their being on a four-day week, a figure that is in marked contrast to the 1.5 positive statements averaged by their more satisfied cohorts. In addition, these men averaged about 2.5 times as many negative comments as those men more positively oriented to their schedule. However, the only complaints mentioned more than once concerned the length of the workday and the added pressure for overtime (eight times and two times, respectively). Perhaps these men felt they received little in the way of compensation for the extra strain they experienced at work.

Workers' Perceptions of Why the Firm
Adopted the Four-Day Workweek

A potentially important determinant of worker response to innovations in work patterns is the reasons given by management for instituting the change in the first place.* Inquiry was therefore made

---

*The extent of worker involvement in the decision to switch schedules and the procedures employed to actually bring the change about have also been cited as important determinants of the schedule's success (Sprague 1970; Wheeler and Bogdonoff 1970). Information pertaining to these factors, however, was not gathered in sufficient detail in this study to warrant reporting.

into the four-day men's perception of why their employers decided to adopt a nonconventional work schedule. The answers they gave are presented in Table 4.2, as are the levels of schedule satisfaction associated with each. Several points are worth noting. First, only 11.3 percent of the men felt their employers adopted the four-day workweek for the benefit of their employees. Among those holding an opinion, factors affecting the company's profit-and-loss picture accounted for the majority of answers. Second, and perhaps more important, there appears to be a relationship between schedule satisfaction and perception of who principally benefits from the change in schedule. Those workers who believed that management's decision to convert to the four-day week was motivated by reasons largely beneficial to the firm expressed significantly greater dissatisfaction with the schedule than did those men holding no opinion, who saw the switch as an attempt by management to organize more rationally their employee's work activities, as well as the firm's own practices, or who believed management's motivation to be basically humanitarian in nature (2.12 versus 1.49 respectively, $p < 0.01$). Unfortunately, the direction of causation in this relationship cannot be determined from available data. Many reasons, therefore, can be cited to explain this finding. Perhaps management conducted the decision-making and conversion processes in an unwise fashion, thereby leaving many workers with the impression that the company was trying to put something over on them—a form of insidious coercion for greater productivity,

TABLE 4.2

Four-Day Workers' Perceptions of Why Company
Adopted Compacted Schedule,
and Related Schedule Satisfaction
(N = 160)

Reason	Percent So Responding	Related Schedule Satisfaction Score
Reduce absenteeism	3.8	2.50
Increase productivity	5.0	2.13
Increase profits, reduce expenses	38.8	2.08
Union pressure	3.1	2.20
Better for workers	11.3	1.72
More rational work schedule	18.1	1.31
Other	4.4	1.57
Don't know	15.6	1.52

Source: Compiled by the author.

for example. If so, these workers could have been negatively disposed toward the four-day week from the start. There is, on the other hand, at least one other equally plausible explanation, which reverses the hypothesized direction of causation. It is quite possible that those workers who grew to dislike this schedule for reasons totally unrelated to the motivations of their employers, nonetheless directed their unhappiness toward the firm—using it as a scapegoat, so to speak, for their own negative experiences. In either case, the relationship between the workers' satisfaction with their nonconventional work schedule and the conversion process warrants being examined in greater depth than was done in this study.

Demographic Predictors of Schedule Satisfaction

Three basic demographic variables that the literature often associates with acceptance of innovation are income, education, and age. Concerning acceptance of alternate, compacted work schedules, the argument with respect to the first two variables is that the greater one's income and/or education, the greater the personal resources for making effective use of free time. Age, on the other hand, should be negatively related to satisfaction with the four-day week due to increased fatigue caused by working the longer ten-hour day.

When family income and the workers' education were related to schedule satisfaction, no essential differences were uncovered between men on the two schedules other than what was found above; four-day workers consistently expressed greater satisfaction. However, there was a tendency, though not statistically significant, for the wealthier and/or better educated five-day men (over \$15,000 and/ or some college education) to report relatively greater dissatisfaction. This pattern did not appear among four-day workers.

Figure 4.1 shows the relationship between age and satisfaction with one's work schedule. It clearly demonstrates the existence of interaction between this demographic variable and work schedule. Unlike their five-day counterparts, for whom increasing age is generally associated with greater schedule satisfaction, four-day workers are almost uniformly satisfied with their hours of work. With the possible exception of the oldest group of workers, there is scant indication here that fatigue, or for that matter, anything else associated with age, adversely affects attitude toward the four-day work schedule. But even if there were, these men still reported somewhat greater satisfaction with their schedule than did their cohorts working a shorter day.

FIGURE 4.1

Schedule Dissatisfaction by Age

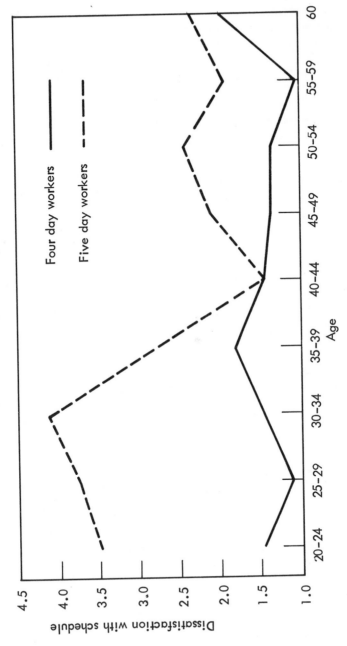

Source: Compiled by the author.

85

Discussion and Summary

There are several points here worth summarizing. First and foremost, the overwhelming majority of four-day workers sampled gave a clear indication of being relatively more satisfied with their nonconventional schedule than did the control group with their standard workweek. Concomitantly, at least 12 percent of the four-day men felt sufficiently dissatisfied with their schedule to express a desire for a return to the five-day week. The fact that this number of men feel this way is not at all surprising. What is somewhat surprising is that more of the workers did not desire a return to the standard workweek. Innovations that result in major changes in peoples' routines and behavior patterns generally run up against significant opposition, at least in that portion of the population most directly affected. Therefore, either the four-day workweek is not perceived by those affected as constituting a major change, or it represents the type of environmental change whose time has arrived. Both factors are probably operating. As will be demonstrated in the discussion to follow, the four-day schedule's impact appears to occur most commonly at the margins of workers' attitudes and patterns of behaving. It serves, thereby, either to facilitate and help legitimize existing life-styles or to accentuate and exacerbate already present adjustment difficulties. Either way, the consequences are real but not radical, and their net impact on adjustment is beneficial for the majority of working men.

Four-day workers provided a variety of reasons for looking favorably on their nonconventional hours of labor and leisure. Among the most often cited are having more time to spend with the family, the ability to do more work around the house, having more opportunity for putting in overtime, and, most commonly, having an extra day-off each week. With respect to the latter reason, it is unclear whether the men like the longer weekend principally because of what they are able to accomplish during this time or because they now spend one less day on the job, that is, because it affords them some additional escape from the frustrations associated with work and the work setting. Given findings still to be presented, it is undoubtedly the result of the complex interaction of both factors.

Reflecting the fact that most four-day workers are at least moderately satisfied with their schedule, relatively few negative comments were made. Three, however, stand out. The first is the perception of several workers that management is using the four-day week to induce, and at times to compel, their employees to put in unwanted overtime. This possibility was previously mentioned as one reason for organized labor's opposition to the four-day 40-hour workweek (Chapter 1). The second and third negative comments are closely related. As expected, many four-day workers expressed a strong dislike for their ten-hour workday, stating that it forced them to get up too early, cut into the time they had to do errands, and interfered with their social life. These consequences appear to constitute the primary explicit reasons why men gave a generally low response to their working a four-day, 40-hour week. Finally, and unexpectedly, only one four-day worker specifically mentioned a negative impact within the family when listing his reasons for liking and disliking the compacted schedule. While more such comments were certainly anticipated, it must be recognized that making adverse statements concerning one's family life runs contrary to social norms. Several of the negative comments do, however, have implications for adjustment in the family context, specifically those pertaining to the length of the workday. Moreover, as will be demonstrated in Chapters 5 and 6, the four-day workweek influences adjustment in this setting via a complex, interactive chain of causation, and both marital and role-performance adjustment, in turn, influence the worker's affective response to working a four-day week.

In view of the analyses that follow, interest in the income and education variables is reduced. Though these variables are undoubtedly related to the quality of the individual's adjustment in his various life domains, their impact seems to occur irrespective of the schedule worked. Factors other than these appear to be more powerful predictors of adjustment. Specifically, the length of the workday, the use of discretionary time, and the issue of overtime loom significant as sources of dissatisfaction with the compacted schedule. These variables will be important when the ramifications of the four-day week within the work and family settings are discussed.

The data presented in the previous sections go beyond describing the attitudes of four-day and five-day workers toward their respective work schedules. They provide several important insights into setting-specific consequences of working this alternative to the standard week, and into the dynamics underlying these consequences. And this, as much as the men's general reactions to their experiences with it, is the concern of this study. In the analyses to follow, a wide variety of variables relevant to several life domains are examined in some depth. Several variables, however, are of particular interest either because of the importance assigned them in this study or due to their significance in previous studies. To some extent, data analysis here was guided by hypotheses and arguments concerning the reciprocal relationship between work-schedule satisfaction and these variables. They are (1) satisfaction with the use of free time, (2) job satisfaction, (3) work fatigue, (4) whether the individual works the amount of overtime he desires—overtime/overtime-wanted, (5) conjugal role-performance satisfaction, (6) parental role-performance satisfaction, and (7) overall marital satisfaction. The last three measures are employed in this study as rough indicators of adjustment in the family context. The three work-setting variables have often been cited in conjunction with work-schedule innovations, while the free-time satisfaction measure is included because of its significance with respect to the arguments advanced by proponents of nonconventional work schedules.

Before turning to the discussions of the effect of the four-day workweek in the context of work, family, and the use of discretionary time, the relationship of the above seven variables to the workers' response to their compacted schedule warrants presentation. Table 4.3 shows the strength of these associations. The results displayed in the table assume the predictor variables relate to work-schedule satisfaction in an additive rather than in an interactive manner. As will be seen throughout subsequent analyses, this assumption is inaccurate. The truth of the matter is that interactive relationships are the rule, with additive ones being the exception. Consequently, the use of an additive model masks opposing relationships among variables in the different subgroups. It also results in the underestimation of

TABLE 4.3

Multiple Classification Analysis Summary Statistics
for Seven Predictors of Work-Schedule Satisfaction,
for Four-Day Workers (N = 209)

Variable	Eta^2	$Beta^2$
Satisfaction with use of free time	.36	.54
Satisfaction with job	.17	.08
Satisfaction with conjugal role perf.	.16	.18
Satisfaction with marriage	.13	.02
Fatigue	.05	.05
Satisfaction with parental role perf.	.03	.11
Overtime/overtime-wanted	.03	.02
Multiple R^2	.47	

Note: The eta-squared coefficients indicate the proportion of variation in the dependent variable explainable by each variable, taken by itself, with all the classification details maintained. The beta-squared coefficients, on the other hand, measure the relative importance of each variable in explaining variation with the remaining variables held constant. These coefficients are not meant to sum to R-squared.

Source: Compiled by the author.

the importance of the association between each predictor-dependent variable pair. Nonetheless, the data shown in Table 4.3 do provide a useful, if rough, estimate.

It is clear from the table that satisfaction with the use of free time is the most powerful predictor of work-schedule satisfaction. Taken by itself, job satisfaction would be next, followed closely by conjugal role performance and overall marital satisfaction. When the other variables are held constant, however, the two marital role-performance variables become relatively important while both job and marital satisfaction appear less so. Using either measure of association, fatigue and overtime/overtime-wanted have no signifi-cant additive relationship to schedule satisfaction. Perhaps more informative than any of these separate coefficients are the findings when the beta-squared coefficients are summed with others relevant to the same setting. When this is done, one sees that the three family-setting variables contribute twice as much to explained variance in work schedule satisfaction as do the three work-setting variables when taken as a group (0.31 and 0.15, respectively). While the poten-tial for reading too much into this finding certainly is present, the result does provide some support for the contention that adjustment in the family context is a potentially important determinant of worker response to nonconventional schedules. It is also in agreement with the findings of other studies, and with the arguments made earlier, as to the relative unimportance of the schedule's impact on the indi-vidual's behavior and attitudes within the work setting when it comes to evaluating the four-day workweek's long-run viability and accept-ability.

Nevertheless, response within the work setting is significant and of considerable intrinsic interest. Therefore, it is with adjust-ment in this setting that we now concern ourselves in the balance of this chapter. Attention then turns, in Chapters 5 and 6, to the conse-quences of working a four-day week in the family setting. Finally, in Chapter 7, four-day and five-day workers are compared on how they use their time, and differences in their utilization of, and reaction to, their use of discretionary (or free) time are discussed.

IMPACT WITHIN THE WORK SETTING

A primary conclusion drawn from the arguments presented in Chapter 2 was that if working an official four-day week had any signi-ficant impact upon workers' lives, it would occur mainly outside the work setting. To be sure, ramifications within this setting are to be anticipated—greater fatigue and more overtime for example. Yet, because this shift in the hours of work implies no meaningful change in the basic nature of the jobs, it was concluded that the workers' job-related attitudes would be affected only at the margin. The time has now come to put this argument to the test. The balance of this chapter is devoted to an examination of selected affective and behavioral responses to the four-day workweek. In particular, it is concerned with this schedule's effect upon job satisfaction, fatigue, and overtime.

Job Satisfaction

It was hypothesized in Chapter 3 that—contrary to the expectations of those managers and employers who view the four-day workweek as a mechanism for boosting their employees' work morale—job satisfaction would, at best, remain unaffected. So long as workers are able to separate their feelings with regard to their work schedule from those pertaining to the job itself, their positive response to the former should not generalize to the latter to any great extent. Since the schedule is probably particularly salient for workers on a nonconventional one, this would seem to be a fairly safe assumption. Not to be discounted, however, is the decided possibility that such factors as fatigue, or a reevaluation of the relative value of job-related and leisure-related gratifications, could adversely influence the worker's attitude toward his job.

When the men sampled were queried about their satisfaction with their jobs, the basic hypothesis had to be rejected; the "average" four-day worker did, in fact, report greater job dissatisfaction than his five-day counterpart ($\overline{X}_4 = 2.48$, $\overline{X}_5 = 2.11$, p < 0.05). Table 4.4

TABLE 4.4

Job Satisfaction by Work Group
(percent)

Work Group	Completely Satisfied*	Moderately Satisfied*	Dissatisfied*
Four-day workers (N = 169)	37.3	35.5	27.3
Five-day workers (N = 50)	30.0	64.0	6.0

*The original response alternatives consisted of a seven-point Likert scale. These responses were combined to form three categories: complete satisfaction (1), moderately satisfied (2-3), and dissatisfied (4-7).

Source: Compiled by the author.

displays a pattern of responses that recurs several times in the study. At least in comparison to five-day workers, the affective levels reported by four-day workers tend to the extremes of the range of possible response alternatives. In this instance, a greater percentage of these men expressed complete satisfaction with their jobs, while significantly more reported being dissatisfied ($z = 2.18$, $p < 0.05$).*

In an effort to explain these findings, job satisfaction was initially examined in terms of the worker's age, perception of the firm's reason for adopting the compacted work schedule, and number of years he had worked this schedule. The first two variables are interesting because of their relationship to schedule satisfaction. The third was included due to the possibility that adjustment in the work setting to the four-day week might improve as one's experience with it increases. Neither the workers' opinions as to why the schedule was changed nor the length of experience with it, however, was related to job satisfaction. Age, on the other hand, was a different matter. Looking first at workers under age 35 in both work groups, though the pattern pointed out in Table 4.4 is repeated, no significant difference was found in their mean job satisfaction. On the average, these younger four-day and five-day workers were equally disenchanted with their jobs. But the same cannot be said of those aged 35 and over. Older four-day men were found to be significantly more dissatisfied with their jobs ($t = 2.99$, $p < 0.01$).

This result is noteworthy in that these men expressed more, not less, satisfaction with their schedule than their five-day counterparts (see Figure 4.1). Based on these findings, an interesting conclusion can be advanced for consideration. It appears that the psychological process of job "habitation"—the reconciling of oneself to one's occupational position and the conditions thereof—occurs to a lesser extent among four-day workers. These men are both dissatisfied with their jobs and satisfied with their compacted work schedule almost irrespective of age. Why this happens is unclear, but one can speculate that perhaps the enhanced opportunity to engage in valued activities outside work highlights the paucity of intrinsic work gratifications to the point that these gratifications look pale in comparison to those now obtainable at home and during free time. If this is in fact the situation, then, despite claims to the contrary, many jobs do

---

*It does not appear likely, however, that the four-day workers' greater job dissatisfaction is translated into relatively more job-seeking behavior. When the men in both work groups were asked "Taking everything into consideration, how likely is it that you will make a genuine effort to find a new job within the next year—very likely, somewhat likely, or not at all likely?"—the distribution of responses was nearly identical.

"deaden the will." The individual's potential for self-development is being insidiously hampered by a work routine that interferes with his participation in more psychologically rewarding endeavors. With time, the worker comes to accept, with equanimity, things as they stand, including disagreeable aspects of the job. Increasingly, he grows unaware of the deprivation and frustration he felt when he was younger. With a growing lack of basis for making comparisons, his critical judgment diminishes. The saliency of working a four-day week, on the other hand, makes such comparisons unavoidable—between the schedule one has and alternative schedules, between work gratifications and leisure gratifications, between one life-style and another, and so on. At least for the men in this sample, the result is that most four-day workers are more satisfied with their schedules than with their jobs. To be sure, this is only speculation; other explanations abound. For example, fatigue may be a serious problem for older four-day workers. Nevertheless, until disproved, the above argument should not be rejected out of hand; there is a good deal of support for it in the literature.

Fatigue

When the four-day week, ten-hour day is discussed, the question of fatigue is invariably raised. To explore this concern, the men studied here were asked "When you come home from a day at work, how tired do you usually feel—very tired, somewhat tired, or not at all tired?" The distributions of answers for four-day and five-day workers are recorded at the top of Table 4.5. Nearly three times as

TABLE 4.5

Relationship between Work Fatigue and Overtime Hours

Variable: Work Group	Very Tired	Somewhat Tired	Not at All Tired
Percent So Responding:			
Four-day workers (N = 167)	22.2	67.1	10.8
Five-day workers (N = 50)	8.0	80.0	12.0
Mean Number of Overtime Hours in Past Month:			
Four-day workers (N = 167)	33.73	27.85	35.72
Five-day workers (N = 50)	31.29	21.86	35.17

Source: Compiled by the author.

TABLE 4.6

Mean Job Satisfaction and Work–Schedule Satisfaction
By Work Fatigue

Variable: Work Group	Very Tired	Somewhat Tired	Not at All Tired
Mean Job Satisfaction:			
Four-day workers	2.43 (N = 37)	2.58 (N = 112)	2.00 (N = 18)
Five-day workers	2.43 (N = 4)	2.16 (N = 40)	1.58 (N = 6)
Mean Schedule Satisfaction:			
Four-day workers	2.46 (N = 37)	1.90 (N = 112)	1.28 (N = 18)
Five-day workers	1.00 (N = 2)	2.57 (N = 34)	1.90 (N = 5)

Source: Compiled by the author.

many four-day workers said they usually felt very tired when they returned home from a day at work ($z = 2.25$, $p < 0.05$). It appears, then, that the length of the workday does indeed result in something of a fatigue problem. Thinking then that fatigue might be related to age, the fatigue levels reported by workers in different age brackets were examined. While a greater percentage of four-day than five-day workers in all age brackets did report feeling very tired when they returned home, no significant relationship between age and fatigue was found within either work group.

The second set of figures in Table 4.5 shows that the fatigue experienced was most likely due to factors other than the number of overtime hours worked; less than six hours per month separate the "very tired" four-day workers from their cohorts who indicate a lower level of fatigue. Moreover, the men who reported feeling no tiredness averaged the most overtime. The same general pattern was found to hold for five-day workers.

The data in Table 4.6 relate job satisfaction and work–schedule satisfaction to fatigue. As can be seen, there is little or no association between job satisfaction and work fatigue for men on the compacted week, but an inverse relationship for five-day workers ($Gamma_4 = -0.07$, $p = NS$; $Gamma_5 = -0.44$, $p < 0.05$). On the other hand, when fatigue is related to satisfaction with one's work schedule, the pattern is reversed; schedule satisfaction is significantly associated with fatigue among the four-day men and not related for those working a five-day schedule (Gamma$_4$ = 0.43, p < 0.01; Gamma$_5$ = -0.04, p = NS).

The first point to be noted about these findings is that they indicate the workers do distinguish their work schedule from their jobs affectively as well as conceptually. Second, apparently men working the standard schedule ascribe their work fatigue more to their job activities than to the arrangement of the hours of work. Consequently, the more tired they feel, the greater the dissatisfaction with their job but not their schedule. Among four-day workers, however, the organization of work hours, particularly the ten-hour day, is highly visible. Not unexpectedly, therefore, they tend to associate work fatigue with their longer hours of daily labor rather than to the nature of their jobs themselves. They express their dissatisfactions accordingly. Finally, while problems with fatigue and its related consequences may partially account for some men's negative attitude toward the four-day week, this brings us no closer to an understanding of why four-day workers were more satisfied with their compacted schedule than the control group with their standard five-day workweek.

Overtime

Overtime, like fatigue, is an issue that inevitably gets raised when the notion of a compacted work schedule is broached. Will the workers use their larger blocks of free time for leisure pursuits or will they allocate additional time to overtime? What role do overtime hours play in determining the men's satisfaction with their hours of work and leisure? It is often argued that workers desire more overtime and not more free time and that it is this that motivates the drive for alternative hours of work. If this is the case, then the data should show that four-day workers want to, and do, put in more overtime than five-day workers. Those who advocate the compacted workweek as a means to escape from the work setting, on the other hand, would anticipate a greater percentage of the men on a four-day week to work the amount of overtime they desired, but not necessarily that they would desire more overtime. To be sure, given the probability that most of their friends work a standard five-day week, there could occur a slight accretion in overtime hours due to the attractiveness of working a full day of overtime on the extra free day. However, a wholesale increase in the average number of overtime hours worked should not be found. For if it were, then one of three possible conclusions would have to be drawn: (1) the drive for a four-day or otherwise altered work schedule is largely motivated by a desire for overtime rather than free time; (2) as disagreeable as the work setting may be, compared to the alternatives, it is the best game in town; or (3) employers are using this schedule as a mechanism for encouraging more overtime. No matter which of these conclusions, or combination thereof, comes closer to the truth, the stance of four-day workweek advocates would be seriously undermined, and perhaps blue-collar workers would be better served by social innovations of a different kind.

When asked how many hours of overtime they worked in the month preceding the interview, four-day men reported working an average of 29.65 hours as against 24.38 hours for the control group. This difference, however, is not statistically significant. Therefore, it is tentatively concluded that most men on the four-day week are not motivated toward substantially greater overtime.* Of equal, if not greater interest is the fact that, when overtime hours are correlated with job satisfaction and schedule satisfaction separately for both work groups, the results are totally insignificant. Job and schedule satisfaction thus are not, at least directly, related to the number of overtime hours worked. This, however, tells only part of the story. Far more important is the extent to which the men are able to work the amount of overtime they desire and the influence this has, in turn, on the attitudes they hold with respect to their jobs and their work schedules. The relevant data are presented in Table 4.7.

This table displays several findings directly relevant to the central concern of this study—determining the affective and behavioral impact working a four-day week has upon blue-collar men. First, more than two-thirds of these men felt they worked the amount of overtime they wanted, while less than half of the men on the standard schedule felt the same way (z = 3.05, p < 0.01). Second, assuming the overtime data for the past month to be representative, we cannot realistically attribute this discrepancy to differences between the two groups in the amount of overtime worked. Though in all three of the overtime/overtime-wanted categories, the average number of hours for four-day workers exceeded those for their five-day counterparts, especially among those who reported working the right amount of overtime, none of the differences is statistically significant. It appears, then, that while four-day workers do not work much, if any, more overtime than men on a standard week, they nonetheless are more likely to work the amount of overtime they want. Just why this paradox should occur is unclear. Perhaps the overtime policies of

---

*When overtime as measured by the time-budget diary was calculated, four-day workers were found to have worked less overtime than the five-day men (Chapter 7). This result reinforces the assumption in the following discussion that four-day workers do not put in more overtime.

TABLE 4.7

Relationship Between Overtime/Overtime Wanted
And Number of Overtime Hours

Variable: Work Group	Less Overtime Than Wanted	Right Amount of Overtime	More Overtime Than Wanted
Percent so Responding:			
Four-day workers			
(N = 163)	19.6	66.9	13.5
Five-day workers			
(N = 50)	30.0	48.0	22.0
Number of Overtime Hours in Past Month:			
Four-day workers			
(N = 163)	15.00	31.74	42.50
Five-day workers			
(N = 50)	13.80	23.60	40.50

Source: Compiled by the author.

TABLE 4.8

Mean Job Satisfaction and Work-Schedule Satisfaction
By Overtime Wanted

Variable: Work Group	Less Overtime Than Wanted	Right Amount of Overtime	More Overtime Than Wanted
Mean Job Satisfaction:			
Four-day workers	2.97	2.36	2.23
	(N = 32)	(N = 109)	(N = 22)
Five-day workers	2.13	1.81	2.73
	(N = 15)	(N = 24)	(N = 11)
Mean Schedule Satisfaction:			
Four-day workers	1.56	2.12	1.68
	(N = 32)	(N = 109)	(N = 22)
Five-day workers	3.36	2.03	2.25
	(N = 11)	(N = 22)	(N = 8)

Source: Compiled by the author.

four-day companies made it possible for more of their employees to work the number of hours they wished, no matter what this figure may be.* Maybe the greater flexibility inherent in the four-day schedule enables these workers to achieve a better balance between overtime and free-time activities irrespective of the number of overtime hours worked. Whatever the reason, the four-day workers did express greater satisfaction with their overtime hours.

The data in Table 4.8 relate both job satisfaction and work-schedule satisfaction to the number of overtime hours worked. For both groups of workers, lack of opportunity for overtime negatively affected job satisfaction. Considering that access to overtime is a salient evaluative aspect of most blue-collar jobs, this finding was certainly to be expected. The data for men who worked more overtime than they wanted are somewhat more informative. Four-day workers here are more satisfied with their jobs than their five-day counterparts, though the difference is not statistically significant. This is a reversal of the pattern found in the other two overtime/overtime-wanted categories. In addition, while the four-day men in this category were as satisfied with their jobs as their cohorts who felt they put in the right amount of overtime, their five-day counterparts indicated significantly greater job dissatisfaction than their "brothers in schedule" who reported overtime satisfaction (t = 3.02, p < 0.01). Since four-day and five-day workers in this category averaged the same number of overtime hours during the past month, it would appear that the compacted schedule made it possible for the former to adjust relatively better to excessive, and occasionally coerced, overtime. By so doing, the adverse impact of unwanted overtime upon the four-day workers' attitude toward their jobs is held to a minimum. One can speculate that by allocating most of the overtime to their extra free day, four-day workers are able to collect their additional premium pay and still have two largely unencumbered weekend days left over. Perhaps the added income in some measure compensates for the undesired loss of free time. Unfortunately, this solution is not available to five-day workers. Though they are at somewhat greater liberty to work overtime during the week due to their shorter workday, extensive overtime can only be accomplished at the expense of free time on their shorter weekend. Thus, unwanted overtime almost inevitably intereferes with the opportunities these workers have for participating in other valued activities. This cannot help but reflect adversely upon their jobs.

Turning to the second set of figures in Table 4.8, we can see that when four-day and five-day men are able to work the amount of

---

*One of the four-day firms did adopt an overtime incentive program when they switched work schedules.

overtime they desire, they are equally satisfied with their respective schedules. Among those less fortunate, however, the situation is decidedly otherwise. The pattern displayed was quite unexpected. Four-day men who worked either more or less overtime than they wanted are more satisfied with their schedule than the men who indicated they worked the right amount of overtime, with the latter group being significantly more so ($t = 2.28$, $p < 0.05$). The situation is just the opposite among five-day workers. For them, working other than the desired amount of overtime associates with greater schedule dissatisfaction, with the difference between the men who worked less and those who worked the right amount of overtime attaining statistical significance ($t = 2.36$, $p < 0.05$). Finally, when the two work groups are compared within response categories, those four-day men who worked less than the number of overtime hours they desired are found to be significantly more satisfied with their schedule than their five-day counterparts ($t = 3.24$, $p < 0.01$).

These findings constitute the first set of results that help to explain why four-day workers expressed greater satisfaction with their nonconventional schedule than the control group with their standard workweek. Among men who worked less overtime than they would have preferred, those on the four-day week are apparently in a relatively better position vis-a-vis their schedule to obtain more than adequate compensatory gratification from nonwork activities, especially during their longer weekends. Just what these activities are is discussed in some depth in Chapter 7. For men who worked what they considered to be an excessive number of overtime hours, the speculation made above in the context of job satisfaction appears equally applicable. Working a compacted four-day week enables men to accommodate better the overtime demands directed at them. With overtime interfering relatively less with their participation in other valued activities, these four-day workers also found themselves in a situation conducive to expression of greater schedule satisfaction.

One work-related by-product of the four-day week remains. As noted earlier, slightly over 7 percent of the four-day workers felt they were being pressured into unwanted overtime. When their responses are compared to those provided by the balance of the four-day sample, one finds these men to have indeed worked more overtime in the past month, though the difference is not statistically significant. Surprisingly, when the 7 percent were asked whether they worked their desired amount of overtime, there was little to distinguish the distribution of their answers from those of the other four-day workers. They did, however, indicate somewhat greater work fatigue. More than 45 percent of them, compared to 20.5 percent of the other four-day men, reported feeling very tired after work ($z = 1.93$, $p < 0.10$). Blaming the four-day week for the increased overtime pressure and their resultant fatigue, they naturally expressed more dissatisfaction with this schedule than their cohorts who did not feel themselves subjected to any such coercion (2.85 versus 1.80 respectively, $p < 10$). Despite this, they were not significantly less satisfied with their jobs and no more likely to look for a new job in the foreseeable future.

Discussion and Summary of Job Satisfaction

The discussion in this chapter concerned specifically with changes in the work setting opened with the hypothesis that working a four-day week should have little or no impact here. In particular, it was expected that job satisfaction would be unaffected or affected only at the margin. The data presented bring this hypothesis into question. Though four-day workers were no more likely than their five-day counterparts to look for a new job in the foreseeable future and did not work significantly more overtime, they nonetheless experienced greater work fatigue and expressed greater job dissatisfaction. Cause can only be speculated upon. Certainly, age is a factor, for those four-day workers aged 35 and over expressed significantly greater job dissatisfaction than their five-day counterparts. Yet the expected reason, greater work fatigue, was found not to apply. To be sure, the ten-hour day contributed to their feeling tired at the end of the workday and, no doubt, accounted for some of the dissatisfaction with the compacted schedule. But fatigue was a problem for four-day workers regardless of age. Moreover, it was found to be unrelated to job satisfaction. Thus, while fatigue does constitute an outcome of working the longer day that needs to be considered in evaluating this nonconventional schedule, it does not appear to account, at least not directly, for the decline in job satisfaction. The suggestion was made earlier that the compacted schedule somehow interacts with age to negate the typical pattern of job habituation.

The same general pattern was uncovered among those four-day workers who experienced unwanted pressure for overtime; work-schedule satisfaction dropped while job satisfaction remained largely unaffected. On the positive side, the four-day week does associate with greater satisfaction with the number of overtime hours worked and, probably, in a more satisfying arrangement of work and leisure time. Finally, contrary to expectation and the results of previous studies, neither the length of time the worker has been on the four-day schedule nor his perception of why the firm adopted it in the first place was found to relate to job satisfaction.

In conclusion, there is little that can be concluded. The variables measured did not adequately explain why the four-day workers were relatively dissatisfied with their jobs. Nor could it be determined whether this dissatisfaction was, in fact, due to the four-day schedule at all. The results do, however, show that while work-setting-related consequences of changes in the arrangement of work time, especially with regard to overtime, constitute a partial explanation for the four-day workers' greater schedule satisfaction, much of the difference here remains unaccounted for. What compensations outside the work setting, for example, are available to four-day workers who work more overtime than desired that are not equally available to five-day men? It has been suggested here that if the four-day workweek were to prove beneficial, the changes would be found to occur in settings outside the work place. The time has now come to focus attention on the ramifications of the four-day workweek in the life domain most salient for the majority of individuals—the family context.

In Chapter 1 it was argued that satisfaction with the four-day workweek would often depend on the individual's adjustment within the family context. In this and the next chapter, the impact of the four-day schedule on family roles and relationships is explored. The objectives are to determine the extent to which role performance and marital adjustment are affected by working this nonconventional schedule, describe selected aspects of the dynamics involved, and relate the men's marital motivations and other family variables to their satisfaction with the four-day schedule.

The four-day week at once contains the seeds for not only increased marital satisfaction but also increased marital discord. The larger blocks of discretionary time may serve to improve the male worker's chances for effectively fulfilling his family role functions and for enhancing the quality of his family relationships and, thereby, result in better marital adjustment. On the other hand, an inappropriate or nonproductive use of the extra discretionary time or too radical changes in the role demands directed at the individual by other members of his family could result in the breakdown of familial relationships and a reduction in the individual's satisfaction with his family life. These opposing possibilities suggest that, before turning to the relationships of marital motivations and other family variables to schedule satisfaction, it would be well to answer two other kinds of questions.

The first set of questions concerns the influence of the four-day schedule upon family role performance and general marital satisfaction. Specifically, as a result of the compacted workweek, does the worker perceive that his conjugal and parental role performances and/or the satisfaction he derives from his marriage have been enhanced or damaged?

Second, the person-environment hypotheses discussed in Chapter 3 relating marital motivations to marital satisfactions and family pressures need to be tested independently of their relationships to other family variables and to schedule satisfaction. Though the hypotheses were suggested as part of the concern with adjustment to the four-day workweek, they can stand on their own. The extent to which they are confirmed is then seen to constitute further indication of the construct validity of the present approach to the conceptualization and measurement of conjugal and parental motivations, regardless of how they relate to other family variables and schedule satisfaction. Of greater importance, this examination will provide added insight into the dynamics of adjustment to the four-day week within the family setting.

MARITAL SATISFACTION AND SATISFACTION WITH CONJUGAL AND PARENTAL ROLE PERFORMANCE

Due to the greater flexibility in organizing their family-related activities, it was hypothesized that four-day workers would express greater satisfaction with their conjugal and parental role performances and with their marriages in general than would a comparable group of five-day workers. The findings displayed in Table 5.1 show that these predictions are not, in fact, borne out by the data. There is virtually no difference between groups as to mean satisfactions for the three dependent variables. This does not mean, however, that the four-day work schedule is unrelated to adjustment in the family setting. While on the average four-day and five-day men expressed equal satisfaction, there are marked differences in the distribution of their responses on the measures of satisfaction with conjugal role performance and marriage.

Five-day workers indicated feeling moderately satisfied with their marriages. Four-day workers, on the other hand, tended to give more extreme responses (p < 0.02). Of particular significance here is the finding that 50.8 percent of all four-day men, compared to only 35.1 percent of those on a standard work schedule, expressed complete satisfaction (p < 0.05). At the other extreme, the portion of workers in each group who were dissatisfied with their marriages is nearly equal. Yet, within this category, somewhat more of the four-day men reported complete or near complete dissatisfaction (4.5 percent versus 1.8 percent). In addition, within the "moderately satisfied" category, four-day men once again tend toward the negative end of the continuum. A similar response pattern also occurs on the conjugal role-performance variable. Relative to those given by their five-day counterparts, the responses of four-day workers tend toward both ends of the continuum (p < 0.05). Approximately 11 percent more of the four-day workers indicated they felt completely satisfied with their role performance, while the percentage of them who expressed dissatisfaction was nearly three times as great as among five-day workers (12.1 percent versus 4.3 percent).

The reason for the identical mean satisfaction scores of both groups on these two dependent variables seems fairly straightforward. It is due not to a lack of impact of the four-day schedule on adjustment in the family context, but to its differential effect on different people. This being the case, any attempt to evaluate the four-day work schedule's impact within the family context based solely on measures of "average" adjustment would lead to an erroneous, and potentially

TABLE 5.1

Satisfaction with Conjugal and Parental Role
Performances and with Marriage

	Completely Satisfied*	Moderately Satisfied*	Dissatisfied*	Mean Satisfaction (Ungrouped)
Conjugal Role-Performance Sat.				
Four-day workers (N = 166)	37.4%	50.6%	12.1%	2.11
Five-day workers (N = 46)	26.1	69.6	4.3	2.12
Parental Role-Performance Sat.				
Four-day workers (N = 149)	36.2	54.4	9.4	2.09
Five-day workers (N = 40)	37.5	60.0	2.5	1.96
Marital Satisfaction				
Four-day workers (N = 199)	50.8	36.2	13.1	2.02
Five-day workers (N = 57)	35.1	54.4	10.5	2.01

*The seven-point codes used in each of the three satisfaction measures were collapsed as follows: completely satisfied—1, moderately satisfied—2 and 3, dissatisfied—4 to 7.

Source: Compiled by the author.

dangerous, conclusion: that the four-day workweek has no significant adjustment consequences in the family setting. The danger derives from its potential influence on planning endeavors undertaken in conjunction with conversions to the four-day workweek, or, for that matter, to any other nonconventional work schedule. Reliance on this erroneous conclusion may induce planners to ignore the schedule's implications for family adjustment and may thereby result in the designing of programs ill-equipped for effectively coping with possible social problems associated with what appears here to be a real, albeit modest, potential for an increase in the number of married men experiencing adjustment difficulties.

MARITAL MOTIVATIONS, PRESSURES, AND SATISFACTIONS

Marital Motivations and Adjustment in the Family

Two distinct sets of relationships between marital motivations and intervening variables that might account for the four-day workers' relatively greater schedule satisfaction were proposed. The first set of hypotheses posited marital satisfaction and satisfaction with role performance as intervening variables. It was predicted that marital motivations would be positively correlated with marital gratifications among four-day workers and zero to negatively correlated among five-day workers. In other words, both companionate and traditional role status motivations were expected, on the average, to be easier to gratify when working a four-day as opposed to a five-day week. As corollaries of these predictions, marital motivations should have near zero or slightly positive correlations with P-E Fit, marital satisfaction, and satisfaction with role performance among four-day workers and near zero to negative correlations with P-E Fit, marital satisfaction, and role-performance satisfaction among five-day workers.

The data lend only partial support to these predictions. As is evident in Table 5.2, the motivations associate positively with their corresponding gratifications in both work groups. The two exceptions are the relationships between conjugal companionship motivation and its gratification for four-day workers, and between traditional status motivation and its corresponding gratification for men on the standard schedule. While the latter noncorrelation was expected, the former was predicted to be positive. Particularly surprising, however, are the fairly strong associations of the conjugal and parental companionship motivations with their corresponding gratifications for men on the five-day schedule ($r = 0.25$ and $r = 0.46$, respectively).

TABLE 5.2

Correlations of Marital Motivations with Corresponding
Gratifications, Marital Satisfactions,
and Opposite Gratifications

Motivation	Four-Day Workers		Five-Day Workers	
Endogomous Variable	N	Correlation	N	Correlation
Conjugal Companionship Motivation with:				
Conjugal compan. gratification	160	-.03	43	.25
Conjugal role performance	161	.20	46	.06
Parental role performance	144	.25	39	.01
Marital satisfaction	159	.14	45	.20
Parental compan. gratification	141	.18	37	.17
Traditional status gratification	143	.01	38	-.15
Parental Companionship Motivation with:				
Parental compan. gratification	144	.48	37	.46
Conjugal role performance	159	.06	45	-.27
Parental role performance	146	.14	38	.03
Marital satisfaction	155	.15	44	-.03
Conjugal compan. gratification	158	.04	42	-.24
Traditional status gratification	147	.16	38	-.06
Traditional Status Motivation with:				
Traditional status gratification	141	.15	36	.04
Conjugal role performance	153	.25	43	-.10
Parental role performance	140	.16	37	-.16
Marital satisfaction	150	.25	43	-.15
Conjugal compan. gratification	152	.03	40	-.10
Parental compan. gratification	138	.08	35	.34

Source: Compiled by the author.

The correlation of the three motivation variables with marital satisfaction and satisfaction with conjugal and parental role performance, on the other hand, are just about as predicted. Among the four-day men, these associations are all positive, with several attaining statistical significance. For their five-day counterparts, the correlations are either near zero or negative, the single exception being that between conjugal companionship motivation and satisfaction with the marriage in general ($r = 0.20$). It appears, therefore, that the three family motivation variables relate as expected to individual adjustment to the four-day schedule in the family context, but that the effects of the intervening gratification variables do not. What follows is a brief interpretive discussion of the results.

It was originally hypothesized that the stronger the four-day worker's family motivations, the more likely he will be to take advantage of his new opportunities for obtaining family gratifications. Accordingly, for four-day workers, it was predicted that the correlations between each motivation and its corresponding gratification would be positive. Since five-day workers' opportunities for family gratifications are more limited, near zero correlations between their motivations and gratifications were predicted. In fact, the data indicate that, with respect to conjugal companionship motivation, rather than making it easier for highly motivated persons to obtain their desired level of gratification, the four-day schedule serves to facilitate the obtaining of conjugal companionship gratifications for all four-day workers, highly motivated or not. Even if those men less motivated toward conjugal companionship worked extensive overtime, say their extra day-off each week, two complete free days would still remain, and most of that time would be spent in the family setting. With access to these family rewards made easier, the relationship between motivation and gratification cannot help but be weakened. And so, the near zero correlation found between conjugal companionship motivation and gratification for men on a four-day schedule is not too surprising.* The situation is different for men on the standard schedule because for them overtime and normal role obligations (such as household repairs) cut deeper into discretionary time, particularly on weekends. As hypothesized, the receipt of conjugal

---

*To some extent, this finding is also an artifact of the measurement technique employed—a five-point Likert scale. Objectively, highly motivated four-day men may well receive more conjugal companionship gratifications than do their less motivated cohorts, but having a limited selection of response alternatives and with both higher and lower motivated men receiving a greater than "normal" supply of such rewards (relative to men on a standard schedule) the responses of these men naturally tend to crowd the positive end of the response scale.

companionship gratifications is relatively more problematic for these men. Receipt of these rewards depends more, therefore, on the individual's taking active steps to obtain them. Thus, the stronger the five-day worker's conjugal companionship motivation, the greater should be his supply of such gratifications, thereby resulting in the positive correlation found between these variables for men in this work group.

The high positive, and nearly identical, associations between each parental companionship motivation and its corresponding gratification found for both work groups can be attributed mainly to the fact that, regardless of their father's work schedule, most children attend school five days a week. In addition, while the four-day worker is in a position to accomplish his family chores, work overtime, and so forth on the third free day, and thus has more time left unencumbered to spend with his children on nonschool days, his children set up their own activity schedules with limited attention to their father's available discretionary time. Further, the four-day worker's weekend advantage is partly offset by the ten-hour length of his regular working day. Consequently, whether the individual works a standard or a compacted week, his chances for experiencing parental companionship rewards are about the same. The level of parental companionship gratifications obtained should, therefore, be roughly in proportion to his motivation toward their receipt. The relationship between these two variables will, therefore, be positive for both the four-day and five-day work groups. This interpretation is consonant with the statements made by those New York employees of the Chrysler Corporation who voted to discontinue their four-day workweek experiment. One of the principal reasons given was that, with their children returning to school, a primary benefit of the compacted schedule—the opportunity to take trips and do other things with the entire family—no longer existed.

Part of the explanation for the associations between motivations and family satisfactions lies in the relationship of each motivation with its two opposite gratifications (for example, conjugal companionship motivation with parental companionship gratification and traditional status gratification). Notice that both four-day and five-day workers who are motivated toward conjugal companionship also receive parental companionship rewards ($r_4 = 0.18$ and $r_5 = 0.17$). This finding is not surprising given that in this society many conjugal companionship activities are often done in the presence of, or actively involve, one's children as well. This pattern probably accounts for some of the positive relationship found between this motivation and satisfaction with parental role performance among four-day workers ($r = 0.25$).

Turning next to the relationship between traditional status motivation and parental companionship gratification, one sees a near zero correlation for four-day workers and a significantly positive correlation for five-day workers ($r_4 = 0.08$ and $r_5 = 0.34$). This result is not readily susceptible to simple interpretation; it will, therefore, be examined closely when the entire model is tested. At this point, it is sufficient to note that five-day men so motivated obtain parental companionship rewards that for some reason are unavailable to, or are withheld from, their four-day counterparts. Observe that in this instance the compacted schedule is viewed as being a decided disadvantage. This is in contrast to those relationships discussed just above where a near zero correlation for four-day workers was interpreted as an indication that all four-day men receive gratifications regardless of the strength of their motivation.

The last relationship to be discussed concerns that of parental companionship motivation and conjugal companionship gratification. The correlations here are 0.04 and -0.24 for the four-day and five-day groups, respectively. The simplest and most plausible interpretation of these results is that, given the smaller blocks of discretionary time available to the five-day worker, especially if he puts in a significant number of overtime hours, a strong desire for companionship with his children interferes with, or supplants, opportunities for conjugal companionship gratification. Among four-day workers this conflict appears far less prevalent—if it exists at all. Perhaps four-day workers use part of their extra free day to interact companionately with their spouse, thereby making it less costly to leave time for their children on the remaining two nonwork days. This explanation is consistent with the observed correlations between parental companionship motivation and the expressed levels of conjugal role-performance satisfaction ($r_4 = 0.06$ and $r_5 = -0.27$).

Marital Motivations and Family Pressures

It was posited in Chapter 3 that the four-day work schedule would influence the level of family pressure these men experience. To test this possibility, five distinct multi-item pressure indexes were constructed: (1) qualitative role overload, (2) quantitative role overload, (3) responsibility overload, (4) role ambiguity, and (5) role underload, or boredom. These measures were then combined to form a composite index of total family pressure.

It was hypothesized that as marital motivation increased, the four-day workers would experience less total family pressure. The reason for this is familiar. Highly motivated four-day workers not only have the inclination to reduce their perceived strain, they also have the temporal resources needed to mitigate the pressure. Their five-day counterparts, on the other hand, have fewer temporal resources and so are less able to alter their stressful environment.

Consequently, a negative correlation was predicted between motivation and total pressure for men working a compacted schedule, and a near zero to positive correlation was predicted for men working a standard five-day week. These predictions do not necessarily imply, however, that four-day men will, on the average, experience relatively less family pressure. The possibility remains that, because they may tend to spend more time in the family setting, additional demands may be directed toward them by the other family members. While, other things being equal, highly motivated four-day men should be able to cope with these demands, those less motivated will tend to initiate fewer coping actions. They may, therefore, find themselves experiencing relatively greater family pressure than like-motivated men on the standard workweek. If this situation should, in fact, occur, it is to be anticipated that these men would report experiencing greater role ambiguity, greater role-responsibility overload, and, possibly, greater qualitative role-performance overload.

Total family pressure does indeed correlate negatively with the conjugal companionship, parental companionship, and traditional status motivation measures for four-day workers (-0.34, -0.24, and -0.19, respectively). The correlations between these three motivations and family pressure for five-day workers are also in the expected direction. The two companionship motivations are both unrelated to total family pressure, while that between traditional status motivation and total family pressure is moderate and positive (-0.09, 0.09, and 0.24, respectively). These results clearly support the hypotheses.

When the associations between each of the motivations with the five component pressure indexes are examined, modest support for the above-stated expectations is found. Both conjugal and parental companionship motivations correlate most strongly with responsibility overload for four-day workers (-0.29 and -0.31, respectively) and are unrelated or weakly related for five-day workers (0.02 and -0.10, respectively). Likewise, conjugal companionship motivation and qualitative role overload, and parental companionship motivation and role ambiguity are moderately related for four-day and not for five-day workers (-0.26 and -0.20 versus 0.07 and -0.05 for four-day and five-day men, respectively). Traditional status motivation also correlates strongest, and negatively, with qualitative role overload among four-day workers and positively among five-day workers (-0.26 and 0.18, respectively). Interestingly, the two companionship motivations also correlate stronger with the boredom index (role underload) among four-day men than is the case among men on a standard workweek (-0.29 and -0.17 versus -0.15 and 0.11 for four-day and five-day men, respectively). Perhaps a lack of drive for these gratifications, combined with a lack of effort toward mitigating family pressures, leaves four-day workers with unwanted free time.

The two work groups were also compared on their average levels of family pressure. No significant differences were found between groups for any of the component pressure indexes or for the level of total family pressure reported. Indeed, the pair of averages for each pressure index was nearly identical in all cases. In general, then, it appears that the four-day workweek does not reduce subjectively perceived family pressure. Rather, it provides the opportunity for reducing the level of pressure experienced for those willing to make the necessary effort. For those not so inclined, it offers the strong possibility of their experiencing yet additional family pressures. Particularly susceptible are those individuals little motivated toward conjugal and parental companionship. These men may not only find themselves subjected to additional responsibility demands and role uncertainty but may also suffer from increased boredom.

CAUSAL MODEL

Specifying Causal Relationships

There are two kinds of causal relationships that the hypotheses in Chapter 3 did not specify: (1) that of each motivation with the two opposite gratifications and (2) that between each gratification variable and family pressure. It is quite plausible that these two sets of relationships account for a significant portion of the obtained correlations of motivations with the two role performance and the marital satisfaction variables.

Table 5.2 showed that conjugal companionship motivation associates positively with parental companionship gratification for both four-day and five-day workers. It was argued that this relationship is due to the tendency of husbands and wives to include their children in many of their conjugal companionship activities. These variables, however, are not viewed here as being causally related, but only as associated positively. This is because men who are motivated toward conjugal companionship tend also to be motivated toward parental companionship. The level of parental companionship gratification received is thus posited as being causally unrelated to the worker's conjugal companionship motivation. Parental companionship motivation, on the other hand, was found to correlate negatively with the level of conjugal companionship rewards obtained by five-day workers. The argument raised here is that, given his relatively limited companionship opportunities, efforts directed toward obtaining parental companionship rewards interfere with the five-day worker's chances for companionship with his wife. Thus, a high level of parental companionship motivation is viewed as possibly being responsible for some loss of conjugal companionship rewards among five-day, but not among four-day, workers. Turning to the cross-effect of traditional status motivation, here again the only significant association involved men on a standard work schedule. This motivation correlated positively with parental companionship gratification. In this instance, no explanation was specified, but it was felt that working a four-day schedule somehow operates to the detriment of those men with a strong traditional status desire. It is, therefore, posited that the higher the five-day worker's level of traditional status motivation, the greater his level of obtained parental companionship gratifications.

It was assumed in Chapter 3 that there would be a negative association between the gratification variables and total family pressure, but no causal relationship was specified. Past research and logic, however, dictate that there should indeed be a negative causal relationship here—that is, the receipt of gratifications should result in a decrease of subjectively perceived total family pressure. For example, conjugal companionship should, other things being equal, provide a husband and wife with an opportunity to work out their interpersonal and role conflicts; the more time they spend companionately, the more opportunities they have for working out any problems they may have. Consequently, a negative relationship is anticipated between conjugal companionship gratification and total family pressure. This logic applies equally for the relationship between parental companionship gratification and total family pressure. A negative relationship should also occur between traditional status gratification and pressure, but for a different reason. Holding a high-status position implies being in a position of relative power, and power can be used to reduce pressure, if only by fiat. Therefore, to the extent that men receive family status gratifications, they are able to overcome, or otherwise circumvent, family pressure.

Each of the above four hypotheses are, in fact, supported by the data. The discussion accompanying Table 5.2 covered the data pertaining to the relationship of each motivation with the two opposite gratifications. Of concern here are the associations between the gratifications and total family pressure.

The three family-related gratifications all correlate negatively with family pressure among the men in both work groups. Thus, as was hypothesized, the greater the supply of gratifications, the less the perceived family pressure. It is interesting to note that the correlations between family pressure and both conjugal companionship gratification and traditional status gratification are weaker for four-day than for five-day workers (-0.21 versus -0.40; and -0.20 versus -0.36). These findings are in line with the argument made earlier in this chapter concerning the relative ease of obtaining conjugal companionship and traditional status rewards when working a four-day week.

The correlation between parental companionship gratification and total family pressure, on the other hand, is stronger for four-day workers (-0.42 and -0.21). This again is to be expected, considering the inhibitory effect of parental companionship motivation on obtaining conjugal companionship gratifications among five-day workers. The data show that obtaining parental companionship gratifications is more strongly associated with the receipt of conjugal companionship gratifications among four-day and five-day workers (0.52 and 0.34). Since most family pressure felt by the husband emanates from the wife, to the extent that parental companionship motivation blocks receipt of conjugal companionship gratification, it weakens the mitigating effect of parental companionship rewards on total family pressure. This is because while receipt of parental companionship rewards operates to reduce pressure, motivation toward parental companionship simultaneously tends to reduce conjugal companionship gratification, which, in turn, operates to increase pressure. Accordingly, one would expect the negative relationship between parental companionship gratification and total family pressure to be weaker among five-day than four-day workers.

Given these specifications and the previously discussed modifications of the original theory and hypotheses, we can now turn to Figure 5.1. This figure is a path diagram specifying a series of hypothetical causal relationships among variables.* The principal utility of path analysis is that it provides a means for working out certain implications of a hypothetical causal model within the constraints imposed by cross-sectional data. To be sure, it cannot be employed either to prove or disprove the validity of the causal model posited. Rather it is used to determine whether the causal structure specified is consistent with the data.

The single-headed arrows in the figure indicate hypothesized relationships between variables, also known as causal "paths." Each variable in the system is viewed as being causally determined by each of the causally prior variables connected to it by a path arrow, and by other variables not specifically included in the model (such as income, family task and decision-making structure, and other characteristics of the person or his environment). The arrow pointing to a variable from outside the system represents the effects of these unspecified, or residual, variables, and of variance due to random error. The causal logic of the model starts with one variable or set of variables (termed exogenous) whose determinants remain unanalyzed. These variables may, as in this case, be correlated (indicated by a curved,

*See Land (1969) and Kerlinger and Pedhazur (1973) for a discussion of path diagrams and path analysis.

FIGURE 5.1

Path Diagram for Family Motivations, Gratifications, Pressures, and Satisfactions

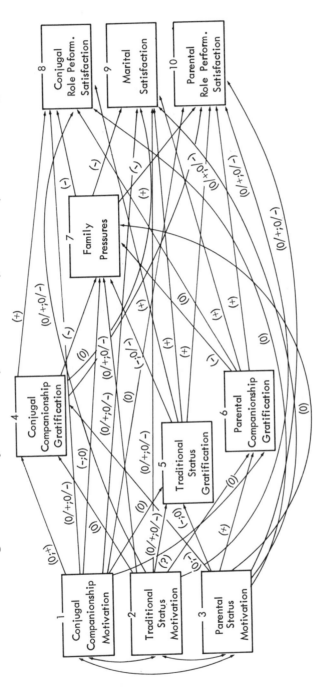

Note: The signs (+, 0, -) indicate the hypothesized direction of each causal relationship. Where different predictions are made for four- and five-day workers, they are indicated before and after the semicolon, respectively. A compound sign (e.g., 0/+) indicates a prediction of either one or the other of the two signs.

Source: Compiled by the author.

113

double-headed arrow). All the remaining variables (termed endogamous) are considered as being "caused" by the exogenous variables and/
or by other variables in the system.

The model displayed in Figure 5.1 postulates that the three
marital motivation variables are causally prior to all other variables.
Therefore, they operate as possible determinants of the supply of conjugal and parental companionship gratification, and of traditional status
gratification. These latter three variables are not ordered causally.
Next, the three motivation and the three gratification variables are
considered to be causally prior to perceived family pressure. Finally,
all the variables in the system are viewed as possible determinants of
conjugal and parental role-performance satisfaction and satisfaction
with marriage as a whole.

Placed next to each arrow are signs (+, 0, -) that indicate the
hypothesized direction of each causal relationship.* In some instances
a compound sign (0/+ or 0/-) is given to represent the expectation of
a weak relationship in the direction of the sign following the slash.
Where different predictions are made for four-day and five-day workers, the sign(s) preceding the semicolon applies to the former, with
those following the semicolon applying to the latter. It should be noted
that these predictions are not really being "tested" with the present
data since the model was partially formulated in light of certain findings emerging from the data. However, this determination is only
partial and was done in this way in an attempt to formulate the most
logical theory for guiding subsequent research endeavors. Moreover,
as will be seen, not all the predictions are confirmed by the present
data.

Testing the Model

The path diagram in Figure 5.1 represents a respecification of
the theory to account for major findings thus far. The technique of
path analysis is employed to test the fit between this model and the
data. Two virtues of path analysis make this technique particularly
useful for this purpose. First, it enables us to consider the effect of
one variable on another with all other relevant variables held constant.
Second, it allows us to decompose the correlations between motivations and family satisfactions in order to determine the extent to
which these relationships are mediated through intervening variables.
As stated earlier, it is considered plausible that the relationship of

---

*The predicted relationship between any two variables is a net
partial relationship (the other variables causing the dependent variables held constant).

each motivation to gratification and family pressure is crucial to an understanding of the impact of the four-day workweek on men's adjustment in the family. The method of decomposing correlations makes it possible to put this notion to the test.

Path coefficients measure "the fraction of the standard deviation of the endogamous variable (with appropriate sign) for which the designated variable is directly responsible," all causally prior variables, including residual variables, being held constant (Land 1969, p. 9). In this study, the path coefficient estimates are computationally identical to the standard regression coefficients (betas) obtained by regressing a given variable on all of its potential causes. This study makes no claim for the precision of these estimates due to the small number of cases involved. It is felt, however, that the estimates provide a rough indication of whether, in fact, the predicted relationships exist, and of their direction.

The results of the path analysis are summarized in Table 5.3, which displays the expected direction of each relationship in the two work groups and the obtained path coefficients. On the whole the results support the predictions, though not perfectly. When the relationship is clearly predicted to be positive (+) or negative (-), coefficients that do not have the expected sign or that have the expected sign but are not greater than their standard error are underlined. When a zero (0) prediction is given, coefficients that exceed their standard error in either direction are considered to have violated the prediction. Where a compound (0/+ or 0/-) prediction is made, coefficients that have the wrong sign (- or + respectively) and exceed their standard error are likewise considered to be a violation.*

When we examine Table 5.3, the results show clear support for the hypotheses relating the three exogenous motivation variables to conjugal companionship gratification (lines 1-3). None of the motivations relates to this gratification in the four-day group, while the two

---

*Path coefficients are normally considered as significant when their value exceeds approximately twice their standard error ($p < 0.05$). The criterion described above was selected for two reasons. First, due to the small number of cases involved, a coefficient that exceeds its standard error deserves some credence. Second, the principal interest of this study is with the direction and size of the relationship rather than with its statistical significance. Consequently, when a clear positive (+) or negative (-) prediction is made, the criterion makes it easier to reject the null hypothesis of no relationship between the variables. However, notice that where either a zero (0) or a compound (0/+ or 0/-) prediction is given, the criterion is even more stringent than usual.

TABLE 5.3

Summary of Hypothesized and Obtained Relationships (Path Coefficients)
Among Marital Motivations, Gratifications, Family Pressures, Role
Performance Satisfaction, and Marital Satisfaction, by Work Schedule

Dependent Variable	Four-Day Workers (Minimum $N = 138$)		Five-Day Workers (Minimum $N = 35$)	
Independent Var.	Hypoth.	Result	Hypoth.	Result
Conjugal Companionship Gratification with:				
1. Conjugal compan. motiv.	0	-0.06	+	0.41^b
2. Parental compan. motiv.	0	0.06	-	-0.36^b
3. Traditional status motiv.	0	0.04	0	-0.08
Multiple R^a	0.07		0.44	
Parental Companionship Gratification with:				
4. Conjugal compan. motiv.	0	0.00	0	0.00
5. Parental compan. motiv.	+	0.49^b	+	0.39^b
6. Traditional status motiv.	?	-0.04	?	0.20^c
Multiple R	0.48		0.50	
Traditional Status Gratification with:				
7. Conjugal compan. motiv.	0	-0.09	0	$\underline{0.21^c}$
8. Parental compan. motiv.	0	$\underline{0.16^c}$	0	-0.16
9. Traditional status motiv.	0/+	0.14^c	0	0.03
Multiple R	0.21		0.21	
Family Pressure with:				
10. Conjugal compan. motiv.	-	-0.26^b	0	-0.09
11. Parental compan. motiv.	-	$\underline{0.07}$	0	0.06
12. Traditional status motiv.	0/-	-0.13^c	+	0.30^c
13. Conjugal compan. gratif.	-	-0.21^c	-	$\underline{-0.20}$
14. Parental compan. gratif.	-	-0.44^b	-	$\underline{-0.21}$
15. Traditional status gratif.	-	0.25^c	0/-	-0.09
Multiple R	0.53		0.49	
Conjugal Role-Performance Satisfaction with:				
16. Conjugal compan. motiv.	0/+	0.06	0/-	0.04
17. Parental compan. motiv.	0	$\underline{-0.10^c}$	0	$\underline{-0.29^c}$
18. Traditional status motiv.	0/+	0.20^b	0/-	0.04
19. Conjugal compan. gratif.	+	0.33^b	+	$\underline{0.03}$
20. Parental compan. gratif.	0	0.04	0	$\underline{0.11}$
21. Traditional status gratif.	+	$\underline{-0.21^c}$	+	0.31^c
22. Family pressure	-	$\underline{-0.39^b}$	-	-0.37^b
Multiple R	0.54		0.70	
Parental Role-Performance Satisfaction with:				
23. Conjugal compan. motiv.	0	0.08	0	$\underline{0.22^b}$
24. Parental compan. motiv.	0/+	-0.03	0/-	-0.28^b
25. Traditional status motiv.	0/+	0.07	0/-	-0.26^b
26. Conjugal compan. gratif.	0	0.09	0	$\underline{-0.23^c}$
27. Parental compan. gratif.	+	$\underline{0.03}$	+	$\underline{-0.57^b}$
28. Traditional status gratif.	+	$\underline{-0.12}$	+	0.38^b
29. Family pressure	-	-0.48^b	-	-0.37^b
Multiple R	0.53		0.90	
Marital Satisfaction with:				
30. Conjugal compan. motiv.	0/+	-0.02	0/-	-0.11
31. Parental compan. motiv.	0/+	0.09^c	0/-	0.19
32. Traditional status motiv.	0/+	0.17^b	0/-	-0.13
33. Conjugal compan. gratif.	+	0.47^b	+	0.31^c
34. Parental compan. gratif.	+	$\underline{-0.13^c}$	+	$\underline{-0.10}$
35. Traditional status gratif.	+	$\underline{-0.09}$	+	$\underline{0.17}$
36. Family pressure	-	-0.34^b	-	$\underline{0.01}$
Multiple R	0.57		0.40	

Notes: Those coefficients that violate the prediction are underlined (for criteria, see p. 115).
aMultiple R for regression equation of dependent variable on independent variables, presumed to be causally realted to it.
bUnstandardized regression coefficient twice its standard error (F > 4.00, p < 0.05).
cUnstandardized regression coefficient greater than its standard error (F > 1.00).
Source: Compiled by the author.

116

companionship motivations strongly relate to conjugal companionship gratification among five-day workers (0.41 and -0.36 for the conjugal and parental motivation variables respectively). The hypothetical causal structure to parental companionship gratification also receives support, with parental companionship motivation being strongly related to its corresponding gratification in both work groups (0.49 and 0.39, line 4). The relationship between traditional status motivation and parental companionship gratification, which was left unspecified, turns out to be near zero for four-day workers and positive for their five-day counterparts (-0.04 and 0.20, line 6). The figure for the five-day group is somewhat smaller than the gross correlation between traditional status motivation and parental companionship gratification shown in Table 5.2 (0.34). This indicates that the size of the correlation coefficient is in part due to the correlation of traditional status motivation with parental companionship motivation (0.37).

Violations of the predictions first appear in the relationship of traditional status gratification with the three exogenous variables. The path coefficient between conjugal companionship motivation and traditional status gratification is slightly negative in the four-day group, as expected, but it is moderately positive in the five-day group (-0.09 and 0.21, line 7). Traditional status rewards also appear to be a function of the level of one's parental companionship motivation, though the motivation variable has an opposite effect in the two groups (0.16 and -0.16, line 8). It seems that in a situation characterized by limited and inflexible discretionary time, a strong parental companionship motivation affects the attainment of tradition status rewards somewhat adversely, while it facilitates gaining these rewards when such time and flexibility are more abundant. This finding will have a bearing on the interpretive discussion of the results given below.

By and large, the predictions made for the potential causes of perceived family pressure are borne out (lines 10-15); one major and three minor violations are to be found here. The minor violations concern the relationships between pressure and parental companionship motivation in the four-day group and between pressure and both companionship gratification variables in the five-day group. Regarding the former, a near zero path coefficient resulted where a positive one was expected (0.07, line 11). Considering the sign and size of the gross correlation between parental companionship motivation and pressure (-0.24), it appears that most of the impact this motivation has on pressure is indirect, through its corresponding gratification. Notice that both the gross correlation coefficient and the path coefficient between parental companionship motivation and its corresponding gratification are large and positive (0.48 and 0.49 respectively) and the path coefficient between this gratification and pressure is large and negative (-0.44, line 14). Thus the indirect effect of parental companionship motivation on family pressure through parental companionship gratification is -0.21 for four-day workers. The two discrepancies between the model and the data in the five-day group are not due to the presence of an incorrect sign. Both the conjugal and parental companionship motivation variables relate to family pressure negatively, as anticipated (-0.20 and -0.21, lines 13 and 14 respectively). However, due to the relatively small sample size for this group, the results failed to attain statistical significance.

The major violation in this portion of the hypothesized causal structure concerns the effect of traditional status gratification on family pressure among men working a compacted week. A positive path coefficient (0.25, line 15) is found where a negative relationship, based on both the logic of the model and the obtained gross correlation coefficient between these two variables (-0.20) was predicted. Clearly the correlation greatly reflects the impact of the other causally prior variables and, to a much lesser extent, the intercorrelation among the exogenous motivation variables themselves. In other words, the correlation coefficient masks conflicting effects. This finding is significant for two reasons. As the first, though by far the less important reason, it accounts for the slight discrepancy between the gross correlation of traditional status motivation with pressure (-0.19) and its associated path coefficient (-0.13). Far more significant is the fact that this is the first indication of the existence of a pattern of relationships among variables that serve to explain, if only in part, why relatively more four-day than five-day workers expressed dissatisfaction with their conjugal role performances and with their marriages in general.

The results of the path analysis for satisfaction with conjugal role performance provide some, though not overwhelming, support for the model (lines 16-22). For both work groups, perceived family pressure predicts most strongly to performance satisfaction (-0.39 and -0.37, line 22). Parental companionship motivation relates modestly, and negatively, to this satisfaction among four-day men. It is, however, a far weaker association than that for five-day workers (-0.10 and -0.29, line 17). Both these figures run counter to the zero relationship predicted. Conjugal companionship gratification operates as a fairly significant "cause" of conjugal role-performance satisfaction for four-day but not for five-day workers (0.23 and 0.03, line 19), with the latter result constituting a violation. The most surprising result, however, is that traditional status gratification relates negatively to this satisfaction for those working a four-day schedule, and positively for those on a five-day workweek (-0.21 and 0.31, line 21).

Four discrepancies between the causal model posited and the data obtained are to be found among the path coefficients leading to satisfaction with parental role performance. Conjugal companionship motivation has a positive influence on satisfaction in the five-day group rather than the zero relationship predicted (0.22, line 23). Interestingly, its corresponding gratifications have a decidedly negative impact on parental role-performance satisfaction for the same workers (-0.23, line 26). This second figure differs markedly from the 0.53 correlation coefficient shown between conjugal companionship gratification and its corresponding role-performance satisfaction. To some extent, this discrepancy can be closed by taking the gratification variable's indirect effect, through family pressure, into account. Mostly, however, it is attributable to the overpowering contrary effect of the remaining two gratification variables and of the conjugal companionship motivation variable. The third misfit occurs in the relationship between parental companionship gratification and satisfaction with parental role performance among four-day workers, which is near zero rather than positive. Notice in particular that this relationship is far stronger when men work a five-day schedule (0.03 and 0.57, line 27). Finally, traditional status gratification has a negative impact on this satisfaction variable among four-day workers, while these variables relate positively for five-day workers (-0.12 and 0.38, line 23).

The majority of predictions made for the potential determinants of marital satisfaction are borne out. Conjugal companionship motivation is unrelated to marital satisfaction in both work groups, as are the parental companionship and traditional status motivation variables for five-day men. These two motivation variables are modestly related to this satisfaction for men working a four-day week (lines 30-32). The most potent variable in both work groups is conjugal companionship gratification (0.47 and 0.31, line 33). Violations occur in the relationships of parental companionship gratification and traditional status gratification with marital satisfaction. The former gratification variable relates weakly, and negatively, to satisfaction among both four-day and five-day workers, instead of being positively related, as was predicted (-0.13 and -0.10, line 34). Traditional status gratification once again is found to relate negatively to a dependent variable among four-day men and positively among five-day workers, but in this instance the relationships failed to attain statistical significance (line 35). Perhaps of greatest surprise is the near zero effect of family pressure on marital satisfaction for those men working a standard week. This is in sharp contrast to the negative effect this "cause" has on marital satisfaction for the men working a four-day week (-0.34 and 0.01, line 36).

To summarize the results of the path analysis, moderate support was found for the causal structure diagramed in Figure 5.1. A decided majority of the predictions, particularly among those made for men working a four-day week, were borne out by the data. Several additional path coefficients for men in the five-day work group were also in the right direction but had smaller than anticipated effects. Where major violations occurred, they tended to fall into two areas: (1) the impact of traditional status gratification on family pressure and satisfaction were consistently opposite to that predicted for four-day workers, and (2) the impact of each companionship motivation and gratification variable on role-performance satisfaction in the opposite role was not sufficiently taken into account for five-day workers. In general, however, the data are consistent with the model, and they provide additional evidence of the construct validity of the present approach to the conceptualization and measurement of marital motivations.

The second advantage of path analysis is that it allows for the decomposition of correlations between motivations and family satisfactions in order to determine the extent to which these relationships are mediated through intervening variables. The direct effect of conjugal companionship motivation on marital satisfaction can then, for example, be compared to its indirect effect through the parental companionship and traditional status gratification variables and the pressure variable. Considering that the four-day workweek is viewed in this study as influencing adjustment in the family context through its impact on obtained gratification levels and family pressure, to the degree that satisfaction is a function of the indirect effects of motivation, there is further support for the model. Moreover, to the extent that both direct and indirect effects differ between work groups, greater understanding is gained concerning the dynamics of adjustment to the four-day workweek in the family context.

Table 5.4 displays the results of this decomposition analysis. From an examination of the data, it is apparent that the men's responses on the three family satisfaction variables are indeed significantly influenced by the indirect effects of the exogenous motivation variables. The proportion of the correlation attributable to indirect effect ranges from a high of 0.80 for conjugal companionship motivation on marital satisfaction among four-day workers, to a low of 0.03 for parental motivation on conjugal role-performance satisfaction among five-day workers. Only five of the 18 Total Indirect Effect (TIE) values account for less than one-third of the total effect of the motivation on satisfaction. These results clearly support the interest of this study with indirect effects.

Several conclusions may be drawn from the data in the table. Turning first to the results for four-day workers, one finds that both role-performance-satisfaction variables are moderately influenced by conjugal companionship motivation and traditional status motivation, and that both direct and indirect effects are positive. Parental companionship motivation, however, has no effect on these men's conjugal role-performance satisfaction (-0.01), and only a modest effect on their level of satisfaction with the quality of their parental role performance (0.09). This is due to the fact that the direct and indirect effects of this motivation on satisfaction are opposite for both role-performance-satisfaction variables. In both instances, the parental companionship motivation's adverse direct effect (strong motivation leads to dissatisfaction) is compensated for by its positive influence through the intervening variables, particularly as it operates to reduce family pressure. Like the two role-performance variables, marital satisfaction is also influenced by traditional status motivation (0.23). Unlike them, however, it is only affected by conjugal companionship motivation (0.06), with parental companionship motivation in the middle (0.12). Much of the effect of both companionship motivations on marital satisfaction thus results from their positive indirect relationship with marital satisfaction through family pressure. This is especially true of the conjugal companionship motivation.

The last point to be raised with respect to the finding for four-day workers concerns the influence of traditional status motivation on satisfaction, as mediated through family pressure, and the mediating role played by its corresponding gratification. The three satisfaction variables are all moderately influenced by this motivation. Notice, however, that in all cases its effect through family pressure is somewhat less than that of parental companionship motivation and is approximately half that of conjugal companionship motivation. This finding constitutes a fair indication that traditional status motivation is a less significant factor in the reduction of family pressure. When we combine the finding that its corresponding gratification mediates negatively between the three motivations and each of the satisfaction variables with the data in Table 5.3, which indicate that the traditional status gratification variable "causes" increased family pressure, a pattern begins to form. A strong traditional status motivation is conducive to satisfaction in the family context so long as concern for the companionship aspect of family living (affection, affiliation, communication) does not fall below some minimum threshold. When the drive for status rewards operates in a manner that sufficiently slights these aspects, it may reduce the individual's ability effectively to work out an understanding with the other members of the family regarding the demands they make on him. This assumes, of course, that his wife and children do not permit him to dismiss their demands by fiat. If this interpretation is correct, then those men who are highly motivated toward traditional status are fortunate in that their schedule makes it relatively more difficult for them to ignore com-

TABLE 5.4

Decomposed Correlations of Marital Motivations
with Conjugal and Parental Role-Performance
Satisfactions and Marital Satisfaction,
by Work Schedule

Dependent Variable Effects	Four-Day Workers (Minimum N = 138)		
	Conjugal Companionship Motivation	Parental Companionship Motivation	Traditional Status Motivation
Conjugal Role-Performance Satis.			
Gross correlation	0.20	0.06	0.25
Total net effect[a]	0.19	−0.01	0.26
Direct effect	0.06	−0.10	0.20
Indirect effects through:[b]			
Conjugal compan. grat.	−0.01	0.01	0.01
Parental compan. grat.	0.01	0.02	0.00
Traditional status grat.	−0.00	−0.03	−0.03
Family pressure	0.13	0.09	0.07
TIE[c]	0.14	0.08	0.09
Parental Role-Performance Satis.			
Gross correlation	0.25	0.14	0.16
Total net effect[a]	0.24	0.09	0.15
Direct effect	0.08	−0.03	0.08
Indirect effects through:[b]			
Conjugal compan. grat.	−0.00	0.00	0.00
Parental compan. grat.	0.01	0.02	0.00
Traditional status grat.	−0.00	−0.02	−0.02
Family pressure	0.16	0.12	0.09
TIE[c]	0.17	0.10	0.10
Satisfaction with Marriage			
Gross correlation	0.14	0.15	0.25
Total net effect[a]	0.06	0.12	0.23
Direct effect	−0.02	0.09	0.17
Indirect effects through:[b]			
Conjugal compan. grat.	−0.01	0.02	0.02
Parental compan. grat.	−0.02	−0.06	−0.01
Traditional status grat.	−0.00	−0.01	−0.01
Family pressure	0.11	0.08	0.06
TIE[c]	0.09	0.09	0.07

Dependent Variable Effects	Five-Day Workers (Minimum N = 35)		
	Conjugal Companionship Motivation	Parental Companionship Motivation	Traditional Status Motivation
Conjugal Role-Performance Satis.			
Gross correlation	0.06	-0.27	-0.10
Total net effect[a]	0.15	-0.30	-0.00
Direct effect	0.04	-0.29	0.04
Indirect effects through:[b]			
Conjugal compan. grat.	0.01	-0.01	-0.00
Parental compan. grat.	0.02	0.05	0.04
Traditional status grat.	0.05	-0.02	0.01
Family pressure	0.03	-0.03	-0.09
TIE[c]	0.11	-0.06	-0.06
Parental Role-Performance Satis.			
Gross correlation	0.19	-0.03	-0.16
Total net effect[a]	0.38	-0.02	-0.12
Direct effect	0.22	-0.28	-0.26
Indirect effects through:[b]			
Conjugal compan. grat.	-0.06	0.06	0.02
Parental compan. grat.	0.12	0.27	0.20
Traditional status grat.	0.06	-0.02	0.01
Family pressure	0.03	-0.03	-0.09
TIE[c]	0.21	-0.00	0.13
Satisfaction with Marriage			
Gross correlation	0.01	-0.03	-0.15
Total net effect[a]	-0.03	0.06	-0.18
Direct effect	-0.11	0.19	-0.13
Indirect effects through:[b]			
Conjugal compan. grat.	0.08	-0.07	-0.03
Parental compan. grat.	-0.02	-0.04	-0.03
Traditional status grat.	0.03	-0.01	0.01
Family pressure	0.00	0.00	0.00
TIE[c]	0.10	-0.08	-0.06

[a]The total net effect (direct plus indirect) does not equal the overall correlation due to the omission of effects through the other motivations, and due to rounding errors.

[b]These are estimates of indirect effects of motivation through each intervening variable as it acts on each dependent family satisfaction variable (a three-variable chain).

[c]TIE = Total indirect effects through the two other gratifications and through family pressures.

Source: Compiled by the author.

123

panionship opportunities, due to its influence on amount of time they spend in the family setting. As will be seen, like-motivated men working a standard five-day week are less fortunate.*

Turning to the five-day work group, one finds a different pattern of direct and indirect effects. As is the case with four-day workers, conjugal and parental role-performance satisfaction among five-day men is positively influenced by conjugal companionship motivation, both directly and through intervening variables. Once again, its impact through family pressure is the largest of the indirect effects. Also, as for their four-day counterparts, the influence of parental companionship motivation on parental role-performance satisfaction nets out to near zero (-0.02) due to the presence of equal, and opposing, direct and indirect effects. This motivation, however, has a strong negative direct influence on conjugal role-performance satisfaction, which is not compensated for by its effects through intervening variables (-0.29). It appears, therefore, that the argument presented earlier in this chapter is valid. A strong parental companionship drive does not lead to the gaining of parental companionship rewards due to the problematic nature of these rewards, but when they are obtained, they result in greater parental role-performance satisfaction. A strong parental companionship motivation, however, does cause the individual to forgo conjugal companionship gratifications (see Table 5.3), which results in a decrement of this gratification variable's mediating effect and contributes to marital and conjugal role-performance dissatisfaction. Notice further that the indirect effect of this motivation on all three family satisfactions through pressure is negative or zero, instead of being positive, as it is for four-day workers.

The last point to be raised concerns the effect of traditional status motivation. This variable has the largest direct effect on parental role-performance satisfaction (-0.26) and the greatest net effect on marital satisfaction (-0.18). Clearly, being motivated toward traditional status when working a schedule that provides for a relatively nonfunctional arrangement of activities operates to the individual's decided disadvantage. Except for its moderately positive effect on the individual's level of satisfaction with his parental role performance through parental companionship gratification (0.20), the motivation

---

*In Chapter 7, where the results of the time-budget diary are presented and discussed, it is shown that the four-day workers spend somewhat more time in the family setting than do five-day workers. Moreover, they allocated considerably more time to companionship activities with their children and to the performance of household tasks traditionally considered their responsibility (for example, yard work, home repairs).

serves only to heighten dissatisfaction. Notice, for example, its consistently negative effect on the satisfaction variables through family pressure. Rather than being a positive contributer to satisfaction by reducing pressure, as is the case for high traditional-status motivated four-day workers, among five-day workers it has no mitigating effect on pressure.

Interpretation of the Path Analysis

The results of the path analysis clearly indicate that the dynamics of adjustment in the family context differ with a four-day as opposed to a five-day workweek. The compacted schedule increases the individual's satisfaction with his role performance and with his marriage by making it easier for him to meet his family obligations and to participate in companionate relationships with his wife and children. While it was originally expected that four-day men oriented toward traditional status rewards might experience difficulties in this setting, this seems either not to be the case or to occur only among those men who ignore the companionship aspects of their family life. It was also expected that men who desire conjugal, and to a lesser extent, parental companionship would be especially advantaged by working a compacted schedule. Again, this expectation was not borne out by the data. Conjugal gratifications appear to be equally available (at least as perceived subjectively) to all four-day workers, regardless of the strength of their motivation toward these rewards. Parental companionship gratifications, on the other hand, seem to remain problematic, thus necessitating effort for their attainment. Such effort, however, does not interfere with obtaining other family-setting gratifications. Thus, working a four-day week operates to enhance marital satisfaction and satisfaction with parental role performance among men motivated toward parental companionship.

The most significant findings appear when one compares the two work groups. The advantages of working a four-day week accrue primarily to those men who are motivated toward parental companionship and/or a traditional status position in the family. When men have a strong parental companionship need and work a standard week, the motivation operates in a fashion that significantly reduces conjugal role-performance satisfaction while providing only minimal, if any, compensation in the form of increased parental role-performance or marital satisfaction. Among four-day workers, on the other hand, this motivation is unassociated with conjugal role-performance satisfaction and is conducive to heightened parental role-performance and marital satisfactions. These data are interpreted here as indicating that a strong parental companionship desire interferes with the individual's willingness and/or ability to meet the companionship demands of his wife, regardless of schedule (notice that this motivation's direct effect on conjugal role-performance satisfaction is negative for both groups). Working a four-day week, however, provides the individual with additional opportunities sufficient for overcoming this gratification conflict and for reaching accord with his wife and children on what they expect of him. As Table 5.4 shows, the total indirect effect of this motivation on each of the three satisfaction variables is negative for five-day workers but positive for four-day workers. Thus, the principal advantage of the four-day workweek for men so motivated is that it tends to improve their conjugal relationship and to increase their capacity for coping with family pressures. *

Being highly motivated toward a traditional status position results in a not insignificant decrease in marital and parental role-performance satisfaction among five-day workers. It proves, however, to be surprisingly conducive to increased conjugal and parental role-performance satisfaction and satisfaction with the marriage in general, among four-day workers. Apparently, the opportunities for doing additional household chores and for engaging in a companionate relationship with one's wife when working a four-day week turns this motivation from a liability into a decided benefit. Perhaps the four-day workers so motivated feel they are better able to fulfill the "traditional" expectations and obligations of marriage and fatherhood, thereby resulting in their expressing a high level of satisfaction with their conjugal and parental role performances, and with the way things are working out in the family setting. Where problems arise, they seem to occur when traditional status gratification (which tends to reflect status differentials in the family) either hinders discourse aimed at reducing pressure or engenders antagonism and yet additional pressure.

---

*The above interpretation is consistent with two distinct hypotheses relating parental companionship motivation and satisfaction with one's conjugal role performance. First, in some cases, parental companionship may indeed be the "cause" of poor performance in the conjugal role due to the slighting of conjugal role obligations. Second, many men may compensate for an unpleasant conjugal relationship by turning their attention toward their children. In a sense, they come to look upon their children, and the gratifications they may receive from a close relationship with them, as substitutes for what they miss in their conjugal relationship. The above interpretation, therefore, implies either that the four-day workweek minimizes the chances of slighting the wife's conjugal companionship needs or that it facilitates reconciliation between husband and wife. Possibly it does both. Either way, the four-day workweek proves advantageous.

To conclude, the four-day workweek appears to be at least modestly beneficial to adjustment in the family context for the majority of men. A remaining task, to be taken up in Chapter 6, is to determine the extent to which the three measures of adjustment associate with, or contribute to, the men's expressions of satisfaction with their weekly work schedule. The study now turns to an examination of selected factors and characteristics of the worker's family environment. These will be related to the variables already discussed in the present chapter in an effort to account for the four-day worker's tendency to have either better or worse marital adjustment and his expression of greater work-schedule satisfaction.

CHAPTER

6

THE INFLUENCE OF
SELECTED CHARACTERISTICS OF
THE FAMILY ENVIRONMENT

It has been demonstrated that the four-day workweek has consequences for adjustment in the family context. The questions that now arise concern whether these effects are reflected in the men's attitudes toward their work schedule and whether selected aspects and characteristics of the family environment interact with their work schedule to affect marital adjustment and schedule satisfaction. The objective here is to gain further insight into those characteristics of the person and his environment that may influence the workers' perception of, and satisfaction with, this important life domain and, thereby, influence their response to working the nonconventional four-day schedule. These questions are focused upon in sequence, starting with the issue of whether the better adjustment of four-day workers associates with increased work-schedule satisfaction.

MARITAL ADJUSTMENT AND
WORK-SCHEDULE SATISFACTION

Proponents of the four-day workweek argue that, in theory, this schedule should provide workers with greater opportunities both for valued gratifications and for engaging in self-validating and self-defining behaviors. As was discussed in Chapters 1 and 2, in contemporary Western society, the family serves as a central determinant of individual identity and happiness. This being the case, satisfaction with the four-day workweek should relate significantly to measures of marital adjustment and, especially, to overall satisfaction with marriage. Table 6.1 displays the relevant data.

TABLE 6.1

Correlation of Schedule Satisfaction
with Conjugal and Parental Role-Performance
Satisfactions and Marital Satisfaction

	Conjugal Role-Performance Satisfaction		Parental Role-Performance Satisfaction		Marital Satisfaction	
	N	Correl.	N	Correl.	N	Correl.
Four-day workers	166	.26*	149	.02	199	.33*
Five-day workers	38	.03	32	-.08	49	-.07

*$p < 0.01$.
Source: Compiled by the author.

None of the satisfaction measures correlate significantly with schedule satisfaction in the five-day work group.* The results indicate, however, that the attitude that four-day workers hold toward their nonconventional schedule may be partially attributable to their adjustment in the family. As can be seen, work-schedule satisfaction associates moderately both with conjugal role-performance satisfaction and with marital satisfaction in the four-day group, but it is unrelated to parental role-performance satisfaction. Men who are satisfied with their performance as husbands and with their marriages tend to look favorably upon the four-day workweek while those less satisfied express a less favorable view. At the very least, this finding shows that the perceived quality of family life is a more salient factor in evaluating one's hours of labor and leisure when working this nonconventional schedule. Equally important, the data extend a conclusion drawn in the previous chapter concerning the schedule's impact in the family setting; the schedule not only appears to contain the seeds for both increased marital satisfaction and marital discord in the view of this researcher but is also thus perceived by the workers themselves. This has obvious implications for the four-day workweek's acceptance by workers and, therefore, for its viability as an

---

*The nonsignificant correlations for five-day workers are not surprising when one remembers that their knowledge of options to the standard work schedule is limited. Considering their schedule to be the normal state of affairs, they are less likely than their four-day counterparts to associate marriage and role performance satisfaction with their hours of daily labor.

alternative to the standard five-day workweek. If workers perceive the four-day schedule as influencing their satisfaction with their family life, then, to the extent it results in improved adjustment in the family setting, the more willing will they be to accept this nonconventional arrangement of work and leisure hours as their own.

Since improvements in both marital adjustment and schedule satisfaction are associated with working a compacted week, it is important to determine whether there are factors in the family environment that interact with workers' hours of labor and leisure to explain these associations. This is the topic of discussion for the balance of this chapter.

FACTORS AFFECTING MARITAL ADJUSTMENT

The Power to Decide and the Division of Labor Between Husbands and Wives

In order for a marriage to work, decisions must be made and tasks have to be performed. This section is concerned with the twin questions of whether working a four-day week causes a change in the balance of decision-making power in the family or a change in the responsibility for performing everyday tasks. It would not be surprising to find differences between the four-day and five-day work groups on either set of family functions. As will be shown in the next chapter, four-day workers do tend to spend somewhat more total time in the family setting. However, any changes that occur are not expected to be major, for while these men spend a greater proportion of their total time in the family setting, they also are away from it more during the workweek. Of perhaps greater importance, a radical change in decision-making and task performance patterns would violate traditional sex-role norms, as unstable as they may currently be. Moreover, the power to make decisions reflects the personal characteristics and relative resources that each partner can mobilize with respect to the decisions being made (Blood 1972). Neither of these factors is significantly altered by working a compacted schedule. Thus, while changes in "who decides" and in "who does what" are possible, the extent of change should be small and its direction uncertain.

To measure precisely the balance of power between spouses, one would have to assess their relative influence in all family decisions over a considerable period of time. Such an exhaustive undertaking would tax the capabilities of husbands' and wives' memories, not to mention the practical limitations of this study. Since a record of this kind is unobtainable, a subset of decisions is needed for estimating the relative balance of power. For this purpose, the eight decisions studied by Blood and Wolfe (1960), with slight modifications, were chosen. These were selected, in the words of the authors, "because they are all relatively important (compared to deciding whether to go to a movie tonight). They are also questions which nearly all couples have to face. . . . The remaining criterion for these questions was that they should range from typically masculine to typically feminine decisions—but should always affect the family as a whole" (pp. 19-20). All discussions of the power to make decisions are in terms of the relative balance of power between husbands and wives.* The eight decisions are as follows:

1. What job the husband should take
2. What car to buy
3. Whether or not to buy life insurance
4. Where to go on a vacation
5. What house or apartment to take
6. Whether or not the wife should go to work or quit
7. What doctor to have or where to go when someone is sick
8. How much money the family can afford to spend per week on food.

As in the case for decisions, the researcher must be satisfied with studying a small subset of family tasks when forming an index of overall division of labor. Here also, this study employs the questions developed by Blood and Wolfe (1960). These are the following:

1. Who repairs things around the house
2. Who mows the lawn
3. Who shovels the sidewalk
4. Who keeps track of the money and the bills
5. Who does the grocery shopping
6. Who gets the husband's breakfast on work days[†]
7. Who straightens up the living room when company is coming
8. Who does the evening dishes

---

*This measure was constructed by converting the total scores for the eight decisions into a ten-point scale that reflects the amount of influence exerted by the husband. The weights used in the process are as follows: husband always (5), husband more (4), husband and wife equally (3), wife more (2), and wife always (1).

†Unfortunately, the responses to the item "Who gets the husband's breakfast on work days?" could not be included in these measures. Too many men said they do not eat breakfast at home.

It is well known that the division of labor covers a wide variety of concepts. Reflecting this, the tasks studied here were combined in a number of ways to construct different measures of task performance and organization. The first combination concerns the amount of work done at home by each partner. This measure is referred to as the relative task participation of the spouses; it is equivalent to the balance of power in decision making. Scores were combined in terms of the husband's mean task performance, using the same weights as for decisions.

Three of these tasks are traditionally done by men, and three are typically allocated to women. The degree of adherence to male roles refers to the extent to which the husband does the repairs, the mowing, and the shoveling. The degree of adherence to female roles refers to the extent to which the wife takes responsibility for the grocery shopping, the living room, and the dishes. These two measures were then combined to form an index of adherence to traditional sex roles. Following Blood and Wolfe (1960), keeping track of the bills and money was omitted from this index because of uncertainty as to whether it should be considered a traditionally masculine or feminine function.

Three other measures were constructed concerning how many tasks are done exclusively by one partner and how many are shared equally by husband and wife. The first of these measures the degree of role stereotype, that is, how many of the seven tasks are done exclusively by the partner to whom they are traditionally assigned. Closely related is the extent of role specialization, which measures the number of tasks performed exclusively by one partner, though not necessarily by the traditional partner. Lastly, an index of role sharing was formed to indicate the number of tasks that are done by both spouses "exactly the same."

Little was found to distinguish between the two work groups with regard to either their relative decision-making power or the various facets of their division of labor. Four-day workers seem to wield slightly less power vis-a-vis their wives, but the difference is not significant. With respect to the seven facets of task performance, marginally significant differences appear on only two—"adherence to traditional sex roles" and "role-sharing" ($p < 0.10$, one-tailed t-test). It is four-day and five-day workers, respectively, who score higher on these two measures. The four-day workers also score consistently higher on the five other task facets, though, once again, the differences between groups are slight.

These results make it appear that working a four-day week has little influence either on who makes the decisions or on who carries out normal family tasks. But this does not necessarily imply that performance of these functions is unrelated to work schedules. As will be shown below, the schedule that a man works interacts with several other family variables to affect the family's pattern of decision making and task performance, and it does so in a manner associated with discrepancies between work groups on role-performance satisfactions, marital satisfaction, and satisfaction with work schedule. Before turning to an examination of these other variables, however, two additional sets of indexes need to be introduced.

Companionship, Sociability, and Tension

Viewing happiness in marriage as a function of the balance between the satisfactions and tensions experienced in the family setting, Orden and Bradburn (1968) developed three distinct indexes designed to measure "the contributions of environmental factors to adjustment in marriage" (p. 718). These measures are companionship between spouses (five items), sociability with others as a pair (four items), and tension (nine items). Each of these measures lists a set of activities or occurrences, and the respondent is asked to indicate which of them he has experienced recently.* In this study, the time period was the two weeks prior to the interview.

When the scores for four-day and five-day workers on these indexes are compared, no significant differences are found in either the mean number of companionate activities ($\overline{X}_4 = 4.22$, $\overline{X}_5 = 4.15$) or the mean number of sociability activities ($\overline{X}_4 = 2.65$, $\overline{X}_5 = 2.86$). Notice, however, that what differences do exist are in the expected direction. That is, four-day men report more companionate activities, presumably because they spend more time at home, and five-day men report more sociability, perhaps because of their fewer hours of work per day. On the tension index, there is a significant difference. The mean score for four-day men is 1.33, while for five-day men it is the relatively high 1.75 ($p < 0.10$). This result is of some interest in that several researchers in addition to Orden and Bradburn have reported a strong relationship between the overt expression of hostility and poor marital adjustment (for example, see Hawkins 1968). This finding offers some support, albeit slight, for one of the original contentions of this study: Working a four-day week enhances marital satisfaction by facilitating the reduction of family-related stress.

---

*Orden and Bradburn (1968) found that each of these indexes related significantly to a general measure of marital happiness: companionship ($r = 0.44$), sociability ($r = 0.20$), and tension ($r = -0.36$).

Time Away from the Family

The availability of discretionary time to spend as one wishes without other members of the family being present is a variable whose importance should not be overlooked. Time away from both family and job not only enables the male worker to do things he wants to do but also constitutes a necessary mechanism for relief from role responsibilities and pressures and provides a temporary escape from constant association with wife and children. This study assessed the worker's access to these gratifications with a three-item index measured in the same manner as the ten marital motivations and gratifications.

When the two work groups are compared, no difference is found in the mean strengths of their desire to have time away from their family. A significant difference does, however, appear on the corresponding gratification index ($\overline{X}_4 = 6.14$, $\overline{X}_5 = 4.76$, $p < 0.01$). Clearly, four-day workers are better able to allocate part of their discretionary time to activities not involving other members of the family. As will also be seen in the next chapter, four-day workers report devoting somewhat more time to such activities as hunting, fishing, and gardening. These activities are often done either alone or with friends, rather than with other family members.

The remainder of this chapter is concerned with the interaction effects of work-schedule and selected characteristics of the worker and his family environment. These interactions are either conducive to, or disruptive of, marital adjustment, and are associated with satisfaction with the four-day workweek. Attention is focused on the following variables: (1) stage in the life cycle, (2) wife's employment status, and (3) wife's attitude toward the four-day workweek as perceived by the husband.

Since it is based more on the pattern of relationships among variables than on their statistical significance, much in the discussion that follows is interpretive and speculative rather than conclusive. Further research support is needed before the findings presented below can be accepted with confidence.

DIFFERENCES OVER THE LIFE CYCLE

It was demonstrated in Figure 4.1 that age is significantly related to satisfaction with work schedule among four-day but not among five-day workers. Though they overlap operationally, life cycle and age are neither synonomous conceptually nor identical in their relationships to other variables. Figure 6.1 shows the effect of life-cycle stage upon satisfaction with one's work schedule.

FIGURE 6.1

Schedule Dissatisfaction by Stage in Life Cycle

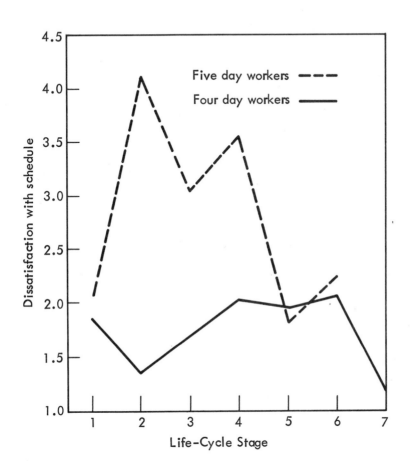

Key:
    1. Other (generally divorced or separated; has children but not at home)
    2. Under age 45; married; no children at home
    3. Married; children; youngest under age five
    4. Married; children; youngest aged 5-14
    5. Married; children; youngest aged 15 or over
    6. Over age 45; married; no children at home
    7. Over age 45; divorced or separated; children at home
Source: Compiled by the author.

Satisfaction with work schedule differs greatly according to the worker's stage in the life cycle and the schedule worked. Those four-day workers still in the "honeymoon" stage of their family life, or whose children have not yet reached the "flight" stage, are far more positively oriented to their hours of work and nonwork than are their five-day counterparts. Once the children start to disengage themselves from the family, however, or if the worker has no spouse or young children, there is little to distinguish four-day from five-day men with respect to schedule satisfaction. But can the greater satisfaction of those four-day workers still in the honeymoon stage or who have young children at home be attributed to differences in the family context? Very tentatively, yes. Several family environment factors and patterns of interpersonal relationships were found to be at least partially responsible for their relatively high regard for the four-day week.

Research into marital adjustment over the life cycle has consistently found a general decline in marital satisfaction and adjustment through the years. For example, Gurin, Veroff, and Feld (1960) report that, while indexes of marital inadequacy and the incidence of marital problems and tensions decline over time, so do scores on a measure of marital happiness. Pineo (1961) conceptualized this trend as "disenchantment." Rollins and Feldman (1970) found those stages in the life cycle that are associated with child bearing and child rearing to be particularly problematic. "Both husbands and wives," they wrote, "suffered loss of positive companionship experienced at the beginning of the marriage and a leveling off through subsequent stages. Later stages of the life-cycle seem to bring increases in satisfaction, especially after the children have left home" (p. 26; also see Burr 1970). In view of these findings, to the extent that working a four-day week attenuates the decline in marital satisfaction associated with the arrival of children, there is support for the argument that the four-day work schedule is beneficial to adjustment in the family context.

Figure 6.2 displays the results for those men whose marriages are intact. As can be seen, men in both work groups who have no children express equal satisfaction with their marriages. Then, once children arrive, the expected decline occurs. Notice, however, that this decline is less sharp among four-day workers. Indeed, among those four-day men whose children have entered adolescence, marital satisfaction even increases, while among the comparable five-day men, it retains its previous level. The result for men whose children have left the home comes somewhat as a surprise; at this point in the life cycle, four-day workers are significantly less satisfied with their marriages than their five-day counterparts ($\overline{X}_4 = 2.49$, $\overline{X}_5 = 1.55$, $p < 0.05$). Undoubtedly, some of this difference is due to their feeling less satisfied with their conjugal role performance ($\overline{X}_4 = 2.39$, $\overline{X}_5 = 1.55$, $p < 0.05$).

FIGURE 6.2

Marital Dissatisfaction by Stage in Life Cycle

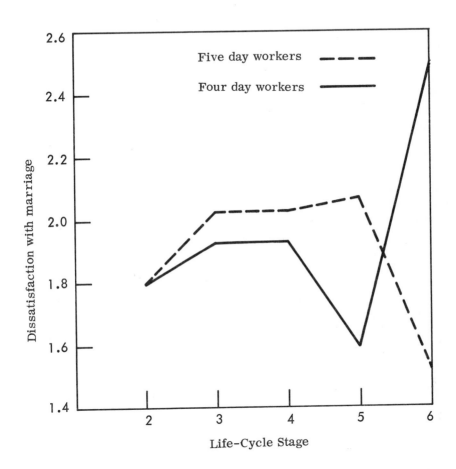

Key:
2. Under age 45; married; no children at home
3. Married; children; youngest under age five
4. Married; children; youngest aged 5-14
5. Married; children; youngest aged 15 or over
6. Over age 45; married; no children at home
Source: Compiled by the author.

137

Apparently, working a four-day week does serve to keep the characteristic decline in marital satisfaction during the child-bearing and child-rearing stages to a relative minimum, but it operates in a fashion that reverses the increase in satisfaction that typically occurs consequent to the children leaving home. To what can these findings be attributed? Turning first to the men still in the honeymoon stage of married life, while no differences in marital satisfaction were uncovered, there are dramatic differences between the work groups on their expresed satisfaction with their work schedule. Equal satisfaction with marriage in this stage is not at all surprising; "disenchantment" has not set in to these young conjugal relationships. Four-day men in this early stage do, however, report receiving significantly more conjugal companionship gratifications ($p < 0.01$), stronger adherence to traditional sex roles, having more family power, less family pressure, and being subjected to fewer hostile acts ($p < 0.05$). It appears, therefore, that while the four-day schedule does not change one's overall marital satisfaction, it does alter the organization of family functions, enhances the four-day worker's access to salient gratifications, and improves the general atmosphere of the family setting. For these reasons, it is hardly surprising that these men are more satisfied with their work schedule.

Among men whose youngest child is less than 15 years old, there are few differences between work groups. Among men whose youngest child is under five, the work groups are distinguished by a noticeable difference on the tension index, with four-day men reporting less hostility. By far the most important difference, however, occurs when one compares work groups on their availability of time to do things without other family members being present. Four-day workers in these two life-cycle stages (youngest child under age five; aged five to 14) are able to escape significantly more than their five-day cohorts ($p < 0.02$). This ability would appear to be a function of the work schedule and undoubtedly contributes decidedly to the four-day men's relatively greater schedule satisfaction. Presumably, it is also a factor conducive to marital adjustment.

For men whose children have all reached later adolescence but are still living at home, several differences between work groups are evident. Four-day workers report doing relatively more of the household tasks, are more active in their performance of the traditional male role, and receive significantly greater parental companionship gratifications than their five-day counterparts (only the latter relationship attains significance at the 0.05 level). They also report a significant reduction in decision-making power relative both to four-day men in earlier life-cycle stages ($p < 0.01$) and five-day workers in the same life-cycle stage ($p < 0.02$). However, despite the decline in their decision-making power, these men experience greater marital satisfaction, which may, in part, be due to their greater involvement in family activities. Another variable, namely, the wife's employment status (discussed more fully below), was found to play an important role here. This is hardly surprising, for in this stage of the family life cycle, many mothers return to work or commence full-time employment.

The clearest pattern occurs among men whose children no longer live at home (life-cycle stage 6). To review previous findings for this group: Four-day workers express slightly greater schedule satisfaction than their five-day counterparts, but they are far less satisfied with their marriages. Several family context variables stand out here. Four-day workers receive significantly less conjugal companionship gratification ($p < 0.01$) and traditional status gratification ($p < 0.05$) than do five-day workers in the same life-cycle stage. In addition, they engage in fewer social activities as couples ($p < 0.01$). They also wield somewhat less power in decision making and comprise the only stage wherein four-day couples adhere relatively less to traditional sex roles* and experience a relatively greater number of hostile acts.

Due to the small sample of five-day men in this stage of the life cycle, any conclusions drawn from these findings are particularly tentative. With this reservation, when the two work groups are compared, an interesting picture emerges; the four-day men seem to experience more rapid disenchantment with their marriages. Freed from their parental responsibilities, perhaps four-day workers see their position in the family as weakened, both in absolute terms and relative to their peers on other work schedules. Because they spend more time at home but enjoy this time less, their disenchantment with their conjugal relationship and their conjugal role performance accelerates, resulting in a marked rise in marital dissatisfaction.

WIFE'S EMPLOYMENT STATUS

In recent years, there has been increased research interest in the impact of the wife's employment status on marital adjustment. Blood (1972), for example, found differences in the marital structures

---

*In a study of age-sex roles in the family, Neugarten and Gutmann (1968) found that older couples commonly show signs of both a switch in the traditional decision-making power of the marriage partners and a breakdown of the traditional sex-based division of labor. In the present study, both four- and five-day men in the sixth life-cycle stage have less power in the family than do men in any other stage of the life cycle. The principal thing to note is that the change appears either to be greater or to occur sooner when men work a four-day week.

of families in which the wife is employed and those in which she is not. Working wives were found to gain greater leverage over their husbands, and the balance of power was shifted more in the wife's direction, especially in economic matters. Also, husbands were found to help out more around the house, especially with traditionally masculine tasks, though the wife still bore the major share of the work. At the same time, several authors also report marital adjustment to be worse in those families where the wife is employed. This is particularly true when the husband's economic function is jeopardized by unemployment (Nye 1961; Axelson 1963). In view of such findings, it is quite possible that men's satisfaction with the four-day work schedule may be influenced by their wives' employment status.

Table 6.2 presents the mean conjugal and parental role-performance satisfaction scores and the mean marital satisfaction scores of four-day and five-day workers, dichotomized according to

TABLE 6.2

Mean Conjugal and Parental Role-
Performance Satisfaction and Marital Satisfaction,
According to Whether or Not Wife Works

Satisfaction	Wife Is Employed		Wife Is Not Employed	
Work Group	N	Mean	N	Mean
Satisfaction with Conjugal Role Perf.				
Four-day workers	69	2.17	96	2.12
Five-day workers	21	2.56	26	1.77
Satisfaction with Parental Role Perf.				
Four-day workers	54	2.07	92	2.11
Five-day workers	16	2.16	24	1.83
Marital Satisfaction				
Four-day workers	81	1.96	116	1.95
Five-day workers	28	2.20	30	1.85

Source: Compiled by the author.

whether one's wife is or is not employed.* From even a cursory examination, a pattern is readily apparent. There is little or no difference on any of the family satisfaction variables between those four-day men whose wives hold jobs and those whose wives do not. In contrast, five-day men with working wives consistently express less satisfaction than do five-day men whose wives are not employed. On conjugal role-performance satisfaction, the difference attains statistical significance (2.56 versus 1.77, $p < 0.01$). Five-day men with working wives also express somewhat greater dissatisfaction with their performance of roles and with their marriages than do four-day men with working wives. On the other hand, when a comparison is made between four- and five-day husbands of career housewives, the latter tend to score higher on the measures of satisfaction. Apparently, working a four-day week somehow mitigates the tendency toward increased role-performance and marital dissatisfaction in families where the wife holds a job. Surprisingly, four-day workers whose wives do not work are relatively dissatisfied.

There are several factors within the family environment to which these findings may be attributed. Perhaps the most interesting is that it is the five-day worker and not the four-day worker who does relatively less of the everyday household duties when his wife is not employed. Concomitantly, the five-day worker tends to take on more of these chores when she is employed. Five-day couples with working wives also adhere least to traditional sex roles and specialize less in their role performances. Several additional family environment variables follow a similar pattern. Five-day men with working wives report receiving less parental companionship and traditional status gratifications than either their cohorts whose wives stay home or their four-day counterparts whose wives work. In addition, they experience by far the greatest number of hostile acts, particularly compared to four-day men with employed wives.

It appears that at least part of the explanation why other studies have found a reduction in marital adjustment of husbands whose wives work is that, despite (or possibly because of) their doing more to help around the house, these men perceive themselves as experiencing a reduction in their level of traditional family status. Moreover, they may well receive fewer parental companionship gratifications. The

---

*A "working wife" is considered here as any wife who works for pay, full- or part-time, in or outside the home. Aggregating all working wives in this way undoubtedly masks certain differences related to differences in their work schedules and the nature of the jobs. This aggregation was necessary, however, because of the small sample size.

longer workday of the four-day schedule, on the other hand, makes it less feasible for husbands to relieve their wives of many of their daily chores, a fact that most wives probably recognize. Consequently, the self-image of four-day workers is less threatened by the presence of a working wife. This would help explain both the relatively poor scores of five-day men with working wives on the three family satisfaction measures, and the equivalency of family satisfaction scores among four-day workers, irrespective of the wife's employment status. While the four-day workweek does not serve to enhance the husband's adjustment in the family context, if his wife works, the compacted schedule appears to minimize the loss of gratifications, the incidence of hostile acts, and the occurrence of situations threatening to his self-image.

THE WIFE'S DISPOSITION TOWARD
THE FOUR-DAY WORKWEEK

With the family constituting the male worker's most significant primary group, his response to the four-day week cannot help but reflect the dispositions of other members of the family. The disposition of the worker's wife should be a particularly important determinant. By giving or withholding gratifications and by altering the nature and degree of her demands on his time, she is in a strategic position to influence both the quality of her husband's marital adjustment and, thereby, his satisfaction with working a nonconventional schedule. It has already been demonstrated that both the life-cycle variable and the wife's employment status interact with the individual's arrangement of work time to affect his adjustment in the family context and his level of satisfaction with work schedule. Neither of these family environment variables, however, provides much insight into the role played by the wife, and they provide no insight concerning the impact of her attitude toward the four-day workweek on her husband's marital adjustment and work-schedule response.

Four-day workers were asked to assess their wives' disposition toward their compacted work schedule. Table 6.3 displays the distribution of responses to this question. The results are fairly conclusive. Fully 69 percent of the four-day workers perceive their wives to be favorably disposed toward their working a four-day week, while only 14.5 percent report that their wives dislike it. Clearly, the compacted work schedule does not constitute a bone of contention in the families of most four-day men included in this study.

What, then, are some of the reasons given by these men for their wives either liking or disliking the schedule? Tables 6.4 and 6.5, respectively, list the pros and cons that wives, in one way or

TABLE 6.3

Wife's Disposition Toward Four-Day Workweek,
As Reported by Husband
(percent; N = 200)

Doesn't Like It at All	Dislikes It Somewhat	Neither Likes Nor Dislikes It	Likes It Somewhat	Likes It Very Much
3.0	11.5	16.5	19.5	49.5

Source: Compiled by the author.

TABLE 6.4

Reasons Given by Four-Day Workers for Wives'
Favorable Disposition Toward Four-Day Work Schedule

Reason	Number of Mentions	Percentage of Respondents
Husband is home more; spends more time with family	89	44.3
Can get husband to do more work around the house	37	18.4
More time for trips	25	12.4
Wife likes the long weekend	13	6.5
Wife accepts schedule	13	6.5
More money	4	2.0
Wife can make fewer lunches	4	2.0
Hasn't changed family activities	4	2.0
Other	7	3.5
Don't know	5	2.5
Total	201	100.1

Source: Compiled by the author.

TABLE 6.5

Reasons Given by Four-Day Workers for Wives'
Unfavorable Disposition Toward Four-Day Work Schedule

Reason	Number of Mentions	Percentage of Respondents
Work hours are too long	16	25.0
Husband and wife have conflicting work schedules	10	15.6
Husband works too late	7	10.9
Husband is away from home more	7	10.9
Husband gets too tired	6	9.4
Interferes with nightlife on workdays	4	6.3
Hasn't improved wife's life-style	4	6.3
Other	10	15.6
Total	64	100.0

Source: Compiled by the author.

another, have transmitted to their husbands. For men who gave multiple reasons for their wife's disposition, only the first two mentions
were coded for inclusion in each of these tables. Seventy-five percent
offered positive mentions; only 27 percent provided negative ones.

Not surprisingly, by far the largest number of favorable responses concern the husband's being at home more, which enables
him to spend more time with the family (44.3 percent) and to do more
work around the house (18.4 percent). The increased opportunity to
take trips on weekends is the one other frequently mentioned reason.
The remaining responses are distributed among such vague and passive factors as the following: The wife likes her husband having a
longer weekend, she accepts the schedule, and the four-day schedule
has brought no changes in family activities. A few men indicated
their wives like the schedule either because it enables him to earn
more money or because she is now required to make fewer lunches.

As for the reasons given why wives dislike having their husbands working a four-day, 40-hour week, the majority of responses
pertain directly to the length of the workday. Twenty-five percent of
the workers plainly stated that their wives feel that their working ten

hours a day is too much, with an additional 10.9 percent and 9.4 percent, respectively, saying their wives complain about their working too late or coming home too tired. Interference with evening activities is yet another reason, which is related to the length of the workday. Nearly 16 percent of the men mentioned the conflict between their own and their wife's work schedule as a cause for her dislike. However, it is debatable whether or not this complaint has much to do with the four-day schedule per se, or whether or not any schedule at variance with the wife's would be problematic. The final negative response given by more than one four-day husband concerns the failure of this schedule to live up to the wife's expectations that it would somehow improve her life-style.

To summarize these results, it is clear that from the wife's point of view (at least as transmitted by the husband) the main benefit of the compacted, four-day schedule is the husband's increased presence in the family setting on weekends. Weighing against this are the various problems associated with the longer workday. Apparently, few wives find the drawbacks sufficiently consequential to tarnish their overall favorable disposition toward the four-day workweek.

But does the wife's attitude toward her husband's four-day work schedule in fact influence his own attitude toward it? The answer is, unhesitatingly, affirmative. The data show the attitudes of husband and wife to be strongly, and positively, related: the more favorable the wife's disposition toward the four-day schedule, the more favorable the worker's own response ($r = 0.49$, $p < 0.01$). To be sure, the direction of causation cannot be determined with certainty. In addition, there are many factors in the marriage partners' common environment that may similarly influence their respective attitudes. Nonetheless, it would contradict neither logic nor what is known about the dynamics of close human relationships to hypothesize that their respective attitudes are casually related and that the direction of causation runs from the wife to husband as well as the other way around.

If we make this assumption, do the data offer any lead concerning the dynamics involved? Again, the answer is affirmative, but this time with a measure of hesitation. The wife's attitude toward the four-day workweek correlates modestly with several of the other family variables in ways that were anticipated prior to analysis. First, with respect to the various facets of the division of family labor, her attitude correlates significantly with adherence to male roles (0.16), adherence to female roles (-0.15), and the extent of role sharing (0.24). Second, both conjugal companionship gratification and traditional status gratification correlate with the wife's disposition toward the four-day workweek (0.34 and 0.28, respectively), as does the worker's perception of family pressure (0.16). Last, her attitude relates to her husband's conjugal role-performance satisfaction and his marital satisfaction (0.17 and 0.28, respectively).*

There emerges from these findings at least an outline of the dynamics involved. When the husband works a compacted week, his wife may expect him to use part of his newfound discretionary time in ways that provide her with additional discretionary time. In particular, she expects him to be of greater assistance around the house. Consequently, to the extent he lives up to the male's traditional household responsibilities and/or relieves his wife of some of her traditional duties, the more favorable will be her attitude toward the four-day work schedule. One by-product of this realignment of tasks is greater role sharing and a reduction in perceived pressure from other family members. Concomitantly, in return for his help, the wife rewards her husband with conjugal companionship and traditional status gratifications, thereby enhancing his satisfaction with both his conjugal role performance and the marriage in general.†

SUMMARY

In this and the previous chapter, the interrelationships among a fairly wide variety of family variables and their unique and interactive influences on the worker's adjustment in the family context and to his work schedule have been examined in some detail. It has been shown that the schedule a person works does affect his marital adjustment and that the dynamics differ according to whether one is on an official four-day or five-day workweek. Contrary to what was hypothesized, the mean level of adjustment (as measured by conjugal and parental role-performance satisfaction and marital satisfaction) was found to be approximately equal for the two work groups. However, this result is attributable to the fact that relatively more four- than five-day men expressed either complete satisfaction or dissatisfaction with the way things were going in their families. Part of the explanation for this pattern of responses was expected to lie in the interactive relationship between the men's marital motivations and their hours of work and nonwork. It was originally hypothesized that, due to their greater flexibility in the scheduling of family activities, four-day workers would receive relatively more marital gratifications, report

---

*All correlations mentioned are significant at the 0.05 level or beyond.

†This proposition helps account for the near zero path coefficient connecting the four-day worker's level of conjugal companionship motivation to its corresponding gratification (see Table 5.3). Desire for such gratification does not ensure its receipt; gratification must be earned.

less family pressure, and, consequently, indicate greater marital adjustment. These hypotheses were supported only in part.

When we combine the results of the two family chapters, it is apparent that while the four-day worker's opportunities for receiving conjugal companionship and traditional status gratifications may increase, actual receipt of these rewards is significantly mediated by his wife's disposition toward the nonconventional work schedule. More specifically, the level of gratifications that the worker receives appears to be determined by his ability to live up to his wife's expectations concerning his helping out around the house during his discretionary time. To the extent that he meets these expectations, he receives gratifications, experiences a reduction in family pressure and tension, and comes to view his role performances and marriage in a better light. Problems may arise, however, when the worker either too strongly enforces, or otherwise comes to occupy, a traditional family status position that makes it difficult for him to deal effectively with family pressure. Though not specifically examined, it is reasonable to assume that these men tend to be the ones who help out least around the house, with greater marital conflict and poorer marital adjustment resulting. This problem appears to be particularly prevalent among those four-day workers whose children no longer live at home.

An unanticipated finding concerns the interactive effect of parental companionship motivation and work schedule on the receipt of conjugal companionship gratifications. Five-day workers so motivated appear to experience parental companionship by forgoing opportunities for receiving conjugal companionship. The outcome is increased tension and reduced adjustment in the conjugal role, if not the entire marriage. Four-day workers, on the other hand, experience no such conflict. By one means or another, they are better able to satisfy both their own companionship needs and those of their wife and children. This factor is reflected in the relatively greater marital satisfaction of four-day workers who still have children at home. This represents one of the most significant potential benefits of the four-day workweek.

Several additional variables were found to associate differently with marital adjustment for four- and five-day workers. Two stand out in particular. Being married to a working woman apparently has little impact on adjustment among four-day workers but has significant, and negative, consequences for men on a standard schedule. Because they arrive home later on workdays than their five-day counterparts, four-day workers are able to shoulder relatively less of the daily household chores. Consequently, they experience far less of a threat to their masculine self-image and traditional family status. The second variable of note is the worker's opportunity for time to himself, away from his family. Four-day men report having significantly more such time than five-day men.

To conclude, adjustment to the four-day week in the family context and, consequently, the individual's response to the four-day schedule itself, result from a highly complex set of interactions among various characteristics of the focal person and factors in his family environment. This study delineates only a few of these. The general picture that appears shows most four-day workers benefiting from their compacted schedule, particularly before their children have grown up and struck out on their own. The enhanced opportunities that the schedule provides these men for experiencing conjugal and parental gratifications, while maintaining a measure of independence from the family, contribute both directly and indirectly (through family pressure and tension) to increased marital adjustment and schedule satisfaction. Those men experiencing adjustment difficulties and schedule dissatisfaction appear to be either older men for whom the process of marital disenchantment has been accelerated by the four-day schedule or men who fail to involve themselves sufficiently in the everyday operations of the family or who slight the companionship needs of their wives and children.

Whether the four-day schedule serves to enhance or hinder adjustment in the family context, sufficient evidence has been unearthed to lend some justice to the claims made earlier concerning the importance of the family when evaluating the long-run viability of the four-day workweek. To be sure, much of the discussion has been speculative, based on scattered bits of information garnered from a small sample. Nonetheless, a pattern quite definitely exists: Working a four-day, 40-hour week does affect marital interaction and adjustment. These, in turn affect the worker's attitude toward his schedule. True, for most people the consequences are marginal, but for others they are great. At the very least, the results uncovered here warrant giving more serious consideration to both the impact of the four-day workweek within the family setting and to the characteristics of persons and family environments that predispose the individual, by whatever process, to adjust successfully in this setting to innovations in the scheduling of work and leisure.

CHAPTER

7

THE USE OF TIME

Time, and its allocation across the wide spectrum of human endeavor, has long been a subject of significant interest to social scientists and planners. The temporal organization of work activities, the duration and patterns of television viewing, and research into trip-making behavior are three areas of study that have extensively employed time-budget techniques of data generation. Time-use data have also demonstrated their capacity to provide insight into such less clearly defined fields of inquiry as child care (Stone 1972), marital cohesion (Varga 1972), and socioeconomic planning (Patrushev 1972).

The most intensive efforts in the collection and utilization of time-budge information, however, have occurred in two fields of study that, though interpenetrating in their spheres of influence, have usually been examined independently. The first is exemplified by the work of British, French, Bulgarian, and, especially, Soviet industrial sociologists and psychologists who have been active in their use of time-budget surveys as a practical method for developing novel approaches to various labor problems, such as work schedules, rotating shifts, and automation (Szalai 1972). The other area experiencing extensive application of time-budget techniques has been in those studies exploring the intimate relationship between the concepts of "time" and participation in leisure activities.

The time-budget survey is attracting adherents because of its sensitivity as a mechanism for assessing changes in patterns of behavior. With the total supply of time being fixed, increments in the amount of time allocated to one activity, or set of activities, can only be accomplished at the expense of time previously given elsewhere. Therefore, it will tend to reflect changes in the individual's matrix of values. Aggregated across individuals, such data provide valuable insights into ongoing shifts in life-styles and culture more generally, insights not readily available through the use of more traditional measurement techniques alone. Thus, the time-budget survey, whether applied separately or (preferably) in conjunction with other techniques, constitutes a uniquely informative instrument for measuring change. It is not surprising then that the plethora of issues pertaining to leisure not only has provided an impetus to time-budget studies in general but also has transformed this subject-methodology marriage into a fashionable research combination.

The four-day workweek issue offers a natural opportunity for welding the diverse time-budget interests of students of work and leisure with the practical data requirements of planners. Not only do questions concerning the impact of this schedule upon how time is used in the various life domains (and their attendant levels of satisfaction) go to the core of many of the arguments raised either in favor of or against its adoption, but many of these claims, both pro and con, can be effectively evaluated only by using time-budget surveys applied in conjunction with more traditional methods of survey research.

Focusing upon what they view as an unbalanced, often irrational, contemporary temporal pattern—one that distributes time to activities tending to produce feelings of dissatisfaction and frustration at the expense of others yielding potentially more positive effective consequences—advocates of nonconventional work schedules perceive a real need for a radical restructuring of the blocks of time assigned to the various spheres of work and nonwork. Evolutionary changes in cultural values and social orientations, they argue, necessitate the unfreezing of conventional time block dimensions, their allocation rules, and a concomitant legitimization of alternative temporal patterns in closer step with current aspirations. Whether or not such change is accompanied by a simultaneous reorganization of the work place, only by achieving greater flexibility in the use of time will workers be in a better position to allocate and utilize their fixed time resources in a manner commensurate with individual preference in the modern context.

Two general questions concerning the above argument are examined in this chapter. The first pertains to the impact of the four-day work schedule upon how time is used, both within and outside the work setting. If the arguments raised by this schedule's advocates are correct, four-day and five-day workers should differ in the amounts of time allocated to the various work and leisure activities, and/or in the breadth of activities engaged in. Data derived from the time-budget survey of the 96 four-day and 31 five-day workers who completed their diaries are used to explore this question.* These data are presented in Table 7.1. This table also displays a hypothetical

---

*All analyses of time-budget diary data were performed on unweighted cases.

TABLE 7.1

Time Spent in 39 Primary Activities
(in average minutes per day and per week)

Activity	Minutes per Workdays 4-Day Workers (N = 96)	5-Day Workers (N = 31)	Minutes per Days-Off 4-Day Workers (N = 96)	5-Day Workers (N = 31)	Minutes per Hypoth. Week[a] 4-Day Workers (N = 96)	5-Day Workers (N = 31)
1. Main job	557	468	NA	NA	2228	2339
2. Meals at work	30	30	5	2	135	154
3. Work breaks	7	6	b	1	28	32
4. Waiting to start	9	8	2	b	42	43
5. At work, other	1	2	3	1	13	12
6. Overtime	20	71	93	57	358	469
7. Second job	1	—	—	13	4	25
8. Travel to/from job	54	53	10	7	246	280
Total work	679	638	113	81	3,054	3,354
9. Cooking	2	3	8	11	31	35
10. Indoor home chores	4	1	13	15	58	36
11. Outdoor home chores	6	6	21	10	85	47
12. Marketing	7	15	19	20	84	116
Total housework	19	25	61	56	258	234
13. Garden, animal care	18	9	37	32	183	110
14. Errands, shopping	6	4	11	6	57	32
15. Other house	2	4	30	33	98	86
Total other household care	26	17	78	71	338	228
16. Basic child care	6	—	10	2	54	6
17. Other child care	6	2	15	4	69	18
Total child care	12	2	25	6	123	22
18. Personal care	52	56	58	78	382	436
19. Eating (except at work)	52	68	84	72	458	485
20. Sleep	393	388	493	495	3,053	2,932
Total personal needs	497	512	635	645	3,893	3,853
21. Personal travel	14	22	26	34	133	179
22. Leisure travel	11	15	37	45	154	166
Total nonwork travel	25	37	63	79	287	345
23. Study	2	6	3	2	17	33
24. Religion	—	—	6	11	18	22
25. Organizations	—	3	1	b	3	17
Total study and participation	2	9	10	13	38	72
26. Radio	1	3	1	4	7	21
27. TV	75	97	142	125	726	734
28. Read paper	15	11	22	24	124	105
29. Read magazines	—	—	2	b	5	b
30. Read books	b	3	4	1	13	16
31. Movies	2	—	7	4	29	9
Total mass media	93	114	178	158	904	885
32. Social	27	42	99	132	406	475
33. Conversation	13	10	14	25	91	98
34. Active sports	1	8	19	17	60	73
35. Outdoors	5	2	50	30	171	72
36. Entertainment	4	4	10	24	44	68
37. Cultural events	b	5	3	2	11	26
38. Resting, relaxing, doing nothing	11	5	28	17	129	57
39. Other leisure	13	5	41	64	175	154
Total leisure	74	81	264	311	1,087	1,023
Total free time	179	218	489	529	2,183	2,146
Total travel	78	90	73	86	533	625
Total unspecified	14	5	14	21	98	66
Total minutes	1,441[c]	1,440	1,441[c]	1,441[c]	10,080	10,082[c]

[a]The hypothetical workweek was constructed as follows:
   Four-day worker – (workday x 4) + 3-day weekend.
   Five-day worker – (workday x 5) + 2-day weekend.
[b]Less than 0.5 minutes
[c]The minutes do not sum to 1,440 per day or 10,080 per week due to rounding.
Source: Compiled by the author.

151

week, constructed to facilitate comparisons between the two work groups. Only participation in "primary" activities is included in the analysis; issues involving (1) "secondary" activities—those done at the same time as the primary activity (for example, listening to the radio while driving), (2) patterns of interpersonal contact—such as time spent in the presence of relatives or others but not in the interactive mode, and (3) such matters as the temporal arrangement of activities—for example, whether going shopping leads to eating in a restaurant—must await subsequent analysis.

Participation in a wide variety of nonwork activities (such as movies, swimming, shopping) is used to supplement the diary. Responses to these questions were coded in two ways: whether or not the respondent participated in the activity at all during the preceding year (participation) and the extent of participation during that period of time (involvement). Though providing only a rough approximation of overall participation, these data have the advantage of extending the analysis over a longer period of time than is covered by the diary (one year versus three of four days), and of including a greater number of respondents.

The second question concerns whether a compacted work schedule does in fact influence the individual's satisfaction with his activity repertoire, particularly those activities occurring during his free time. Clearly, from labor's perspective, change in the pattern of participation in work and leisure activities, in itself, constitutes insufficient justification for widespread conversion to an alternative work schedule. For it to warrant strong union advocacy, such a schedule shift must be accompanied by a heightening of the worker's level of satisfaction with his daily routine and with his total use of free time. Failure to affirm a significantly positive affective consequence here would go a long way toward demonstrating a lack of empirical validity to the arguments made in support of the four-day workweek.

Several measures of affective response were used in examining this question. Though it was not possible to explore the relationship between these measures and the time-budget diary reports, participation and involvement could be, and were, so related. One of the main goals here was an attempt to replicate Nord and Costigan's (1973) finding that four-day workers who engage in task-oriented activities tended to be more satisfied with their work schedule.

WORKING LIFE

Human activity can be roughly divided into three heuristic categories, their differentiation determined by location along an implicit "underlying dimension having to do with the degree of volition or short-term discretion involved" (Robinson, Converse, Szalai 1972, p. 117). At one extreme are those activities, like sleeping, that permit little individual leeway in terms of time consumption. At the other end of the continuum is that time wherein short-term discretion is at a relative maximum. Activities commonly defined as leisure pursuits fall into place here. Occupying intermediate positions are those activities whose nature cannot be characterized as either absolutely obligatory or as absolutely individually determinable. These activities are more or less socially mandated; they are primarily work activities.

In modern industrial societies, work plays an essential role in the organization of time. So central, in fact, are many work activities (especially one's job) to the maintenance of what we, sometimes generously, refer to as "civilized society," that industrial man has even adjusted many of his biological imperatives to work's routines and rhythms. Consequently, a major change in the official schedule of work has the potential for influencing time allocation patterns in the remaining categories, particularly among those activities in which engagement involves freedom of choice. The allocation of time to work activities is the first topic of this chapter.

Activities Related to Formal Work

Many people oppose nonconventional job schedules on the grounds that rather than opening up new behavioral opportunities in free time, adoption would only lead to the devotion of additional time to the job. This conclusion was not borne out by the data. Though their official working day exceeded that of five-day men by two hours, the four-day workers allocated only three-quarters of an hour more to activities related to formal work on these days. In part, this was because they put in less time than what was officially expected of them. Four-day men also averaged significantly less overtime on their workdays—20 minutes versus 71 minutes. It should be noted, however, that whereas 64.5 percent of all five-day workers recorded overtime hours on their workday, only 19.8 percent of the men on a four-day schedule did so. If we take this difference into account, the discrepancy in time allotted to overtime on workdays is reduced to nine minutes. As expected, four-day workers put in the bulk of their overtime hours on their days-off, largely on their extra free day. In addition, more of them engaged in job-related activities during their weekend than did their five-day counterparts (42.7 percent versus 29 percent respectively). However, when the entire week is considered, four-day workers averaged both less overtime and less total time in activities related to formal work than did the men on a five-day schedule.

A common complaint expressed against the ten-hour workday is that in order to minimize the workers' confinement within the work setting, the amount of time allowed for meals and coffee breaks is often reduced. Interestingly, though discussions with plant managers indicated this to be formally true, the time-use data show otherwise. Both groups averaged a half-hour break for meals and less than a minute difference in their coffee breaks.

A second argument, but this time presented in support of widespread adoption of the four-day week, holds that such a switch would be socially beneficial in that it would reduce the number of work trips, thereby helping to relieve traffic congestion and save fuel. This argument can be contested on several grounds, not the least of which is that by having to make fewer work trips the individual may feel less constrained in his selection of residential location. By moving further away from the work site, he would lengthen his daily work trip time and possibly also extend congestion further out into the suburbs. The study's control over the geographic location of the work sites selected, combined with the similar distribution of the two groups on how many years they have worked their respective schedules, provides a crude test one way or the other. As Table 7.1 showed, there was no significant difference between four-day and five-day workers in their daily travel time to and from work. It appears, therefore, that the four-day schedule may bring about these trip-related social benefits, provided some control is kept over the number of men working overtime on their days-off.

Household Obligations

It is a common convention to consider the time allocated to household obligations as part of the world of work. These duties, assuredly, center around activities necessary for the maintenance of family and home. Yet, for many people, these activities have taken on many characteristics more generally associated with leisure. Determining, for example, when a person's interaction with his children is a function of necessity or volition requires a plumbing of human motivation quite beyond the limited capabilities of this study. Nevertheless, as diverse as the constituent chores may be, distinctions can be made between general types of household obligations.

The first cluster, labeled "housework," is comprised of those activities involved in the preparation of food (grocery shopping and cooking), the washing of dishes, housekeeping, laundry, and basic outdoor chores (excluding lawnmowing). The second group is more concerned with the general upkeep of the residence, though its components include such heterogeneous activities as gardening, animal care, shopping for goods and services other than groceries, the maintenance of heat and water, home repairs, and the care provided elderly or infirm family members. The rough distinction implied here is between those obligations conventionally considered "women's work" as opposed to other activities thought of as either masculine or less clearly defined according to sex role differentiation. The third and last cluster of household-related obligations centers on caring for children.

Differences between four-day and five-day workers on the first cluster (housework) are minimal. While men on the compacted work-week did spend a few less minutes doing these activities on their working day, the reverse was true on days-off. Over the entire week, four-day men spent only 24 more minutes on housework-related activities than did their five-day counterparts. Time allocated to both indoor and outdoor chores on the days-off accounted for most of the discrepancy. If we consider that the demands imposed by housework chores are relatively time-inelastic, finding no significant differences here was expected. While four-day workers have more opportunity to perform such tasks on the weekend, they also have less available time on workdays.

In comparison to housework chores, the functional demands of those activities labeled "household care" are quite elastic. The amount of time allocated to gardening, shopping, and so on, is determined by many factors in addition to necessity or obligation. To be sure, most men have to allocate some minimal period of time to these activities, but their duration is to a large extent subject to factors such as access to modern time-saving conveniences, services for hire, the sheer availability of discretionary time, and the degree of personal satisfaction derived from engaging in these activities. Dumazedier (1967) coined the term semileisure to describe activities such as these.

When compared over the entire week, four-day workers devoted more time to household care chores than did men on a five-day schedule. Time spent in gardening and animal care accounted for most of the difference. While the participation rates of both groups of workers were approximately equal on both workdays and days-off, the average time allocated to these two activities was greater among four-day participants. It appears, then, that as the blocks of discretionary time expand, the desire to do household care chores does not spread to previously uninterested workers. Among those already interested, however, the additional free time affords them the opportunity to become more fully involved.

Child care represents another set of activities that at points merges into leisure. Reflecting this, Table 7.1 subdivides the category into basic and peripheral components. Following the distinction made by Robinson, Converse, and Szalai (1972), basic child care "consists of fulfilling those essential requirements such as feeding, clothing, comforting and caring for the health of children which, while sometimes gratifying as activities, represent minimal and fixed demands on time" (p. 127). Peripheral child care (labeled "other") includes all remaining activities requiring the father to adopt the "interactive mode" of contact with his children. These activities, such as conversation, helping with homework, babysitting, and playing, "tend to have a somewhat greater admixture of the discretionary or leisurely about them" (p. 127).

There is a decided difference between four-day and five-day workers in their allocation of time to child care. Although the difference in basic child care is somewhat exaggerated because of one four-day worker who rushed his daughter to the hospital and subsequently spent a great deal of time with her, further analysis nonetheless indicates that almost twice as many four-day workers are actively involved with their children; this was true equally for workdays and for days-off. Over the entire week, men on a four-day schedule spent 200-300 percent as much time in this mode. On the average, among men who reported any contact with their children, those working a four-day schedule spent over six more hours per week with their children than did their five-day counterparts.

Combining the time requirements of formal work with that of all household and child care tasks, including associated travel, there is little to distinguish between the two groups of workers. As Table 7.2 shows, their socioeconomic obligations took up approximately equivalent portions of their daily and weekly allotments of time. The extra time five-day workers gave to job-related activities was accomplished at the expense of time that would otherwise be devoted to family and home. Although on any given day the four-day men did spend somewhat more time engaged in work activities, the extra day-off served to balance out the total for the week as a whole.

TABLE 7.2

Proportion of Total Workday, Day Off, and Week
Devoted to Working Life

Work Group	Workday	Day-Off	Hypothetical Week
Four-day workers	0.52	0.21	0.39
Five-day workers	0.49	0.17	0.40

Source: Compiled by the author.

PHYSIOLOGICAL NEEDS

As might be expected, there is almost no difference between four-day and five-day workers as to the amount of time allocated to physiological needs. Four-day workers tended to spend somewhat less time eating and in personal care, and somewhat more time sleeping. Perhaps one of the side benefits of working a compacted week is the opportunity it provides for getting in a little additional rest and sleep on the third day-off. From the family perspective, the only difference of possible interest was the lesser amount of time allocated to meals (other than at work) on the weekday by the four-day workers. This quarter-hour difference does, in general, constitute time spent with the family and may partially explain why five-day workers reported less interaction with their children as a "primary" activity. On the other hand, this discrepancy was largely negated by the slightly greater amount of time allocated to meals by four-day workers on their days-off.

FREE-TIME ACTIVITIES

Although men working ten-hour schedules have less free time on their workdays than do men working only eight hours, over the entire week no difference in their relative amount of free time is to be expected. Recognizing this, advocates of the four-day workweek emphasize the increased opportunity to organize activities in a satisfying manner. Table 7.1 verifies that four-day workers did report less time for discretionary activities on their workday. But on weekends, again as expected, these activities accounted for almost seven hours more of their time than for five-day workers. This occurred even though, on "typical" days-off, four-day men worked more overtime. Considering the total week, the differential in free-time activities for the two groups is a scant 37 minutes (2,183 versus 2,146 minutes).

Do four-day workers, then, exhibit a pattern of free-time use noticeably distinct from five-day workers? For instance, do they participate in different activities? Perhaps they distribute their time to the same set of activities but in altered proportions. Or perhaps both. This question is taken up with reference to three broad categories of free-time behavior: (1) mass media usage, (2) social interaction, and (3) participation in leisure pursuits.

Use of the Mass Media

In a cross-national study of time use, Robinson, Converse, and Szalai were impressed "by the degree to which the mass media—newspapers, magazines, books, television, and radio—have come to represent a dominant staple for free time use everywhere. . . . [It] is clear that the media do absorb highly significant portions of free time everywhere, and beyond the media one encounters only a rather diffuse scatter of other types of leisure, so that as a group the media seems to tower over all else" (1972, p. 132). While Robinson et al.'s conclusion is perhaps extreme, few would contest the importance of the mass media, television in particular, upon how time is used in modern societies.

The men included in this study are no exception. As a portion of total free time, excluding time associated with leisure travel, their mass media contact is quite substantial; it occupies more than half their free time on workdays (Table 7.3). Furthermore, the data only measure contact with the mass media as a "primary" activity. If contact with them as a "secondary" activity were included, a far greater proportion of the individual's use of free time would be accounted for.* More significant for this study, however, is that the data show strong similarities in use of media by four-day and five-day workers on workdays as well as on days-off and for the total week.

Turning to the number of minutes actually allocated to media use, Table 7.1 indicates some tendency for four-day workers, relative to five-day workers, to make greater use of the media on their days-off and less on their workdays. Television watching, of course, accounted for the bulk of this time. However, no real difference was uncovered between work groups in the total amount of television watched per week. On the other hand, a slightly larger percentage of four-day workers did read newspapers, magazines, and books and did

TABLE 7.3

Use of Mass Media as Proportion of Total Free Time
(Excluding Leisure Travel Time)
On Workdays, Days-Off, and per Week

	Workday	Day-Off	Hypothetical Week
Proportion of Free Time			
Four-day workers	0.55	0.39	0.45
Five-day workers	0.56	0.33	0.45

Source: Compiled by the author.

---

*Robinson, Converse, and Szalai (1972) found that when use of the mass media as a secondary activity is taken into consideration, estimates of media contact nearly double.

so for long periods of time. These findings are of significance if for no other reason than because they run counter to the expectations of social critics who fear the average man would waste increased leisure time in uncreative free-time pursuits, such as watching television.

Social Interaction

This category of activity includes all forms of communication not captured in mass media usage. Specifically, the survey reports include estimates of the amount of time the respondent spent talking to his wife—labeled "conversation." Second is that time allocated to such social activities as visiting or entertaining friends and relatives, attending parties or other social gatherings, going to bars, cafes, and so on, and playing parlor games—all subsumed under the label "social."

Clearly, the few minutes spent conversing with one's wife as a primary activity only roughly reflect the total extent of verbal communication between the marriage partners. A good deal of conversation between spouses occurs while coping with functional obligations or as an accompaniment to other activities. "Conversation," therefore, implies some degree of sustained dialogue. In this limited respect, there is little separating the two groups. Five-day workers did spend a few more minutes talking to their wives, but without considering secondary conversation, the significance of this finding remains ambiguous, if not meaningless.

Outside of work and the family, the social visit or social gathering constitutes the most nearly "organized" setting for informal communication. One of the most commonly stated criticisms directed against the 4/40 schedule is that the longer workday interferes with the individual's social life on weeknights, a loss that is difficult to recoup on the weekend because of the conflicting five-day schedule adhered to by most workers. To some extent, the data bear out this observation. The ten-hour day did result in less time spent socializing on workdays, a difference not made up over the longer weekend (Table 7.1). Furthermore, while both groups of men socialized in approximately equal proportions on the weekends, a larger percentage of five-day workers did so on workdays (45.2 percent versus 27.1 percent).

Other Forms of Leisure Pursuits

With the examination of attention paid to mass media and the time spent in informal communications, 64 percent and 68 percent of the free time available to four-day and five-day workers, respectively, have been accounted for.* Roughly another 7-8 percent is taken up by travel associated with free-time pursuits.

The balance of the respondents' free time was distributed among a heterogeneous collection of activities, ranging from study and religion, through hobbies and participation in outdoor activities, to time spent "resting" or "doing nothing." Though there is little real difference here between the two work groups, a few points are worth noting. The first concerns the often heard prediction that, rather than leading to better use of free time a compacted work schedule would, so to speak, leave many people "hanging" for want of something to do. They would find themselves saddled with more dead time than desired. The four-day workers did, on the average, report more than twice as much dead time per week as their five-day counterparts. But the amounts of time in question still add up to hardly overwhelming totals (129 minutes versus 57 minutes). Moreover, neither group was plagued with the problem of boredom outside the work setting.

Turning to participation in religious, organizational, or educational activities, there is again little to distinguish the two groups. Only one worker from each group reported spending any time studying, going to special lectures, and so on. Likewise, participation in the affairs of formal organizations was almost universally ignored.[†] Four-day workers also spent relatively less time in religious services. Clearly, any claims that compacted work schedules may yield greater participation in formal, hopefully public, service organizations finds little support in these data.

The third and last cluster of activities of interest is combined under the label "outdoors." This includes such things as hunting, fishing, hiking, cycling, bicycle riding, and walking. Almost 13 percent more four-day workers participated in these activities over the weekend, and, surprisingly, they allocated more time to them on their workdays as well as on their days-off. Significantly, hiking/hunting/fishing accounted for all but 10 minutes of the 99-minute weekly discrepancy between the two groups. Here is another possible instance of a behavioral change attributable to working a different schedule. The longer weekend appears to have facilitated engagement in activities requiring extended periods of time.

---

*Approximately the same percentage of free time was similarly accounted for in a national sample of Americans (Robinson, Converse, Szalai 1972).

[†]Attending "Little League" functions attracted two of the four men who gave time to formal organizations.

SATISFACTION WITH FREE TIME:
RESOLVING A PARADOX

The impact of the four-day workweek is perhaps nowhere more evident than in its effect upon satisfaction with the use of free time. Four-day workers indicated significantly greater satisfaction with how they used their free time than did their five-day counterparts ($\overline{X}_4$ = 2.49, $\overline{X}_5$ = 2.98, $p < 0.01$). Thirty percent of the former, compared to only 12 percent of the latter, reported being extremely satisfied. Yet, as was just discussed, there was little or no difference between the two groups of workers on how they disposed of their free time. What differences did appear tended to occur at the margins. If anything, the data pertaining to the use of free time showed a marked "strain toward consistency." To be sure, these changes could account for some of the difference in the levels of free-time-use satisfaction between four-day and five-day workers, but more convincing reasons must exist elsewhere. To what, then, can four-day workers' greater satisfaction be attributed?

The ability to use one's free time in a satisfying way is, of course, a function of several factors besides the number of minutes a person engages in various activities. Four possible reasons for the four-day workers' greater satisfaction with how they use their free time are briefly discussed—overtime flexibility, recreation and task-oriented activities, the significance of friends, and the importance of the family in the use of free time. Much in the following discussion centers around the importance of having discretion in how time is used.

Flexibility in Overtime

In Chapter 4, the men were trichotomized according to whether they worked less, the same, or more overtime than they desired. Significantly more four-day than five-day workers were found to work the desired amount of overtime. In addition, among those who felt they put in the right amount of overtime in the month preceding the personal interview, the four-day men exceeded their five-day counterparts by approximately eight hours. Yet, despite these differences, the four-day workers indicated no greater satisfaction with their jobs. Where, then, do these findings make their presence felt? Part of the answer, apparently, lies in the workers' satisfaction with their use of free time.

Overtime is generally treated as a relatively pure obligatory activity, one engaged in out of economic necessity. Without doubt, there is much merit to this position. Yet the role played by overtime in the individual's life extends beyond economic survival; it reflects his life-style, his material expectations, and his ability to use free time in a personally satisfying manner as well. Even when compelled to work overtime for economic reasons, the individual still retains a measure of choice over how many hours of overtime he does work and, within limits, over their arrangement. Thus, overtime can legitimately be viewed as a discretionary, as well as an obligatory, activity.

Theoretically, the four-day workweek makes possible greater flexibility in the arrangement of, and in the relationship between, overtime and free time. By virtue of their extra day-off, workers on this schedule can put in extensive hours of overtime, management permitting, without interfering with the two remaining weekend days. In addition, by choosing to work less than a full day of overtime on their extra day-off, men working an official four-day week can expand their supply of free time on the weekend and still accumulate a significant number of overtime hours. The end result is that they should find it easier both to put in the number of overtime hours they desire and to have the amount of free time left over for the leisure activities they value.

Table 7.4 indicates that the potential for harmony between overtime and free time appears often to have been actualized in practice. When the respondent was able to work the desired amount of overtime, working an official four-day or five-day schedule has no significant effect upon satisfaction with the use of free time. But where this fortunate situation did not occur, five-day workers were significantly adversely affected. Clearly, working too little overtime had a more negative effect upon satisfaction with use of free time for both groups than did working too much overtime. Apparently, however, the additional free time made available by working less overtime than desired

TABLE 7.4

Mean Satisfaction with Use of Free Time
by Whether Worker Put in Desired Amount of Overtime

	Four-Day Workers	Five-Day Workers	Significance Level
Less overtime than desired	2.81 (N = 31)	3.53 (N = 15)	$p < 0.05$
Same amount of overtime as desired	2.51 (N = 109)	2.68 (N = 24)	NS
More overtime than desired	2.27 (N = 22)	2.86 (N = 11)	$p < 0.10$

Source: Compiled by the author.

could be put to more satisfying use by men on a four-day schedule. The same pattern also seems to hold for those men who worked excess overtime. But in this case, the ability of four-day workers to put in much of their undesired overtime on the extra day-off appears to have mitigated much of their potential discontent. Indeed, these men reported even greater satisfaction with the use of their free time than did those four-day workers who put in the amount of overtime they desired. Perhaps the additional income compensated them for their loss of free time, or maybe they simply used what free time they had more wisely.

Paradoxically, the above findings can also be interpreted as indicating the inability of four-day workers to use their additional free time in satisfying ways. Consequently, they tend to put in more overtime, and the more overtime the better. This second perspective cannot be dismissed on the basis of the present findings. If subsequent research shows this interpretation to be in fact correct, then it says something not altogether favorable about our society, its values, and its system of education. But this would constitute a conclusion quite separate from the relative merits of the four-day and five-day work schedules. For in either case, the four-day workers' comparatively greater discretion in the use of time (free and otherwise) has the advantages both of (1) greater ability to regulate the amount of overtime so as to preserve the amount of free time they can use effectively and (2) when compelled to work an undesired number of overtime hours, greater flexibility to arrange overtime so it interferes only minimally with their ability to use free time in satisfying ways. Whether they arrange their overtime with the intention of filling time that would otherwise prove dissatisfying or with the goal of making more effective use of additional free time (possibly accompanied by more overtime as well), the four-day workers' enhanced discretion in the use of time results in greater satisfaction.

Task-Oriented and Recreation-Oriented Activities

In their study of workers in a Saint Louis pharmaceutical firm that switched to a 4/40 work schedule, Nord and Costigan (1973) found that after a year's experience with the new schedule, satisfaction with it was related to participation in task-oriented, but not recreation-oriented, activities. In an attempt to replicate their results, the activities on the list used to supplement the diary were categorized according to whether they were task- or recreation-oriented.* These

---

*Task-oriented activities include church attendance, classes, gardening, home repair, car repair, shopping, and helping friends and relatives. Recreation-oriented activities are movies, clubs, at-

two types of activities were then related to satisfaction with both work schedule and use of free time in terms of (1) the number of activities the individual participated in (participation) and (2) the extent of such participation (involvement).

Analysis of these data uncovered no significant relationships between "participation" and the two satisfaction measures for either four-day or five-day workers.* Likewise, the expected relationship between task-oriented activities and satisfaction with work schedule for four-day workers was not replicated when "involvement" was the predictor variable. On the contrary, it was their involvement in recreation-oriented activities that related positively (Gamma = 0.22, $p < 0.05$). Neither activity type associated with satisfaction with work schedule for the five-day workers. On the other hand, when satisfaction with the use of free time was examined with reference to the extent of involvement in the two activity types, a result similar to that uncovered by Nord and Costigan (1973) was found. Among four-day workers, satisfaction here was significantly related to involvement in task-oriented, but not recreation-oriented, activities (Gamma = 0.19 and 0.06, $p < 0.05$ and NS, respectively). However, task involvement was even more strongly associated with free-time-use satisfaction among the five-day workers, though, because of their smaller sample size, the finding did not attain statistical significance (Gamma = 0.26).

Do these findings mean, then, that involvement in task-oriented activities does not play an important mediating role between work schedule and the four-day men's relatively greater satisfaction with their schedule and with their use of free time? Not necessarily. In the discussion of the results of the time-budget diary, task-oriented endeavors, such as those concerning household care, were artificially excluded from the operational definition of free-time activities. But, as pointed out at the time, the extent of individual involvement in these activities is often a matter of personal discretion. Thus, in many minds, these endeavors functionally and psychologically constitute free-time activities and are taken into consideration when evaluating the use of free time. When this enlarged definition of free-time behavior is employed, the results presented above start to form a coherent picture.

_____

tending sports events, fishing/hunting/camping, active sports, boating/swimming, going to bars/night clubs, concerts/fairs, museums, social visits, indoor games, and hobbies. It should be noted that though similar, these lists are not identical to those used by Nord and Costigan.

*The proportion of workers in each of the two work groups who participated in the two types of activities was also nearly identical.

Note that the activities list roughly measured only the number of times a person participated in the various activities, not the amount of time devoted to them. Assuming that satisfaction with the use of free time is significantly, and equally, associated with involvement in task-oriented activities for both work groups, by making it possible for the four-day workers to allocate additional time to these activities the compacted work schedule should, other things being equal, serve to enhance their relative satisfaction. Moreover, we would anticipate these men in fact to allocate most of whatever additional discretionary time their four-day schedule affords them to task-oriented rather than recreation-oriented activities because of their closer association with free-time usage. Data from the time-budget diaries quite strongly suggest that men working an official four-day week did allocate whatever additional discretionary time they had to task-oriented activities; the amount of time spent in recreation-oriented activities remained constant, roughly matching that of five-day workers. With relatively more time spent in those activities associated with free-time-use satisfaction, it comes as no surprise that four-day workers were more satisfied with how they use their free time. Now to carry the argument a step further. Given that satisfaction with one's work schedule is related to satisfaction with one's use of free time, then the four-day workers' greater "time involvement" in task-oriented activities may partially account for their relatively greater satisfaction with their work schedule.

The Importance of Friends

When asked how satisfied they were with (1) the number of friends they had and (2) their friendships in general, the men in both work groups expressed approximately equal levels of satisfaction. Yet, Table 7.5 shows that both variables related considerably stronger

TABLE 7.5

Correlations (r) of Satisfaction with Use of Free Time
with Satisfaction with Number of Friends and
Satisfaction with Friendships

	Four-Day Workers ($N = 168$)	Five-Day Workers ($N = 49$)	Significance Level
Satisfaction with number of friends	0.64*	0.14	$p < 0.01$
Satisfaction with friendships	0.69*	0.05	$p < 0.01$

*$p < 0.01$
Source: Compiled by the author.

to how satisfied the four-day respondents were with their use of free time than they did for the men on a standard work schedule. Unfortunately, this study made few forays into the respondents' friendship patterns. As a result, interpreting these findings is largely a matter of speculation. There is, however, one additional bit of information that might shed some light on what is occurring here. When asked what proportion of their friends their wives knew well, the proportion claimed by four-day workers was significantly higher than that by their five-day counterparts ($\overline{X}_4 = 1.86$, $\overline{X}_5 = 2.29$, $p < 0.01$).* Concomitantly, they also reported knowing more of their wives' friends, though the difference between groups was not significant.

In her study of social networks and the family, Bott (1971) suggested that the greater the "connectedness" characterizing the family's external social relationships (networks), the more influence will these relationships have upon the spouses' emotional satisfactions. "When the person's network is close knit, the members of his network tend to reach consensus on norms and they extend consistent informal pressure on one another to conform to the norms, to keep in touch with one another, and, if need be, to help one another" (p. 60). Two consequences resulting from a closed network are (1) more rigid segregation of conjugal role functions and (2) greater dependence on friends and relatives for gratifications during free time.

Certainly, the extent to which the spouses know each other's friends constitutes a very rough estimate of the connectedness of the family's social network. Nevertheless, it points to the possible existence of relatively more tight-knit networks among the four-day workers, especially when considered in light of their tendency toward greater conjugal role segregation. If this is in fact the situation, then the correlations shown in Table 7.5 have a ready explanation. Spending more time in the family setting, the four-day worker has more opportunity to meet and get to know his wife's friends, and she, his friends. In time, their social network should begin to close, although probably only to a moderate degree. Bounded now by a tighter network, the four-day worker depends more upon friends for emotional satisfactions, including satisfaction with the use of free time. Concomitantly, the more important friendships become, the greater the saliency of those activities involving friends when it comes to evaluating how satisfied he is with his free time. Given that four-day and five-day workers were equally satisfied with the number of friends they have and their friendships in general, the relatively greater affective importance of these relationships for four-day men should, logically,

_____

*The response alternatives provided were the following: all (1), most (2), about half (3), some (4), none (5).

result in greater satisfaction with their use of free time—which was the case. In a sense, they derive more affective intensity for the time invested.

The Family

Though not well documented, the existence of an important relationship between the use of free time and marital satisfaction has long been recognized (Chapter 1). The data presented below point to at least two ways in which the family plays an important mediating role between the arrangement of work hours and satisfaction with the use of free time. Both work to the advantage of men on compacted schedules.

First, given the high value placed on family life in American society, we would anticipate that the greater the discretion an individual has over his use of time, the more time he will spend in the family setting, and, consequently, the greater will be his chances for meeting the demands of his family roles (for example, through the performance of task-oriented activities). In return, the worker will receive more family-sent gratifications, causing him to feel more satisfied with his conjugal and parental role relationships. Considering that much of the person's discretionary time is spent in the presence of other members of his family, better family relationships should result in a heightened feeling of satisfaction with the use of free time. The second family-related cause works alongside the first and is similar to the argument presented in the previous section on friendships. Simply put, the more time spent in the family setting, and the more gratifying these family relationships become, the greater their saliency when the individual evaluates his use of free time. Again, there is a greater affective return for the time and energy invested.

Given the available data, the validity of the above two hypotheses cannot be tested in detail. There is, however, circumstantial evidence that provides some support. When all the minutes distributed among the various discretionary activities, including those labeled "semileisure," are summed, the four-day workers not only had more discretionary time per week (3,055 minutes versus 2,809 minutes), they spent more time both in absolute terms (810 minutes versus 582 minutes) and as a proportion of total discretionary time (0.27 versus 0.21) in house and family-related activities. If this extra 4.75 hours translates into better role performance, four-day workers should be more satisfied with their performance as husbands and fathers, and with their marriages in general. In Chapter 5 this was shown to be the case except for parental role performance, where there was no significant difference. Following the logic further, being more satisfied with these relationships, the four-day men likewise should, and did, express greater happiness with their use of free time. Concomitantly, Table 7.6 shows that satisfaction with one's family role performances and with one's marriage related far more strongly to satisfaction with the use of free time for four-day workers than it did for their five-day counterparts. Apparently, these relationships constitute a more salient aspect of free-time use for men working a compacted four-day schedule. There appears, therefore, to be some support in the findings of this study for both hypotheses linking the dynamics of the family setting to the four-day workers' greater satisfaction with the use of free time.

TABLE 7.6

Correlations between Satisfaction
With Use of Free Time
And Conjugal, Parental, and Marital Satisfactions

	Four-Day Workers	Five-Day Workers	Significance Level
Satisfaction with conjugal role performance	0.69^a (N = 166)	0.37^b (N = 46)	$p < 0.01$
Satisfaction with parental role performance	0.56^a (N = 149)	0.38^b (N = 39)	NS
Marital satisfaction	0.52^a (N = 161)	0.19 (N = 45)	$p < 0.05$

$^a p < 0.01$.
$^b p < 0.05$.
Source: Compiled by the author.

SUMMARY

The focus of this chapter has been on four-day and five-day workers' allocation of time, and on differences in their patterns of time use. The general picture that appears is one of a marked strain toward consistency with respect to both how time is distributed among the various activities and to who participates. Rather than engaging in novel endeavors during their discretionary time, four-day workers tend merely to rearrange their activity schedules. When they find themselves with spare time, these men simply expand the amount of time they naturally allocate to already familiar patterns of behavior, instead of involving themselves in new forms of behavior.

This does not mean, however, that four-day workers do not derive greater satisfaction from how they use their discretionary time or that there are no significant differences in patterns of time usage between work groups. On the contrary, four-day workers did express greater satisfaction with their use of free time than did the men on the standard work schedule, and important differences were found in their respective arrangements of overtime, in the amount of time spent with and caring for children, and in the extent of time given to task-oriented activities in the family setting.

The data show that four-day workers did not work more overtime than their five-day counterparts but that most of what overtime they did work took place during the extra nonwork day. This result is not surprising considering the length of their official workday and the arguments related in Chapter 2. While the data in Chapter 4 do point to the possibility of a slight accretion in overtime hours among four-day workers, the difference between groups was found to be neither significant nor sufficient to interfere with their enjoyment in other valued activities. The ten-hour workday, on the other hand, does somewhat inhibit evening social life and the doing of errands, losses that are not easily recouped on the weekend. Finally, the compacted workweek does not result in a noticeable decrease in travel time to and from the work place due to the number of men working overtime during the long weekend.

The primary benefits gained from working a four-day week appear to be in its effect on time allocated to activities in the family setting. Contrary to expectations, four-day workers as a group do not seem to help their wives by taking on more of the routine housework. They were found, however, to spend additional time doing major household chores such as gardening, errands, and repair work. Of probably greater significance, the average four-day workers allocated more than five times as many minutes to activities involved directly with child care. The opportunity to so engage oneself appears to constitute one of the principal advantages of working a four-day week.

Neither the amount of time available for nor the pattern of participation in activities traditionally associated with leisure differ significantly between work groups. Thanks to their shorter workday, five-day men had more free time (discretionary time minus overtime) during the week, while men on the compacted schedule had more total free time during the weekend, as anticipated. As to what was done during this time, despite the often and loudly stated fears of social critics, no difference in television watching per week was found. Less optimistic, however, was the finding that four-day workers do not take advantage of their greater scheduling flexibility to become more involved in educational or public service activities. The leisure activities that four-day workers apparently turn to most during their free time are those done outdoors, away from the home though not necessarily away from the family. They also spend somewhat more time relaxing or doing nothing. Boredom, however, seems to constitute no more of a problem for men on four-day schedules than for those working a standard week.

Based on these findings, supplemented by the results of previous chapters, several explanations were offered to account at least partially for four-day workers' greater satisfaction with the use of free time and with the work schedule. Flexibility in the arrangement of overtime enhances one's opportunity to work the right amount of overtime. This ability was found to associate significantly with higher levels of satisfaction with schedule and with free-time use. The argument given was that, when one has more control over how one's discretionary time is arranged, overtime is less likely to interfere with other valued activities. Two sets of activities appear most relevant here. First, four-day workers organized their discretionary time to allow them greater opportunity for involvement in task-oriented activities. This type of activity was found to be a factor in determining expression of satisfaction with free time. Second, men working a four-day week reported both a higher level of marital adjustment and spending more time in the family setting. Regardless of whether this additional time leads to heightened adjustment or vice versa, four day workers find themselves both interacting more, and getting along relatively better, with other family members. In particular, they are able to spend more time with their children, and, as shown in Chapter 5, they can do so without forgoing conjugal companionship gratification. In combination, these family-related outcomes cannot help but result in greater satisfaction with the use of free time and in the fostering of a positive disposition toward the four-day workweek.

The final suggestion raised concerns a possible effect that working the compacted schedule has on the family structure. Data were presented that indicate that working a four-day week may cause a modest tightening of the marriage partners' social network. One consequence of such a phenomenon is the placing of greater dependence on friends for emotional satisfaction and free-time gratification. By looking more outside the family for valued gratifications, four-day workers simultaneously heighten the saliency of these outside relationships while reducing the pressures on their wives and children for such rewards. Expecting less from the other members of the family, they are now less likely to feel disappointed in these relationships. They have also expanded the number and scope of people they can turn to for support and assistance when problems crop up. Either way, by tightening the family's social network, the four-day workweek seems to enhance marital adjustment, satisfaction with the use of free time, and work-schedule satisfaction.

CHAPTER

8

FINDINGS, CONCLUSIONS, AND RECOMMENDATIONS

This study has addressed selected issues and potential problems associated with conversion to the four-day, 40-hour workweek. This nonconventional arrangement of work hours has been examined in terms of its impact on blue-collar workers' adjustment in the work place, within their families, and in their use of discretionary time. The main objective was to provide valid, and at times provocative, information that would be of interest and utility to social scientists, planners, and others. The underlying hope was that this might attract more attention to the individual and societal implications of alternate modes of organizing work time and, on a broader level, encourage additional exploration into the dynamic interaction among the spheres of work, leisure, and family life.

The intent of this chapter is first to review a few of the more significant findings and to suggest several specific areas that warrant further research. Next is a general discussion of the wider implications of the findings, along with several recommendations that follow as much from the arguments raised in Chapters 1 and 2 as from the data. Thus, while these recommendations grow directly out of the findings, they go far beyond them. The recommendations reflect the author's interest and concern with the more encompassing issues pertaining to the relationships among work, leisure, and the family and the potentially important mediating role played by policy makers, planners, and researchers in a society characterized by rapid technological development and a growing leisure orientation.

RESEARCH LIMITATIONS

This study has been a preliminary step in what the author hopes will be a series of related efforts directed toward the development of

171

a coherent theory of work and leisure that will be of instrumental as well as intrinsic value. Being a first step, the study had some serious limitations that should be kept in mind as the reader goes through this concluding chapter. A review of these limitations is presented in order to remind the reader that the study was conceived and operationalized as an exploration and to caution the reader against too broadly generalizing the results.

The first qualification is that the findings are based on a relatively small sample (N = 233) chosen according to a decidedly nonrandom selection procedure. As a result, though the findings reported and the conclusions drawn have implications for the viability of the four-day workweek outside the present sample, they can legitimately serve only as rough guides to what may transpire. Further, because it was not possible to obtain the desired control group of workers on a standard five-day week, comparisons between the two work groups are not as reliable as one might wish. Care, however, was taken to report only those differences in which the most confidence could be placed.

Another limitation is that the sample consists entirely of blue-collar men. Naturally this limits the relevance of the study's implications to men who fit this description. Fourth, the issue of marital adjustment was examined solely from the perspective of husbands, thereby providing a partial, one-sided picture of the four-day workweek's impact in the family setting. Because wives of male workers and married female workers were not interviewed, there exists a distinct possibility that important consequences of this nonconventional schedule have been overlooked.

The final reservation derives from the fact that the study was undertaken during a period of economic instability and energy uncertainty. Serious effort was directed toward minimizing the likelihood of these environmental conditions influencing workers' perceptions, behavior, and affective responses—principally by postponing the field-work until the economy appeared to be improving. The inclusion of a control group helps to reduce further the chance of drawing faulty conclusions based on data allegedly pertaining to the four-day workweek's impact but actually measuring the workers' response to economic insecurity. Despite these precautions, however, the possibility remains that then current economic and energy problems may have colored the data.

REVIEW OF THE FINDINGS

In this section are presented a few of the data highlights discussed in Chapters 6 and 7. To avoid repetition, only the most significant or interesting of the findings are reported here, leaving discussion of the interrelationships among variables relevant to different settings to the more detailed chapters.

The paramount finding of this study is that <u>four-day workers express significantly greater satisfaction with their work schedule than workers on a standard five-day week</u>. Despite complaints about such things as the length of the workday, fatigue, and pressure to work additional overtime, few of the 179 four-day men indicated a desire to return to the standard schedule. Further, few of the dissatisfied men felt sufficiently so to search for new jobs. From these findings, one must conclude that, at the very least, workers' response to experience with the four-day schedule is generally favorable. Indeed, their dispositions are sufficiently positive to justify further efforts directed toward convincing management and labor to experiment more with the four-day workweek.

Certainly, the four-day workweek does not entail uniform consequences for all who are directly affected by it. The pattern is one in which the overwhelming majority of men either are unaffected or experience a net benefit, while a not significant minority suffer modest, and at times major, adjustment difficulties. Neither is the impact of the schedule in the same direction in all settings. Comparisons between four-day and five-day work groups show, for instance, that while the compacted schedule is probably conducive to greater satisfaction with the use of discretionary time and may, in certain cases, result in improved marital adjustment, it also associates with a reduction in job satisfaction, and for a few workers, poorer adjustment in the family context. One of the principal motivations of this study was the desire to provide a start at determining just who benefits, 'who suffers, and why, within each setting. What follows is a discussion summarizing the findings for each setting separately.

The Work Setting

In the work setting, the most important consequence of the four-day week is its association with decreased job satisfaction. It is not clear why this occurs, but the data do provide a few leads. First, as a group, four-day men reported greater job fatigue, which was generally unrelated to their age. Second, several men felt management was exerting too much pressure for additional overtime. Even so, four-day workers were not found to put in significantly more overtime than their five-day counterparts, though they did work a few more hours each month. Those who felt overtime pressure worked a few more hours still. Third, while there were no differences in mean job-satisfaction levels between four- and five-day men under age 35, older four-day workers expressed significantly greater dissatisfaction than their counterparts on the standard schedule. Finally, a far larger portion of four-day than five-day workers stated that they worked the amount of overtime they wished.

At least two explanations are suggested by the data. First, though work fatigue was felt equally by four-day workers of all ages, it may be a more salient aspect of the job for those over 35. If this is the case, then these men should indeed have been found to be more sensitive to overtime pressure and to be less satisfied with their jobs than their five-day counterparts. However, when scrutinized, this explanation does not hold up well. If it were true, older four-day workers would express greater, and not merely equal, dissatisfaction with their jobs than their younger cohorts, and would also be less satisfied with the work schedule than either younger four-day men or older five-day men. These conditions, however, were not found. A second explanation is more consistent with the data and with the arguments presented in Chapter 2. Instead of reflecting changes in the nature of work and the energy required to do the job, the greater job dissatisfaction of older four-day workers results, primarily, from interference with the normal tendency toward job habituation. Greater flexibility in the allocation of discretionary time, particularly in how overtime is arranged, causes gratifications received in the work place to pale in comparison to those attainable elsewhere. Job habituation, therefore, finds itself in relatively infertile ground. To be sure, fatigue generated by the ten-hour day and discontent produced by unwanted pressure for overtime contribute to the four-day workers' greater job dissatisfaction. But these extrinsic factors serve largely to exacerbate already unfavorable opinions about their jobs, opinions stemming originally from their frustration with what they do during this time and reinforced by sharp contrasts between available work and nonwork gratifications.

The Family Context

No significant differences in the mean levels of conjugal and parental role-performance satisfaction or in overall marital satisfaction were found between four- and five-day workers. Neither were any significant differences uncovered when these groups were compared on their respective distribution of family-related gratifications, pressures, the balance of decision-making power, and the division of labor in the performance of daily household chores. These findings do not mean, however, that working a four-day week has no impact on what transpires in the family setting, only that its effects vary among subgroups within each work group. One outcome of these differential impacts was that four-day workers tend to extreme scores on the measures of conjugal role-performance satisfaction and general satisfaction with the marriage. Apparently, working a four-day schedule has positive consequences on adjustment in the family context for some men and negative consequences for others. Again, the question is, Who benefits, who suffers, and why?

The data examined provide several interesting leads. Stage in the life cycle appears to be one important determinant. Men with young children at home (under age 15) seem to gain most from working the compacted schedule. They reported greater companionship with their children, along with less family pressure and tension. Though four-day workers still in the "honeymoon" stage were found to be no more satisfied with either their marriages or role performances than their five-day counterparts, they nonetheless reported receiving relatively more conjugal companionship rewards, having greater decision-making power, and experiencing less family pressure and tension. These occurred despite the fact that they took less part in the doing of daily household chores. Turning finally to those men whose children no longer live at home, the situation was reversed. The four-day workers in this life-cycle stage were found to receive fewer conjugal companionship and traditional family status rewards than their five-day counterparts. They also indicated having relatively less decision-making power, that their wives performed more of what are traditionally considered male tasks, and that they engaged in fewer social activities as a marriage pair. Not surprisingly, these four-day men reported somewhat greater family pressure and tension and expressed less satisfaction with both their conjugal role performance and their marriages than five-day men in the same life-cycle stage. Exacerbation or acceleration of the general pattern toward marital disenchantment with increasing age could possibly be responsible for these negative findings. Among younger four-day workers, the chance to spend more time at home with one's wife and children appears to be an important contributor to their better marital adjustment and, thus, to their greater satisfaction with their work schedule.

The wife's attitude toward the four-day schedule and her own employment status are two additional family context variables that influence marital adjustment and worker response to the compacted workweek. Surprisingly, four-day workers with nonworking wives were found to be less satisfied with their conjugal role performance than five-day workers whose wives are not employed. Part of the reason may lie, surprisingly, in the positive association between the amount a man helps his wife around the house and the traditional status rewards he receives from her. Four-day men with nonworking wives were found to help out at home less than five-day men and, presumably, went unrewarded. Paradoxically, though, four-day men with employed wives reported greater marital and conjugal role-performance satisfaction than comparable five-day men, even though they also helped their wives less with housekeeping chores. The data suggest the possibility that, concomitant with helping their wives at home, five-day men perceive a threat to their traditional status in the family. Four-day men seem to have an advantage—because of their longer workday, they typically leave home earlier and return home later than their working wives, giving them an excuse, which their wives apparently accept, for helping out less at home. On their days off, when opportunities to do household chores cannot be ignored, four-day men spend relatively more time performing major, typically masculine jobs and repairs. The nature of their help at home, therefore, minimizes any feeling of threat to their position in the family or to their self-image.

The wife's attitude comes into play in a variety of ways. Two effects, however, seem most important. First, by withholding or dispensing gratifications, she has great control over her husband's marital adjustment. The data indicate that the level of gratification the husband receives depends on his ability to perform his family roles in a satisfactory fashion. This includes his willingness or ability to meet any additional task or companionship demands his wife may make as a result of the extended weekend. The second mode of influence is simply that the wife is the most important other person in the worker's life. Her attitudes and dispositions, therefore, cannot help but be reflected in his own orientation toward the four-day schedule. Whether she makes her feelings known through control over gratifications or simply through her expression of these feelings, she exercises considerable influence.

Extensive time and effort were given to analyzing the dynamics of adjustment to the four-day workweek in the family context. Though the undertaking was only partially successful, several significant findings resulted. The following are the most insightful. First, the four-day workers' receipt of conjugal companionship gratifications appears to be more a function of their ability to fulfill family roles than of the strength of their desire for these gratifications. Obtaining parental companionship gratification was found to be equally problematic for four- and five-day workers. This is thought to be due mainly to the children's own five-day academic schedule and to their nonconcern for when their fathers have time to spend with them. The data do show, however, that four-day workers appear to reap some benefit from their schedule here as well. These men were better able to obtain whatever parental companionship gratification they could without losing opportunities for conjugal companionship. This fact undoubtedly helps explain why the vast majority of these men felt that their wives liked the four-day schedule.

Adjustment to the four-day workweek in the family setting was hypothesized to be a function of the worker's marital motivations, gratifications, and family pressures or stress. The original hypotheses, with some revision, were generally supported. With increased opportunities for effective performance of their family functions and, therefore, for receipt of conjugal companionship rewards, four-day workers motivated toward a companionate husband-wife relationship were better able than their five-day counterparts to cope with the demands (pressure) directed at them by other members of the family. Receipt of such gratifications, and the associated reduction in family pressure, was found, in turn, to be possibly causally related to workers' satisfaction with conjugal role performance and with marriage. Concomitantly, those four-day workers who were little motivated toward conjugal companionship, or who failed to receive these gratifications, experienced greater pressure and showed symptoms of worse adjustment in the family context than comparable men working a standard schedule. Greater family pressure and poorer marital adjustment also associated with those four-day workers occupying a strong traditional status position in the home. Exactly why is not clear, but it can be speculated that too great a status discrepancy between spouses hinders communication and problem solving. Possibly, these men adapt less well to being home for relatively long periods of time. Quite likely they also adapt less well to their wives' heightened demands for a more companionate relationship and for a measure of relief from their housekeeping routines.

In sum, the ramifications within the context of the family of working a four-day week are multiple and complex. A cursory assessment could result in dismissal of its effects, either as minor inconveniences or as important for only a small minority. Both of these conclusions would be unwise. The results of this study clearly indicate that adjustment in the family setting is a potential major determinant of the nature of the worker's response toward, and the ultimate acceptability of, this nonconventional arrangement of work time. It is therefore necessary to gain further insight into who adjusts well, who poorly, and the reasons for these different outcomes. Only once such knowledge is obtained can the four-day workweek's impact on the individual be understood, its long-run viability accurately assessed, conversion to it undertaken, determination made of when and where it may provide the greatest benefit, and, perhaps most importantly, steps taken to minimize attendant adjustment difficulties that may occur in some families subsequent to its adoption.

Use of and Satisfaction with Free Time

At best, only modest support for the benefits advanced by advocates of the four-day workweek was found in the time-budget data. The index measuring satisfaction derived from the activities engaged in during discretionary time offers somewhat greater support. Most encouraging, the four-day workers expressed significantly more satisfaction with how they use their free time than did the men in the control group. Little affirmative evidence, however, was found for the expectation held by many that, if given increased or more functionally arranged discretionary time, workers would demonstrate a greater willingness to participate in educational programs and to involve themselves in civic-minded, public service organizations. Instead, the four-day workers tended to expand their participation in already familiar activities, particularly those that occur in the family setting. Gardening, major household care tasks, and interacting with one's children were the activities that showed the largest gains in allocated time. Participation in such outdoor recreations as hunting and fishing constituted the one area of leisure behavior outside the home that evidenced a marked increase in the number of adherents.

The pessimistic predictions made by more than a few social critics—that larger blocks of discretionary time for blue-collar workers would result in an increase in time allocated to overtime or spent stupefied before the television set—are not borne out by the data. Neither, however, are they strongly rejected. As already discussed, the four-day workers sampled did not put in significantly more overtime in the month preceding their interview than did the men in the five-day control group. Indeed, if one were to base a conclusion solely on the results of the time-budget diary, one could possibly conclude (weakly) that a four-day schedule associates with working relatively less overtime. As for television watching, four-day workers did not spend more time before the television set over the entire week. This last finding is due, however, largely to the length of their official workday. During periods when their discretionary time was greatest (that is, on the three-day weekend), these men did watch more television. On the other hand, four-day workers also tended to spend somewhat more time reading, but the difference between work groups here is hardly overwhelming.

In conclusion, four-day workers used their "improved" discretionary time in ways predicted by Shostak (1969, p. 207)—to resonate existing blue-collar life-styles and culture:

> The impact of specific leisure choices appears restricted to the power to intensify patterns of behavior that are already established. Leisure choices do not seem to have the power to change behavior. Blue-collar attitudes and ideas may be modified, but conversion is unlikely.

Though the four-day schedule enhances the workers' opportunities for involvement in novel, challenging, and creative behavior patterns, these men are unlikely to take anything close to full advantage of them without encouragement from the wider community. Participation in activities of this sort requires the utilization of skills, information, and a repertoire of problem-solving experiences generally lacking among blue-collar men. This deficiency does not reflect a basic character weakness on their part, as the old-style work ethic would have one believe. Rather it is one unfortunate consequence of a society that sanctions jobs that stifle initiative, operates public service organizations geared toward the involvement of the professional and the semiprofessional volunteer, creates cultural and educational institutions designed primarily for satisfying the tastes of the highly educated elite, and condones the financial exploitation of recreational activities. Before blue-collar workers can realistically be expected to experiment with new modes of behavior, society must first decide whether it truly desires them to do so—and then act on that decision.

SUGGESTIONS FOR FURTHER RESEARCH

While a cross-sectional research format can provide much useful insight, a longitudinal approach would supply more extensive and reliable information concerning the dynamics of adjustment to this nonconventional schedule. Workers should be queried at least once prior to their conversion to the four-day workweek, and changes in their perceptions, behavior, and attitudes should be mapped, preferably over a minimum of three years. This time span would allow for a period of passive, as well as active, adjustment, thereby enabling the researcher to determine the long-run stability of attempted solutions to adjustment problems. The data would also permit examination of adjustment through its various phases, facilitate determination of who benefits, who suffers and why, and, finally, provide a good baseline for assessing the total impact of working this schedule. Inclusion of a time-budget survey in a subset of the interview applications is strongly recommended.

The causes of four-day workers' greater job dissatisfaction requires investigation. Omitted from this study, but believed to be of significance, are such factors as the social relationships among workers, the quality of the job supervision, and intrinsic characteristics of the job, especially the opportunities it provides for self-development, self-utilization, and self-expression. This would call for the describing of each job type in some detail and obtaining the worker's reactions to each of these factors.

Subsequent examination of adjustment in the family setting should gather data from the wife as well as the husband. It should include information concerning their mutual expectations and perceptions and their actual patterns of interaction. The motivation, gratification, and pressure indexes developed for this study may provide a starting point.

Of all the areas requiring further investigations, perhaps the most compelling one concerns the influence of job type, specifically, and work, more generally, on adjustment in the family setting and on the use of discretionary time. Before it can be determined whether the four-day or otherwise altered work schedule can fulfill the expectations of its advocates, information of this nature must be available. In the same vein, workers' responses to nonconventional schedules must be assessed against the backdrop of conditions in the wider community. For example, what recreation facilities are provided? Are leisure and family counseling services readily available? Do cultural and educational institutions attempt to meet the interests of all sections of the community, including those of blue-collar workers? Finally, what is the quality of the outreach programs for all of the above, and how much does the worker know about them?

GENERAL CONCLUSIONS AND RECOMMENDATIONS

The work-leisure debate confronts not only the issue of individual behavior and psychological well-being, but also the more ambiguous, thorny issue of the future shape of society. The increasingly leisure-oriented character of modern industrial states could usher in a golden age of individual growth and societal well-being. It could also generate individual frustration, alienation, and anomie resulting in increased social distress and decay. Both paths are open.

When the central issue of general life satisfaction is seen as a function not of the choice between work and leisure but as the consequence of the quality of their synthesis, it becomes clear that work per se does not constitute the basis of the Protestant Ethic. Rather, the basis of that ethic is the sense of being needed and attaining self-dignity. Viewed from this perspective, the challenge before society becomes one of fostering those conditions and sociocultural climates that enable people to feel needed and to obtain dignity in work and in leisure. It is our responsibility, in this unstable age of the artificial, to create our future as best we can.

Leisure behavior is not a random phenomenon, determined by individual wish or whim, but a set of activities bounded by existing social norms. "Individual leisure is highly ordered by a society as a whole. This is true as to the amount of leisure, its timing, and the activities in it" (Clawson 1964, p. 16). The extent of choice is, therefore, limited; it is constantly being massaged by the ubiquitous demands and normative expectations of a work-dominated social structure. Equally pertinent to this discussion, the range of leisure behavior is greatly restricted by public and private decisions about the allocation of resources (and, by implication, values) to alternate packages of work-leisure goods, services, and activities.

The determinants of leisure behavior are many, complex, and, for the most part, beyond the scope of this discussion. There is one notable exception: the role of policy makers, whether they be located in the public or private sector of the economy. Due to the nature of the offices they occupy and their ultimate control over the resource allocation processes of the society, policy makers are in a position to influence which leisure patterns will emerge and which will prevail. What follows is a brief discussion of several mechanisms whereby policy makers manifest their influence, and the presentation of several suggestions as to how the work-leisure challenge may be met.

Through their support or opposition to alternate arrangements of work and nonwork time, persons occupying decision-making positions in labor and management can influence the way time is used and how both work and leisure are perceived. When undertaken in an environment conducive to behavioral innovation and experimentation, adoption of nonconventional schedules has the potential to significantly influence the individual's chances for creating a viable, more satisfying synthesis between work and leisure. Different people, however, are located in different environments, have different life-style aspirations, and vary in their capacity to adjust to major changes in daily routine. One implication is that if the welfare of the worker is truly a principal motivating force behind the decision to switch to a four-day schedule, consideration ought to be given to offering it only to individuals who desire it, and subsequently, to permit those who wish to return to the standard schedule to do so. A second possibility is the adoption of a "flexi-time" schedule, perhaps in conjunction with the four-day workweek. This would enable workers better to tailor their hours of labor to their particular nonwork interests and responsibilities. Either of these arrangements would constitute an improvement for employees, though both would no doubt complicate the employer's production scheduling.

By itself, reorganizing the hours devoted to the job has limited potential for fostering a greater synthesis between work and leisure. Because what transpires in each of these life spheres is interrelated, so long as work activities are designed in a fashion that blocks initiative and stifles learning, innovative behavior and personal growth through engagement in novel endeavors outside the work place are unlikely to occur with any degree of regularity. To be sure, radical changes in the design of jobs and in the organization of the work process entail great expense and are long-term prospects. Nevertheless, such changes must eventuate before the worker can hope to find

the job satisfaction he desires and before he can experience many of
the nonwork benefits sought through flexibility in work time. In short,
adoption of nonconventional work schedules should not be viewed as an
end in itself, but as part of a larger effort directed toward enhance-
ment of the general conditions and opportunities in both work and leisure time presently characterizing workers' lives.

This encompassing approach is all the more important when it
is realized that the fastest-growing occupations are those in the tertiary sector of the economy—which includes such support personnel
as secretaries, clerks, truck drivers, and bookkeepers (Levitan and
Johnston 1973). While this implies that the jobs needing redesign are
becoming less important as a fraction of the labor force, it also
means that people will continue to work at jobs requiring little ability
for coping with rapidly evolving technologies and constantly changing
environments. Workers will continue to lack the skills necessary for
making the most of their leisure. To ameliorate this situation, three
courses of action are suggested:

1. Whenever possible, the work place and the job technology
should be redesigned in order to invest work with greater meaning,
responsibility, and complexity. This would directly result in heightened job satisfaction and indirectly enhance the quality of leisure.

2. Where work place redesign is not practical, improved extrinsic work-setting (financial, hygienic, job-security) rewards
should be offered in compensation. If the job cannot be made intrinsically rewarding, conditions should at least be made as pleasant as
possible.

3. Creative and challenging leisure patterns should be encouraged so as both to compensate for unsatisfying jobs and to serve as a
stimulus for individual experimentation with unfamiliar leisure pursuits. Included here are such things as the development of cultural
and recreational facilities and institutions designed to meet the needs
and interests of all sections of society and the operation of effective
outreach programs for attracting participants into leisure activities,
orthodox and otherwise.

The prospect for the first two suggestions lies largely in the
hands of management and organized labor. Undoubtedly, the many
issues and problems entailed in the adoption or rejection of these
will form the basis of much of the labor-management debate during
the coming years. Adoption of the third suggestion, however, depends
on the actions of policy makers more widely. How may leisure patterns be influenced by policy makers, and how may creative and challenging patterns be fostered by their actions? A few general recommendations can be offered.

The underlying motives that activate the individual's leisure-gratification search behavior (for example, need for safety, need for achievement, need for affiliation) are relatively fixed through time. The specific needs that arise, however, are "second order" or learned. Thus, the individual's desire to engage in such activities as hunting or taking his family to the movies is quite flexible and subject to fairly rapid change—given appropriate inducements. Among all people, those in policy-making positions are unique in their capacity to provide the appropriate inducements. In part, this is because they are the focus of a plethora of competing demands for goods and services, not all of which can be met out of existing resources. By supporting one set of demands over another, policy makers can do much to eliminate certain activities from the list of those open to the individual. One would not, for example, go fishing in an ecologically dead lake. More commonly, policy makers affect the way free time is used by the actions they take that serve to lower or raise the relative total price of a commodity. An excise tax on movies, for instance, would lower the cinema's popular appeal, particularly relative to that of television. Multiply this case by the thousands like it and the importance of price decisions upon the nature and extent of leisure-time use becomes quite clear.

But the impact of policy makers extends beyond control over supply and prices. By their decisions to foreclose certain leisure options or to make others more expensive, policy makers not only increase the relative feasibility of yet other options but may even popularize them. By calling public attention to the goods and services they supply, they encourage participation in those activities most likely to require their utilization. The potential for public and private policy makers to influence the behavior of other persons is, consequently, quite strong (albeit indirect) and wide in scope. (The proliferation of recreational vehicles during the past few years—stimulated by the publicity given to the construction of additional specially designed camping facilities—is an example of the effectiveness of this influence process. Despite the large expense inherent in this mode of recreational behavior for all but the most persistent of travelers, its popularity has grown exponentially.) Because of this potential, it is the responsibility of policy makers to make their decisions with as much, or more, attention to the public good than to private interests. An unwillingness on their part to participate constructively in the process of creating new, more satisfying life-styles would severely diminish the society's capacity for effectively confronting leisure's challenge.

One way in which policy makers may serve the interests of the wider community is by not interfering with how people in tertiary occupations, or on the fringe of society, elaborate their leisure. These workers develop leisure patterns quite different from those of workers in the broad band of manufacturing and extractive industries. They tend to set the pace and develop the commodities for everybody's leisure, though their activities may not always be beneficial to workers in other types of occupations. How can we justify interfering with or exploiting their efforts any more than we do with other social inventions whose consequences may be at once liberating and discomforting? "Rather," as Denney and Riesman suggest, "it makes sense to establish as many centers of innovation as possible, drawing on as many styles and traditions in leisure as possible, so that people in a fluid society may find their way to styles that fit them" (1964, p. 407). Pricing policy and publicity decisions can go a fair distance toward determining the variety and viability of such centers, the scope of their innovations, and, eventually, the distribution of those innovations that prove successful to a waiting population.

Public officials can influence the nature of society's leisure in another, more binding (though not necessarily deliberate) way—through legislative legitimization of social structures and norms. Legislation may be written with the explicit aim, or have the result, of encouraging the further emergence of alternative, fledgling behavior and value systems. It may also provide additional support for those norms and structures already dominant. The history of the standard five-day, 40-hour workweek is a case in point. Though the eight-hour day was not uncommon by the mid-1930s, its position of dominance was held in abeyance until it received strong official support with the passage of the Walsh-Healey Public Contract Act in 1936 and the Supreme Court's approval in 1938 of the Fair Labor Standards Act. The result was a reduction of almost one hour in the length of the average workweek between 1936 and 1940 (Owen 1970). Subsequent legislation reinforced this schedule's status as the dominant mode.

In combination, these statutes markedly improved the working conditions and take-home pay of many employees. But time passes. Conditions and expectations change. In an era characterized by a growing demand for alternate arrangements of work hours, a rigid five-day, 40-hour schedule—locked in by law—may be more of a liability than a benefit. It now constitutes a serious obstacle to the emergence of alternative work-leisure schedules that might be better suited to contemporary and emerging life-styles. For example, the requirement of premium pay for all work in excess of eight hours a day greatly limits the number of firms able to adopt a compacted work schedule such as the 10-hour day, four-day week. Selective legislative change here, accompanied by the development of mechanisms to control the resulting potential for abuse, could significantly affect the arrangement and extent of free time in this country. In so doing, it would influence the uses to which this time is put and the values Americans hold with respect to work and leisure. At the very least, such a step would recognize and legitimize the current drive for meaningful choice among alternate work-leisure schedules.

Public officials can further the synthesis between work and leisure in a variety of other ways. Government could, for example, take the lead in supporting relevant research. There is ample precedent for this as part of its role as the party responsible for the development of general policy to meet newly emerging problems embracing the welfare of more than a single faction of the population. Research institutes that concentrate on work-leisure issues could be established and publicly supported, as they are in almost every country of Europe. As presently mandated, these centers feed data to government and private sectors on such matters as tourism, mass media, and adult education. They also provide broad interpretations of what industrialization, more free time, rising affluence, emerging life-styles, television, and higher levels of education mean to the future of their societies.

The government's role and influence could also be expanded in the realms of recreation and, especially, in the area of education for leisure. There is a growing awareness that industrial man's interests "need awakening, refinement, expansion, and direction [which] points up the necessity for an educational program. . . . Men need training and opportunities to exercise their powers before they are able to have abilities for making profitable use of leisure time" (Weiss 1964, p. 25). Present educational practices, however, inadequately address this objective. The unfortunate consequences of this oversight can now be seen all too clearly in workers' adjustment to retirement. On this problem Maddox writes (1970, p. 18):

> We are increasingly aware that if we wait until a person is in retirement to inquire about how that experience can be made a satisfying one, we have probably waited too long. We will be fighting the wrong battle at the wrong time in most cases. More and more we are realizing that, if the battle for adequate adaptation in retirement is to be fought successfully, it must be fought in the younger years. If we are asking people to be creative in their adaptation to changes in life, we have to provide them not only with skills, both personal and social, to make these adaptations, but we must also give them adequate experience in making these adaptations. . . . What people learn about the use of leisure time during their school years would be a case in point.

Thus, if people are to derive pleasure from and be creative in their use of time during their later years, they must find pleasure and develop creativity in their use of discretionary time during their youth and earlier adulthood. For this, they need training and experience with leisure in their school years, and the skills learned during this time should be refreshed and further developed throughout their lives. The task of aiding the individual in these efforts rightfully falls to the education system. Society, therefore, needs to establish continuing education programs designed to meet the changing needs and aspirations of a shifting population and of all the social categories within it.

The final recommendation is one advanced by Herbert Striner (1972). Viewing education as a national capital investment, he urges the establishment of a "National Economic Security Fund," somewhat like the system in West Germany. This fund could be integrated with existing unemployment insurance funds and be supported by modest, though compulsory, individual contributions. It would be used to enable 1 percent of the labor force to engage in a "self-renewal program" at any given point in time for periods of up to two years. The purpose of such a program would be to reduce the prevalence "of people who remain frozen in their value system or ways of seeing things [for such people] become a retarding force in that society" (Striner 1972, p. vii). These programs must, therefore, be geared to both vocational and humanism-oriented learning and be directed toward all levels and classes in the population.

As an advanced industrial society orders its leisure, so does it increasingly order itself. The shape of our society today is the outgrowth of past decisions based on increasingly antiquated values about work and a long-held belief in the necessity of maintaining the present work system—capital gains taxes, investment credits, depletion allowances, highway construction, a narrow definition of productivity, and so on. Now that we are becoming increasingly leisure-oriented, it is incumbent upon us to realize that past and present decisions (and nondecisions) with respect to leisure also influence the shape of our society. To the extent that policy and decision makers have it within their power to determine the quality of our leisure, they have it within their power to influence the strength and vitality of our culture. The decisions they make and the actions they undertake today concerning the arrangements of work (and simultaneously, nonwork)—which are to be considered standard, and which leisure activities deserve financial and planning support—will go a long way toward determining the character of tomorrow's society.

It is no longer a matter for debate whether this societal ordering process will occur, only whether it shall be done consciously, coherently, and with forethought. This is assuredly not the mode at present. Though many leisure demands are being satisfied, others are being ignored. This oversight is not always because these demands are unimportant or because meeting them would entail negative consequences elsewhere. The social structure simply has little incentive to consider them. Not even the basic issues of how much leisure is advisable or how this time should be ordered have been seriously confronted. People are experimenting with nonconventional work schedules such as the four-day workweek on an ad hoc basis. Minimal information is supplied to the individuals involved, and little is shared among firms, between industry and government, and between the academic and non-academic communities. This is not to say that planning and rational decision making will always, or even usually, succeed. However, forethought and planning may at least enable us to avoid a few of the more obvious pitfalls to be encountered in alternate arrangements of work and leisure time.

BIBLIOGRAPHY

Ackerman, Nathan W. The Psychodynamics of Family Life. New York: Basic Books, 1958.

AFL-CIO. The Shorter Work Week. Washington, D.C.: Public Affairs Press, 1957.

Aller, Florence A. "Role of the Self-Concept in Student Marital Adjustment." Family Life Coordinator 11 (April 1962): 43-45.

American Psychiatric Association. Leisure and Mental Health: A Psychiatric Viewpoint. Washington, D.C.: Committee on Leisure Time and Its Uses, American Psychiatric Association, 1967.

Andrews, Frank; Morgan, James; and Sonquist, John. Multiple Classification Analysis: A Report on a Computer Program for Multiple Regression Using Categorical Predictors. Ann Arbor: Survey Research Center, Institute for Social Research, 1967.

Arendt, Hannah. The Human Condition. Chicago: University of Chicago Press, 1958.

Argyris, Chris. Personality and Organization. New York: Harper and Brothers, 1957.

Avineri, Schlomo. The Social and Political Thought of Karl Marx. London: Cambridge University Press, 1968.

Axelson, Leland J. "The Marital Adjustment and Marital Role Definition of Husbands of Working and Nonworking Wives." Journal of Marriage and the Family 25 (May 1963): 189-95.

Bachman, Jerald G.; Kahn, Robert L.; Mednick, Martha T.; Davidson, Terrence N.; and Johnston, Lloyd D. Youth in Transition, vol. 1. Ann Arbor: Survey Research Center, Institute for Social Research, 1972.

Bacon, William A. "Leisure and the Alienated Worker: A Critical Assessment of Three Radical Theories of Work and Leisure." Journal of Leisure Research 7 (1975): 179-90.

Bauer, Raymond A. "Detection and Anticipation of Impact: The Nature of the Task." In Social Indicators, edited by Raymond A. Bauer, pp. 1-67. Cambridge, Mass.: MIT Press, 1960.

Bell, Daniel. "The Cultural Contradiction of Capitalism." Public Interest (Fall 1970): 16-43.

——. "Labor in the Post-Industrial Society." Dissent (Winter 1972): 163-89.

——. The Coming of Post-Industrial Society: A Venture in Social Forecasting. New York:. Basic Books, 1973.

Bellamy, Edward. Looking Backward: 2000-1887. Introduction by Paul Bellamy. Cleveland: World Publishing Co., 1945.

Bennis, Warren G.; Benne, Kenneth D.; and Chin, Robert. The Planning of Change. 2d ed. New York: Holt, Rinehart and Winston, 1968.

Benson, Purnell. "The Interests of Happily Married Couples." Journal of Marriage and the Family 14 (November 1952): 276-80.

Bernard, Jesse. The Future of Marriage. New York: World Publishers, 1972.

Biddle, Bruce J. The Present Status of Role Theory. Columbia, Mo.: Social Psychology Laboratory, University of Missouri, 1961.

Blalock, Hubert M., Jr. Social Statistics. New York: McGraw-Hill, 1960.

Blauner, Robert. Alienation and Freedom: The Factory Worker and His Industry. Chicago: University of Chicago Press, 1964.

——. "Work Satisfaction and Industrial Trends in Modern Society." In Labor and Trade Unionism, edited by Walter Galenson and Seymour Lipset, pp. 339-60. New York: John Wiley and Sons, 1960.

Blood, Robert O., Jr. Family Life. New York: Free Press, 1972.

—— and Wolfe, Donald M. Husbands and Wives: The Dynamics of Married Living. New York: Free Press, 1960.

Bosserman, Phillip. "Implications for Youth." In Technology, Human Values and Leisure, edited by Max Kaplan and Phillip Bosserman, pp. 131-63. New York: Abingdon Press, 1971.

Bott, Elizabeth. Family and Social Network: Roles, Norms and External Relationships in Ordinary Urban Families. 2d ed. Preface by Max Gluckman. New York: Free Press, 1971.

Brightbill, Charles K. The Challenge of Leisure. Englewood Cliffs, N.J.: Prentice-Hall, 1960.

Brown, Harrison. "Technology and Where We Are." In Technology, Human Values and Leisure, edited by Max Kaplan and Phillip Bosserman, pp. 58-67. New York: Abingdon Press, 1971.

Burch, William R., Jr. "Images of Future Leisure: Continuities in Changing Expectations." In The Sociology of the Future: Theory, Cases and Annotated Bibliography, edited by Wendell Bell and James A. Mau, pp. 160-87. New York: Russell Sage Foundation, 1971.

Burgess, Ernest W., and Wallin, Paul. Engagement and Marriage. Chicago: J.B. Lippincott, 1953.

Burnham, James. The Managerial Revolution. New York: John Day, 1941.

Burr, Wesley R. "Satisfaction with Various Aspects of Marriage over the Life Cycle: A Random Middle Class Sample." Journal of Marriage and the Family 32 (February 1970): 29-37.

Caplan, Robert D.; Cobb, Sidney; French, John P., Jr.; Harrison, R. Van; and Pinneau, S.R., Jr. Job Demands and Worker Health: Main Effects and Occupational Differences, NIOSH Research Report. Washington, D.C.: Government Printing Office, 1975.

Charlesworth, James C., ed. Leisure in America: Blessing or Curse? Philadelphia: American Academy of Political and Social Sciences, Monograph no. 4, April 1964.

Chinoy, Ely. Automobile Workers and the American Dream. New York: Doubleday, 1955.

Clawson, Marion. "The Crisis in Outdoor Recreation." Resources for the Future, Reprint no. 13, from American Forests, March and April 1959.

———. "How Much Leisure, Now and in the Future?" In Leisure in America: Blessing or Curse? edited by James C. Charlesworth, pp. 1-20. Philadelphia: American Academy of Political and Social Sciences, Monograph no. 4, April 1964.

Clements, William H. "Marital Interaction and Marital Stability: A Point of View and a Descriptive Comparison of Stable and Unstable Marriages." Journal of Marriage and the Family 29 (November 1967): 697-702.

Conference Board in Canada. The Altered Work Week: A Symposium Held in November 1973. Ottawa, 1973.

Cronbach, Lee J., and Meehl, Paul E. "Construct Validity in Psychological Tests." Psychological Bulletin 52 (July 1955): 281-302.

Davis, Kingsley. Human Society. New York: Macmillan, 1949.

Dean, Dwight G. "Emotional Maturity and Marital Adjustment." Journal of Marriage and the Family 28 (November 1966): 454-57.

———. "Alienation and Marital Adjustment," Sociological Quarterly 9 (Spring 1968): 186-92.

de Grazia, Sebastian. Of Time, Work, and Leisure. Garden City, N.Y.: Anchor Books, 1964.

Denney, Reuel, and Riesman, David. "Leisure in Urbanized America." In Comparative Social Problems, edited by S. N. Eisenstadt, pp. 401-8. New York: Free Press, 1964.

De Rosis, L. E. "Leisure Time—Burden or Benefit?" New York: Auxiliary Council of the Association for the Advancement of Psychoanalysis, 1951.

Detroit Free Press, September 21, 1974. Sec. B, p. 1.

Driver, Beverly L., and Tocher, S. Ross. "Toward a Behavioral Interpretation of Recreational Engagements, with Implications for Planning." In Elements of Outdoor Recreation Planning, edited by Beverly L. Driver, pp. 9-31. Ann Arbor: University of Michigan Press, 1974.

Dubin, Robert. "Industrial Workers' Worlds: A Study of the 'Central Life Interests' of Industrial Workers." Social Problems 3 (January 1956): 131-42.

———. "Work and Non-work: Institutional Perspectives." In Work and Leisure in the Year 2001, edited by Marvin D. Dunnette. Belmont, Calif.: Wadsworth Publishing, 1972.

Dubos, René, and Pines, Mayan. Health and Disease. Life-Science Library. New York: New York Times, Inc., 1965.

Dumazedier, Joffre. Towards a Society of Leisure. Translated by Stewart E. McClure. Foreword by David Riesman. New York: Free Press, 1967.

———. "Leisure and Post-Industrial Societies." In Technology, Human Values and Leisure, edited by Max Kaplan and Phillip Bosserman, pp. 190-220. New York: Abingdon Press, 1971.

Durkheim, Emile. The Division of Labor in Society. Translated by George Simpson. New York: Free Press, 1964.

Ellul, Jacques. The Technological Society. New York: Vintage Books, 1964.

Federal Register. March 15, 1972. Washington, D.C.: U.S. Government Printing Office.

Fourastié, Jean. Les 40.000 Heurs. Paris: Edition Gouthier, 1965.

French, John R. P., Jr.; Rodgers, Willard; and Cobb, Sidney. "Adjustment as Person-Environment Fit." In Coping and Adaptation, edited by George V. Coelho, David A. Hamburg, and John E. Adams, pp. 316-33. New York: Basic Books, 1974.

Fried, Marc. The World of the Urban Working Class. Cambridge, Mass.: Harvard University Press, 1973.

Friedman, Eugene A. "The Work of Leisure." In Free Time: Challenge to Later Maturity, edited by Wilma Donahue, Woodrow W. Hunter, Dorothy H. Coons, and Helen K. Maurice, pp. 119-31. Ann Arbor: University of Michigan Press, 1958.

Friedman, Georges. The Anatomy of Work: Labor, Leisure and the Implications of Automation. Translated by Wyatt Rawson. New York: Free Press, 1964.

Fromm, Erich. The Sane Society. New York: Rinehart and Co., 1955.

———. Escape from Freedom. New York: Avon Books, 1965.

Furstenberg, Frank F., Jr. "Work Experience and Family Life." In Work and the Quality of Life: Resource Papers for "Work in America", edited by James O'Toole, pp. 341-60. Foreword by Elliott L. Richardson. Afterword by Edward M. Kennedy. Cambridge, Mass.: MIT Press, 1974.

Gabor, Denis. Inventing the Future. New York: Alfred A. Knopf, 1964.

Galbraith, John K. The New Industrial State. Toronto: Signet Books, 1968.

Gerson, Walter M. "Leisure and Marital Satisfaction of College Married Couples." Journal of Marriage and Family Living 22 (November 1960): 360-61.

Giordano, Joseph. Ethnicity and Mental Health. New York: National Project on Ethnic America of the American Jewish Committee, 1973.

Glickman, Albert S., and Brown, Zenia H. Changing Schedules of Work: Patterns and Implications. Kalamazoo, Mich.: W. E. Upjohn Institute for Employment Research, 1974.

Goode, William J. The Family. Englewood Cliffs, N.J.: Prentice-Hall, 1964.

Greenberg, Clements. "Work and Leisure Under Industrialism." In Mass Leisure, edited by Eric Larrabee and Rolf Meyersohn, pp. 38-43. Glencoe, Ill.: Free Press, 1958.

Greenson, Ralph R. "On Boredom." American Psychoanalytic Association Journal 1 (1953): 7-21.

Grinstein, Alexander. "Vacations: A Psychoanalytic Study." International Journal of Psychoanalysis 36 (1955): 177-86.

Gurin, Gerald; Veroff, Joseph L.; and Feld, Sheila. Americans View Their Mental Health. New York: Basic Books, 1960.

Hackman, Ray C. The Motivated Working Adult. New York: American Management Association, 1969.

Hawkins, James L. "Association Between Companionship, Hostility and Marital Satisfaction." Journal of Marriage and the Family 30 (November 1968): 647-50.

Hays, William L. Statistics for the Social Sciences. 2d ed. New York: Holt, Rinehart and Winston, 1973.

Hedges, Janice N. "New Patterns for Working Time." Monthly Labor Review 96 (1973): 3-8.

————. "How Many Days Make a Workweek?" Monthly Labor Review 98 (1975): 29-36.

Heron, Woodburn. "The Pathology of Boredom." Scientific American 196 (1957): 52-56.

Herzberg, Frederick. Work and the Nature of Man. Cleveland: World Publishing, 1966.

Hess, Robert D., and Handel, Gerald. "The Family as a Psychosocial Organization." In The Psychosocial Interior of the Family, edited by Gerald Handel, 2d ed., pp. 10-24. Chicago: Aldine-Atherton, 1972.

Hicks, Mary W., and Platt, Marilyn. "Marital Happiness and Stability: A Review of the Research in the Sixties." Journal of Marriage and the Family 32 (November 1970): 553-74.

Hill, Reuben. Families Under Stress. New York: Harper and Brothers, 1949.

Hoffer, Eric. The Passionate State of Mind. New York: Harper and Row, 1955.

House, James S. "The Relationship of Intrinsic and Extrinsic Work Motivations to Occupational Stress and Coronary Heart Disease Risk." Ph.D. dissertation, University of Michigan, 1972. University Microfilms no. 72-29094.

Howard, Alan, and Scott, Robert. "A Proposed Framework for Analysis of Stress in the Human Organism." Behavioral Science 10 (April 1965): 141-60.

Hurley, John R., and Palonen, Donna P. "Marital Satisfaction and Child Density Among University Student Parents." Journal of Marriage and the Family 29 (August 1967): 483-85.

Kahn, Robert L. "The Meaning of Work: Interpretation and Proposals for Measurement." In The Human Meaning of Social Change, edited by Angus Campbell and Philip E. Converse, pp. 159-203. New York: Russell Sage Foundation, 1972.

—— and Wolfe, Donald M.; Quinn, Robert P.; Smoek, J. Diedrick; and Rosenthal, Robert A. Organizational Stress: Studies in Role Conflict and Ambiguity. New York: John Wiley and Sons, 1964.

Kaplan, Max. Leisure in America: A Social Inquiry. New York: John Wiley and Sons, 1960.

——. "The Relevancy of Leisure." In Technology, Human Values and Leisure, edited by Max Kaplan and Phillip Bosserman, pp. 19-26. New York: Abingdon Press, 1971.

Kasl, Stanislav V. "Work and Mental Health." In Work and the Quality of Life: Resource Papers for "Work in America", edited by James O'Toole, pp. 171-96. Foreword by Elliott L. Richardson. Afterword by Edward M. Kennedy. Cambridge, Mass.: MIT Press, 1974.

Katz, Daniel, and Kahn, Robert L. The Social Psychology of Organizations. New York: John Wiley and Sons, 1966.

Katz, Irwin; Goldston, Judith; Cohen, Melvin; and Stucker, Solomon. "Need Satisfaction, Perception, and Cooperative Interactions in Married Couples." Journal of Marriage and the Family 25 (May 1963): 209-13.

Kelly, John. "Socialization Towards Leisure: A Developmental Approach." Journal of Leisure Research 6 (1974): 181-93.

Kennedy, Edward M. "After Work." In Work and the Quality of Life: Resource Papers for "Work in America", edited by James O'Toole, pp. 395-99. Foreword by Elliot L. Richardson. Afterword by Edward M. Kennedy. Cambridge, Mass.: MIT Press, 1974.

Kerlinger, Fred N., and Pedhazur, Elazar J. Multiple Regression in Behavioral Research. New York: Holt, Rinehart and Winston, 1973.

Kirkpatrick, Clifford. "Measuring Marital Adjustment." In Selected Studies in Marriage and the Family, edited by Robert F. Winch, Robert McGinnis, and Herbert R. Barringer, pp. 544-52. New York: Holt, Rinehart and Winston, 1962.

Kornhauser, Arthur W. Mental Health and the Industrial Worker: A Detroit Study. With the collaboration of Otto M. Reid. New York: John Wiley and Sons, 1965.

Krebs, Juanita M. Lifetime Allocation of Work and Leisure. Research Report no. 22. Washington, D.C.: U.S. Department of Health, Education and Welfare, Social Security Administration, Office of Research Statistics, 1968.

Land, Kenneth C. "Principles of Path Analysis." In Sociological Methodology 1969, edited by E. Borgatta, pp. 3–37. San Francisco: Jossey-Bass, 1969.

La Velle, Mike. "Four-Day Week Gaining, Despite Drawbacks." Detroit Free Press, 18 June 1973, Sec. A, p. 11.

Levitan, Sar A., and Belous, Richard S. "Thank God It's Thursday: Can Shorter Workweeks Reduce Unemployment?" Across the Board (March 1977): 28–31.

Levitan, Sar A., and Johnston, William B. "Job Redesign, Reform, Enrichment—Exploring the Limitations." Monthly Labor Review 96 (1973): 35–42.

Linden, Maurice E. "Preparation for the Leisure of Later Maturity." In Free Time: Challenge to Later Maturity, edited by Wilma Donahue, Woodrow W. Hunter, Dorothy Coons, and Helen K. Maurice, pp. 77–97. Ann Arbor: University of Michigan Press, 1958.

Lubin, Joann S. "The 4-Day Week: Employee Lives Change as More Firms Adopt New Work Schedules." Wall Street Journal, 16 February 1977, Sec. A, p. 1.

Luckey, Eleanore B. "Marital Satisfaction and Its Association with Congruence of Perception." Marriage and Family Living 22 (February 1960): 49–54.

—— and Bain, Joyce K. "Children: A Factor in Marital Satisfaction." Journal of Marriage and the Family 32 (February 1970): 43–44.

Maddox, George L. "Adaptation to Retirement." Gerontologist, Spring 1970, Part II, 14–18.

Maklan, David M. "The Four-Day Workweek: Blue Collar Adjustment to a Nonconventional Arrangement of Work and Leisure Time." Ph.d. Dissertation, University of Michigan, 1976.

Marcuse, Herbert. One-Dimensional Man: Studies in the Ideology of Advanced Industrial Society. Boston: Beacon Press, 1964.

Martin, Alexander R. "The Fear of Relaxation and Leisure." American Journal of Psychoanalysis 11 (1951): 42-50.

———. "Man's Leisure and His Health." Bulletin of the New York Academy of Medicine 40 (1964): 21-42.

Martin, Peter A. Introduction to Leisure and Mental Health: A Psychiatric Viewpoint, pp. 3-9. Washington, D.C.: Committee on Leisure Time and Its Uses, American Psychiatric Association, 1967a.

———. "The Psychiatrist's Role in Free Time and Its Uses." In Leisure and Mental Health: A Psychiatric Viewpoint, pp. 71-82. Washington, D.C.: Committee on Leisure Time and Its Uses, American Psychiatric Association, 1967b.

Marx, Karl. Capital: A Critical Analysis of Capitalist Production. Translated by Samuel Moore and Edward Aveling. Edited by Frederick Engels. London: William Glaisher, Ltd., 1920.

———. "Alienated Labour." In Industrial Man: Selected Readings, edited by Tom Burns, pp. 95-109. Baltimore: Penguin Books, 1969.

Mead, Margaret. "The Pattern of Leisure in Contemporary American Culture." Annals of the American Academy of Political and Social Science 313 (September 1957): 11-15.

———. "The Changing Cultural Patterns of Work and Leisure." Paper Presented at a Seminar on Manpower Policy and Programs, U.S. Department of Labor, January 1967.

Meany, George. "Labor's Basic Position." In The Shorter Work Week, pp. 1-6. Washington, D.C.: AFL-CIO, Public Affairs Press, 1957.

Mesthene, Emmanuel G. "Technology and Human Values." In Technology, Human Values and Leisure, edited by Max Kaplan and Phillip Bosserman, pp. 42-57. New York: Abingdon Press, 1971.

Meyerowitz, Joseph H. "Satisfaction During Pregnancy." Journal of Marriage and the Family 32 (January 1970): 38-42.

Meyersohn, Rolf. "Changing Work and Leisure Routines." In Work and Leisure: A Contemporary Social Problem, edited by Edwin O. Smigel, pp. 97-106. New Haven: College and University Press, 1963.

——. "Leisure." In The Human Meaning of Social Change, edited by Angus Campbell and Philip E. Converse, pp. 205-28. New York: Russell Sage Foundation, 1972.

Mills, D. Quinn. "Does Organized Labor Want the 4-Day Week?" In 4 Days, 40 Hours: Reporting a Revolution in Work and Leisure, edited by Riva Poor, pp. 61-69. Foreword by Paul A. Samuelson. Cambridge, Mass.: Bursk and Poor Publishing, 1970.

Moore, Geoffrey H., and Hedges, Janice N. "Trends in Labor and Leisure." Monthly Labor Review 94 (February 1971): 3-11.

Morse, Jane. "Second Thoughts on the 4-Day Week." Parade Magazine, December 24, 1972, p. 12.

Morse, Nancy, and Weiss, Robert. "The Function and Meaning of Work." American Sociological Review 20 (1955): 191-98.

Mortimer, L. R. The Four Day Week: Recent Trends in Workweek Rescheduling. Washington, D.C.: Congressional Research Service, Library of Congress, HD5106 U.S., 71-215E, September 30, 1971.

Mott, Paul E.; Mann, Floyd C.; McLoughlin, Quinn; and Warwick, Donald P. Shift Work: The Social, Psychological and Physical Consequences. Ann Arbor: University of Michigan Press, 1965.

Nash, William W., Jr. "Implications for Urban America." In 4 Days, 40 Hours: Reporting a Revolution in Work and Leisure, edited by Riva Poor. pp. 123-32. Foreword by Paul A. Samuelson. Cambridge, Mass.: Bursk and Poor Publishing, 1970.

Navran, Leslie. "Communication and Adjustment in Marriage." Family Process 6 (1967): 173-84.

Neugarten, Bernice L., and Gutmann, David L. "Age-Sex Roles and Personality in Middle Age: A Thematic Apperception Study." In Middle Age and Aging, edited by Bernice L. Neugarten, pp. 58-71. Chicago: University of Chicago Press, 1968.

Newsweek, August 23, 1971, pp. 63-64.

Nord, Walter R., and Costigan, Robert. "Worker Adjustment to the Four-Day Week: A Longitudinal Study." Journal of Applied Psychology 58 (August 1973): 60-66.

Northrup, Herbert R. "The Reduction in Hours." In Hours of Work, edited by Clyde E. Dankert, Floyd C. Mann, and Herbert R. Northrup, pp. 1-16. New York: Harper and Row, 1965.

Nye, F. Ivan. "Maternal Employment and Marital Interaction: Some Contingent Conditions." Social Forces 40 (December 1961): 113-19.

——. "Values, Family, and a Changing Society." Journal of Marriage and the Family 29 (May 1967): 241-48.

Orden, Susan R., and Bradburn, Norman M. "Dimensions of Marriage Happiness." American Journal of Sociology 73 (May 1968): 715-31.

Owen, John D. The Price of Leisure: An Economic Analysis of the Demand for Leisure Time. Foreword by Jacob Mincer. Montreal: McGill-Queens University Press, 1970.

Packard, Vance. The Hidden Persuaders. New York: Pocket Books, 1958.

Parker, Stanley. The Future of Work and Leisure. London: MacGibbon and Kee, 1971.

Patrushev, V. D. "Aggregate Time-Balances and Their Meaning for Socio-Economic Planning." In The Use of Time, edited by Alexander Szalai, pp. 429-40. Hague: Mouton, 1972.

Pineo, Peter C. "Disenchantment in the Later Years of Marriage." Marriage and Family Living 23 (February 1961): 3-11.

Poor, Riva, ed. 4 Days, 40 Hours: Reporting a Revolution in Work and Leisure. Foreword by Paul A. Samuelson. Cambridge, Mass.: Bursk and Poor Publishing, 1970.

Quinn, Robert P., and Sheppard, Linda J. The 1972-73 Quality of Employment Survey. Ann Arbor: Survey Research Center, Institute for Social Research, 1974.

Quinn, Robert P.; Staines, Graham L.; and McCullough, Margaret R. "Job Satisfaction: Is There a Trend?" (Manpower Research Monograph no. 30, U.S. Department of Labor, Manpower Administration.) Washington, D.C.: Government Printing Office, 1974.

Reich, Charles. The Greening of America. New York: Random House, 1970.

Renne, Karen S. "Correlates of Dissatisfaction in Marriage." Journal of Marriage and the Family 32 (February 1970): 54-67.

Riesman, David. "Work and Leisure in Post-Industrial Society." In Mass Leisure, edited by Eric Larrabee and Rolf Meyersohn, pp. 363-85. Glencoe, Ill.: Free Press, 1958.

——. The Lonely Crowd. New Haven: Yale University Press, 1961.

Roberts, Kenneth. Leisure. London: Harlow, Longman, 1970.

Robinson, John P.; Athanasiou, Robert; and Head, Kendra B. Measures of Occupational Attitudes and Occupational Characteristics. Ann Arbor, Mich.: Survey Research Center, Institute for Social Research, 1969.

Robinson, John P., and Converse, Philip E. "The Impact of Television on Mass Media Usage: A Cross-National Comparison." In The Use of Time, edited by Alexander Szalai, pp. 197-212. Hague: Mouton, 1972a.

——. "Social Change Reflected in the Use of Time." In The Human Meaning of Social Change, edited by Angus Campbell and Philip E. Converse, pp. 77-86. New York: Russell Sage Foundation, 1972b.

——. "Social Change Reflected in the Use of Time." In The Human Meaning of Social Change, edited by Angus Campbell and Philip E. Converse, pp. 17-86. New York: Russell Sage Foundation, 1972c.

Robinson, John P.; Converse, Philip E.; and Szalai, Alexander. "Everyday Life in Twelve Countries." In The Use of Time, edited by Alexander Szalai, pp. 113-44. Hague: Mouton, 1972.

Rollins, Boyd C., and Feldman, Harold. "Marital Satisfaction and the Family Life-Cycle." Journal of Marriage and the Family 32 (February 1970): 20-28.

Schein, Edgar H. "The Mechanisms of Change." In The Planning of Change, edited by Warren G. Bennis, Kenneth D. Benne, and Robert Chin, 2d. ed., pp. 98-107. New York: Holt, Rinehart and Winston, 1969.

Scheuch, Erwin K. "The Time-Budget Interview." In The Use of Time, edited by Alexander Szalai, pp. 69-87. Hague: Mouton, 1972.

Schlesinger, Arthur. "Implications for Government." In Technology, Human Values and Leisure, edited by Max Kaplan and Phillip Bosserman, pp. 68-91. New York: Abingdon Press, 1971.

Shostak, Arthur B. Blue-Collar Life. New York: Random House, 1969.

Smigel, Erwin O., ed. Work and Leisure: A Contemporary Social Problem. New Haven: College and University Press, 1963.

Sprague, Linda G. "Breaking the 5-Day Mold: Scheduling Issues." In 4 Days, 40 Hours: Reporting a Revolution in Work and Leisure, edited by Riva Poor, pp. 71-78. Foreword by Paul A. Samuelson. Cambridge, Mass.: Bursk and Poor Publishing, 1970.

Steele, James L., and Poor, Riva. "Work and Leisure: The Reaction of People at 4-Day Firms." In 4 Days, 40 Hours: Reporting a Revolution in Work and Leisure, edited by Riva Poor, pp. 105-22. Foreword by Paul A. Samuelson. Cambridge, Mass.: Bursk and Poor Publishing, 1970.

Stone, Philip J. "Child Care in Twelve Countries." In The Use of Time, edited by Alexander Szalai, pp. 249-64. Hague: Mouton, 1972.

Strauss, George. "Is There a Blue-Collar Revolt Against Work?" In Work and the Quality of Life: Resource Papers for "Work in America", edited by James O'Toole, pp. 40-69. Foreword by Elliott L. Richardson. Afterword by Edward M. Kennedy. Cambridge, Mass.: MIT Press, 1974.

Striner, Herbert E. Continuing Education as a National Capital Investment. Kalamazoo, Mich.: W. E. Upjohn Institute for Employment Research, 1972.

Swados, Harvey. "Less Work—Less Leisure." In Mass Leisure, edited by Eric Larrabee and Rolf Meyersohn, pp. 353-63. Glencoe, Ill.: Free Press, 1958.

——. A Radical's America. Boston: Little, Brown, 1962.

Swedner, Harold. "Regulated Time and Leisure Time." Society and Leisure 2 (December 1969): 7-28.

Szalai, Alexander. "Concepts and Practices of Time-Budget Research." In The Use of Time, edited by Alexander Szalai, pp. 1-12. Hague: Mouton, 1972.

Tallman, Irving. "The Family as a Small Problem Solving Group." Journal of Marriage and the Family 32 (February 1970): 94-104.

Taylor, Alexander B. "Role Perception, Empathy, and Marriage Adjustment." Sociological and Social Research 52 (October 1967): 22-34.

Terkel, Studs. Working: People Talk About What They Do All Day and How They Feel About What They Do. New York: Pantheon Books, 1974.

Theobald, Robert. "Thinking About the Future." In Technology, Human Values and Leisure, edited by Max Kaplan and Phillip Bosserman, pp. 27-41. New York: Abingdon Press, 1971.

Tiryakian, Edward A. "A Model of Social Change and Its Lead Indicators." In The Study of Total Societies, edited by Samuel Z. Klausner, pp. 69-97. Garden City, N.Y.: Anchor Books, 1967.

Vance, William. "U.S. No Longer Seeks Delay in Pollution Control." Detroit Free Press, 22 February 1973, Sec. B, p. 5.

Varga, Kanaly. "Marital Cohesion as Reflected in Time-Budgets." In The Use of Time, edited by Alexander Szalai, pp. 357-75. Hague: Mouton, 1972.

Veblen, Thorstein. The Theory of the Leisure Class. Introduction by John Kenneth Galbraith. Boston: Houghton Mifflin, 1973.

Veroff, Joseph L., and Feld, Sheila. Marriage and Work in America: A Study of Motives and Roles. New York: Van Nostrand Reinhold, 1970.

Vincent, Clark E. "Familia Spongio: The Adaptive Function." Journal of Marriage and the Family 28 (February 1966): 29-36.

Walton, Richard E. "Alienation and Innovation in the Workplace." In Work and the Quality of Life: Resource Papers for "Work in

America", edited by James O'Toole, pp. 227-45. Foreword by Elliot L. Richardson. Afterword by Edward M. Kennedy, Cambridge, Mass.: MIT Press, 1974.

Weber, Max. The Protestant Ethic and the Spirit of Capitalism. Translated by Talcott Parsons. Foreword by R. H. Tawney. New York: Charles Scribner's Sons, 1958.

Weiss, Paul. "A Philosophical Definition of Leisure." In Leisure in America: Blessing or Curse? edited by James C. Charlesworth, pp. 21-29. Philadelphia: American Academy of Political and Social Sciences, Monograph no. 4, April 1964.

Wheeler, Kenneth E., and Bogdonoff, Philip D. "How to Handle a 4-Day Conversion." In 4 Days, 40 Hours: Reporting a Revolution in Work and Leisure, edited by Riva Poor, pp. 91-104. Foreword by Paul A. Samuelson. Cambridge, Mass.: Bursk and Poor Publishing, 1970.

Wheeler, Kenneth E.; Gurman, R.; and Tarnowieski, D. The Four-Day Week. New York: American Management Association, 1972.

Wilensky, Harold L. "The Uneven Distribution of Leisure: The Impact of Economic Growth on 'Free Time'." Social Problems 9 (1961): 32-55.

———. "Work, Careers and Social Integration." In Industrial Man, edited by Tom Burns, pp. 110-39. Baltimore: Penguin Books, 1969.

Wilson, James A. "Some Philosophic and Social Implications of the Flexible Work Week." In The Four Day Week: Fad or Future? Proceedings of a Conference Conducted by the Graduate School of Business, University of Pittsburgh. Pittsburgh, November 1971, pp. 1-43.

Wolfenstein, Martha. "The Emergence of Fun Morality." In Mass Leisure, edited by Eric Larrabee and Rolf Meyersohn, pp. 86-96. Glencoe, Ill.: Free Press, 1958.

Work in America: Report of a Special Task Force to the Secretary of Health, Education and Welfare, by James O'Toole, Chairman. Foreword by Elliot L. Richardson. Cambridge, Mass.: MIT Press, 1973.

Wrenn, C. Gilbert. "Human Values and Work in American Life." In Man in a World at Work, edited by Henry Borow, pp. 24-44. Boston: Houghton Mifflin, 1964.

Zuzanek, Jiri. "Society of Leisure or the Harried Leisure Class? Leisure Trends in Industrial Societies." Journal of Leisure Research 6 (Fall 1974): 293-304.

Zweig, Ferdynand. The British Worker. London: Penguin Books, 1952.

ABOUT THE AUTHOR

DAVID M. MAKLAN is a Senior Analyst and Project Director at Westat, Inc. Until 1976, he was a doctoral student at the University of Michigan and at various times taught courses in the university's Residential College and the School of Engineering. He was also a Research Assistant in the School of Natural Research.

Dr. Maklan is a contributing author to Professor John P. Robinson's How Americans Use Time: A Social-Psychological Analysis of Everyday Behavior (New York: Praeger, 1977).

Dr. Maklan holds a B.A. from Carleton University, Ottawa, Canada. He received his Ph.D. in Urban and Regional Planning from the University of Michigan. While a graduate student, Dr. Maklan was a three-time recipient of a Doctoral Fellowship from the Canada Council and was awarded a Doctoral Dissertation Grant from the Manpower Administration, U.S. Department of Labor.

HD
5124
.M3
1977

$8.80

HD
5124
.M3

1977